C0-AVE-578

BY THE EDITORS OF
VIDEO MOVIES MAGAZINE

THE BEST
VIDEO
FILMS

WARNER BOOKS

A Warner Communications Company

CONTRIBUTORS

Carlos Clarens, the author of *The Illustrated History of Horror* and *Crime Movies*, wrote the sections on Gangster Films and Horror Films.

Marcia Froelke Coburn, a frequent contributor to *American Film* and *Film Comment*, wrote Coming-of-Age Films and Melodramas.

Stephanie Arena Drea, a writer/producer for Encyclopedia Britannica, wrote Music Video and Rock 'n' Roll Movies.

David Ehrenstein, a film critic for the *Los Angeles Herald Examiner*, wrote Foreign Films.

Owen Gleiberman, a film critic for the *Boston Phoenix*, wrote Art Films and Cult Films.

Alex Gordon, a former film producer for American International Pictures, wrote Westerns.

Joel Hirschhorn, an Academy-Award-winning songwriter, wrote Love Stories and Musicals.

Randy Lofficier, a frequent contributor to *American Cinematographer* and *Cinefex*, wrote Animated Films and Adventure Films.

Kurt Luchs, a stand-up comedian and free-lance writer, wrote Comedies, Melodramas, and War Films.

Fran McCarthy, a free-lance writer, wrote Great Books.

Joe Menosky, a contributor to *Science '84* magazine and National Public Radio, wrote Family Films, Prison/Escape Films, and Science Fiction Films.

Bob Ottoson, the author of a forthcoming book on AIP films, wrote Mysteries and Spy Films.

Jeff Rovin, the author of numerous books on film and popular culture, wrote Animated Films, Historical Epics, and Sports Films.

WARNER BOOKS EDITION

Copyright © 1984 by Publications International, Ltd. All rights reserved. This book may not be reproduced or quoted in whole or in part by mimeograph or any other printed means or for presentation on radio, television, videotape, or film without written permission from:

Louis Weber, President
Publications International, Ltd.
3841 West Oakton Street
Skokie, Illinois 60076

Permission is never granted for commercial purposes.

Warner Books, Inc.
666 Fifth Avenue
New York, N. Y. 10103

 A Warner Communications Company

Printed in the United States of America

First Printing: December, 1984

10 9 8 7 6 5 4 3 2 1

Cover design: Barbara Clemens

CONTENTS

INTRODUCTION

There are over 7,000 movies available on videotape—a figure that is dwarfed only by the 30,000-odd films that have been made and *not* yet released to the video public. The number that is presently available is staggering, containing nearly all the product seen in movie theaters over the past five years and most of the classic and cult product, to boot. It's a lot of material. And while we'd hesitate to say that there is too much on tape (can there ever be too much?), there is an acute need to structure the material—to make sure that the word gets out on the best of the available fare. That's where this book comes in. *The Best Video Films* is our salute to the best in video programming. It's designed to separate the truly exceptional from the pack. More than that, it's designed to celebrate these titles and celebrate them triumphantly.

There are 24 chapters in this book, each one of them singing the praises of a certain type of film. Whether it be Comedy or Horror or more playful chapters like Coming-of-Age or Prison/Escape, this book is designed to help you with your selection process—to suggest films based on the type of movie you want to see. And you can count on the recommendations. From the classics to the obscure, the authors have hand-picked titles that have proved their worth not only as great films but, more importantly, as great *video* films.

There can be no doubt that the home viewing experience is substantially different than seeing movies in a theater. The most obvious difference is the size of the screen, but certain subtle characteristics may be more important in determining the success or failure of a video film. The home experience provides an atmosphere that the theater could never attempt to reproduce. The intimacy of the home—the fact that the TV may be in your living room, den, or bedroom—has a profound impact on the way these films are received. Intimate subject matter—Love Stories or Melodramas—may play more comfortably at home. Furthermore, broadcast television has been so dominant in certain areas that many films—such as those dealing with sports or animation—

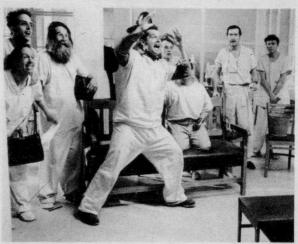

One Flew Over the Cuckoo's Nest. *The inmates of the sanitarium enjoy the antics of their new rabble-rousing buddy, R. P. McMurphy (Jack Nicholson). The image of the rebel is a dominant force in American movies.*

seem more appropriate at home than they do in the theater. Finally, the home provides a setting that can increase enjoyment of certain films simply because of your mobility and freedom to talk. The viewing of a Family Film, for example, can be a greater family experience when everyone can discuss the film while it plays.

Still, the majority of movies in this book were made for the theaters, and a certain loss of quality is unavoidable in the transfer of any film to videotape. The most crucial transfer problem concerns wide-screen films. Because up to half of the image of wide-screen films cannot physically fit within the frame of a television set, much of the image is lost in the transfer process. The only way to compensate for that loss would be to put the film in a "letterbox"—a technique that gets the whole image on the screen but one that necessitates the use of black masking bars above and below the movie. In other words, only part of the television screen actually reproduces the image. (To physically see this process, rent a copy of Woody Allen's *Manhattan*—the only major film to date that uses the "letterbox" technique.) Another problem in the transfer process concerns the black properties of film as opposed to the black properties of videotape. Simply put: Film can recreate a night scene better than videotape. Horror Films are the worst victim of this difference, since much of a Horror Film's action takes place at night. The detail is often lost and the characters are sometimes obscured in the transfer process.

However, video has so many special attributes that comparisons to film, while necessary, become secondary in importance. More often than not, the general visual quality of the videotape is better. The scratches, jumps, and blemishes that inevitably haunt the older films as they travel from theater to theater are often nonexistent in the videotape versions—many of which were struck from the original negatives of the film. And videotape often has the complete unedited versions of the films that played in the theaters. The video version of *Blade Runner* is 10 minutes longer than that played in movie houses. Finally, video gives you a control over the material that the most skilled projectionist would envy. With a press of the button you can slow down the action, repeat memorable or confusing segments, fast forward through scenes that are tedious or unnecessary, or study the art of film through a frame-by-frame advance. Such manipulation of the media may have far-reaching effects on the future course of video programming.

In short, video has provided a control that has been heretofore unthinkable—not merely control over the film, but control over selection of films: choosing what you want to see when you want to see it. *The Best Video Films* is proudly offered as an introduction to the new video. Within these pages are full profiles of the most remarkable and memorable films on tape. If you bought your video recorder to watch movies, you'll find this book to be a valuable companion—a guide, a cohort, and most of all, your host to the revolutionary world of video film.

ADVENTURE FILMS

More people rent Adventure Films than any other type of movie, according to a recent survey of the *Video Movies* readership. Thanks to the quirks of the alphabet, we're able to launch this book with the most popular type of movie. Adventure Films work especially well on tape, for these are movies that rely heavily on action, exploration, and plot—characteristics that translate especially well to the small screen. The word "adventure" could apply to a wide variety of titles, but there is a distinct group of films that are rooted in the matinee "cliffhangers" of old that are the subject of this chapter. The primary quality of these movies is that they're episodic—one action leads to another, which leads to another, usually culminating in a wham-bang, action-packed climax. These are movies with heroes and villains, with good and evil. Other recommended Adventure Films include: *Captain Blood, Excaliber, King Solomon's Mines, Mutiny on the Bounty, The Sea Hawk,* and a slew of adventure serials (look for titles that begin with "Perils of" as in *Perils of the Darkest Jungle*).

Gunga Din. *Adventure* lives *in these three soldiers of fortune (Cary Grant, Victor McLaglen, and Douglas Fairbanks, Jr.). Sam Jaffe plays waterboy Gunga Din.*

THE ADVENTURES
OF ROBIN HOOD

(1938), C, *Directors:* Michael Curtiz and William
Keighley. *With* Errol Flynn, Olivia de Havilland,
Claude Rains, Basil Rathbone, and Patric Knowles.
102 min. *NR.* Tape, CED, Laser: CBS/Fox.

To paraphrase the publicity for a recent Hollywood
release: If adventure has a name, it must be Errol
Flynn. . . .

Flynn's Robin Hood has become so firmly entrenched
in our minds that we have forgotten how large a role his
portrayal had in shaping today's image of the famous
Sherwood Forest outlaw.

This classic 1938 production, which won an Oscar for
its stirring musical score by Erich Wolfgang Korngold,
is staged lavishly, with great production values and
beautiful, vibrant, color photography. In fact, this may
very well be one of Hollywood's *prettiest* pictures.

The tale follows Robin's adventures from the time of
his rebellion against the villainous Prince John to his
triumph when King Richard returns. All the classic
ingredients are here: the recruiting of Little John and
Friar Tuck; the winning of Maid Marian's heart; the
archery contest where Robin splits his opponent's arrow
in two; and the rousing duel with the evil Sir Guy.

Flynn is, as could be expected, superb as Robin. His
rakish grin and lithe form come as close to embodying
the Hollywood hero as any we're likely to see. The other
cast members are also delightful. Olivia de Havilland
gives a lovely and touching performance as Marian;
Claude Rains is a wonderfully slimy Prince John; and
Basil Rathbone as Sir Guy is the perfect foil (literally, in
the famous swordfight-by-torchlight scene) for Robin.

Michael Curtiz, best known for *Casablanca* and a host
of other Flynn pictures, here shares the directorial credit
with William Keighley, who was equally competent at
adventure pictures. The two men's styles blend beautifully, making *The Adventures of Robin Hood* one of the
best and most lighthearted adventure epics ever made.

THE COUNT OF MONTE CRISTO

(1934), B/W, *Director:* Rowland V. Lee. *With* Robert
Donat, Elissa Landi, Louis Calhern, Sidney Blackmer,
Raymond Walburn, O.P. Heggie, Luis Alberni, and
Irene Hervey. **119 min.** *NR*. Tape: Nostalgia Merchant.

The fact that at 119 minutes, this 1934 version of
Alexandre Dumas' rousing yarn seems too short is a
tribute to the excitement it generates.

The well-known story follows Edmond Dantes (Robert
Donat), a sailor unjustly imprisoned at the deadly
Chateau d'If. Dantes eventually escapes with the help of
fellow prisoner Faria (O.P. Heggie), who gives him a
treasure map. After Dantes has found the treasure, he
goes back to Paris under the guise of the Count of Monte
Cristo, to wreak his revenge upon the three villains who
framed him 20 years before.

The film is remarkably faithful to Dumas' novel until
the end, where (for time limitations no doubt) it decides
to wrap up the plot quite abruptly. Nevertheless, kudos
go to the screenwriters Philip Dunne and Dan Totheroh,
who do an outstanding job adapting extremely complicated and difficult material.

Director Rowland V. Lee orchestrates the tale in a
beautiful, evocative black-and-white style. He is well
served by a fantastic cast, headed by Robert Donat as
Monte Cristo. Donat has the cold magnetism and im-
placable strength that the character requires. The three
villains are also excellent, each in his own twisted way,
but the exquisite Elissa Landi as Mercedes, Dantes' old
flame, steals the scenes and inspires love and admiration
for her character.

The Count of Monte Cristo is yet another of the classic
stories that have generated many film and television
adaptations. The versions starring Richard Chamberlain, Jean Marais, or Louis Jourdan may be familiar.
But this, the first "talkie" version, is by far the best.

GUNGA DIN

(1939), B/W, *Director:* George Stevens. *With* Cary
Grant, Douglas Fairbanks, Jr., Victor McLaglen, Sam
Jaffe, Joan Fontaine, Eduardo Ciannelli, Montagu
Love, Abner Biberman, and Robert Coote. **117 min.** *NR.*
Tape: VidAmerica.

Why is *Gunga Din* one of the most endearing pictures
ever made? It was, as a matter of fact, remade twice, once
as *Soldiers Three* (1951), and the other time as *Sergeants
3* (1962), the latter taking place in the Old West,
with Sammy Davis, Jr. as the heroic Indian. And even Steven
Spielberg's recent *Indiana Jones and the Temple of
Doom* pays homage to this small-budget R.K.O. production.

Loosely based on a poem by Rudyard Kipling, *Gunga
Din* follows the adventures of three British Army officers
as they attempt to stop a Thugee revolt in India. The
officers are played by Cary Grant, who is in India mostly
to find gold or emeralds; Douglas Fairbanks, Jr. who,
much to his two friends' dismay, wants to get out of the
Army, marry and become a tea merchant; and Victor
McLaglen, who plays the brave but unimaginative chief
sergeant. Sam Jaffe admirably plays Gunga Din, a
humble water boy who wants to be a soldier. It is he who
saves the day at the end of the film. *Gunga Din* is filled
with swashbuckling acts of derring-do, but it also contains many touching and funny moments that create
real empathy for the characters. And along with its
value as entertainment, *Gunga Din* also makes a strong
case in favor of Indian independence.

Producer and director George Stevens, who would
later direct such masterpieces as *Shane* (1953) and
Giant (1956), demonstrates his talent in the way he
infuses every frame of the film with excitement. In spite
of its low budget, the film has authenticity, another of
Stevens's trademarks. *Gunga Din* came out the same
year as *Gone With the Wind* and *The Wizard of Oz,* and
therefore failed to garner any Oscar nominations. But,
to paraphrase Kipling: You're as good a film as they are,
Gunga Din!

QUEST FOR FIRE

(1981), C, *Director:* Jean-Jacques Annaud. *With*
Everett McGill, Ron Perlman, Nameer El Kadi, and Rae
Dawn Chong. **100 min.** *R*. Tape, CED, Laser: CBS/Fox.

In 1909, French writer J. H. Rosny Aine ("the Elder")
wrote a novel about prehistoric life, *La Guerre du Feu*,
loosely translated into English as *Quest for Fire*.

The 1981 film of the same name was an international
effort, directed by Frenchman Jean-Jacques Annaud,
produced by Canadian Denis Heroux, and filmed in
Kenya, Iceland, and Scotland to obtain a feeling of
authenticity. The latter is the key word to the whole film,
as anthropologist Desmond Morris and linguist Anthony Burgess (author of the novel *A Clockwork Orange*)
were called in to recreate the languages and gestures of
the Stone Age people.

The film follows the plight of a tribe that has lost its
fire, and doesn't yet know the secret of its making. Three
men are sent on a desperate quest to recapture, or steal,
the essential element. After encountering sabertooth
tigers, mammoths, and a tribe more advanced than
theirs, they eventually learn the secret of fire in a scene
that makes us truly understand what a giant step for
mankind it was.

Actors Everett McGill, Ron Perlman, Nameer El
Kadi, and actress Rae Dawn Chong—the daughter of
comic Tommy Chong—are superb in roles that require
wonderful mimicry abilities, as there is no comprehen-
sible dialogue in the film. Annaud and cinematographer
Claude Agostini succeed in raising the lonely enterprise
of the three cavemen to epic proportions, while maintaining a funny, touching, intimate feeling with the
protagonists.

Ultimately, *Quest for Fire's* true hero is Man, portrayed here at his noblest and most touching, in his
desire to learn and to grow. The Quest continues.

Quest for Fire. *Prehistoric tribesmen (Ron Perlman, Everett McGill, and Nameer El Kadi) venture beyond their narrow confines in search of their world's most precious commodity: fire. Like any journey of discovery, the experience brings greater knowledge and maturity.*

Raiders of the Lost Ark. *Indiana Jones (Harrison Ford) with his salty ex-girlfriend Marian (Karen Allen). Long on fistfights and bullwhips and short on scientific method, he's the toughest archeologist you'll ever want to meet.*

RAIDERS OF THE LOST ARK

(1981), C, *Director:* Steven Spielberg. *With* Paul
Freeman, Harrison Ford, Karen Allen, Wolf Kahler,
Ronald Lacey, John Rhys-Davies, and Denholm Elliott.
115 min. *PG.* Tape, CED, Laser: Paramount.

Raiders of the Lost Ark needs little introduction. This
Steven Spielberg (director) George Lucas (producer) film
was *the* blockbuster of 1981, and went on to become one
of the top money-grossing pictures of all time.

With the help of fellow filmmaker Philip Kaufman
(The Right Stuff), and that of screenwriter Lawrence
Kasdan *(Body Heat),* Spielberg and Lucas have embodied adventure in the character of Indiana Jones, a
treasure-hunting archeologist of the 1930s. In this first
picture of the series (the second was released in 1984),
Dr. Jones and a group of properly villainous Nazis, led
by Jones's suave rival, Belloq (Paul Freeman), hunt for
the lost Ark of the Covenant. The secret of the Ark,
revealed at the end of the film, is a triumph for Lucas-
film's Industrial Light & Magic division, and will
delight special-effects fans the world over.

A direct descendant of the Saturday morning matinee
serials and a return to the simpler heroes of the past,
Raiders is built to be a series of cliffhangers that leave
you clinging to the edge of your seat. A good portion of its
success is attributable to its two stars, Harrison Ford as
Dr. Jones and Karen Allen as his spunky, long-lost girl
friend. Ford, in particular, projects an indomitable
spirit, combined with a good dose of tongue-in-cheek
that seems to say, "You and I both know that this is a
movie!"

John Williams's rousing score completes this irresistible concoction that is one of the best adventure movies
ever made. Warning: The finale may cause heart damage.

ROMANCING THE STONE

(1984), C, *Director:* Robert Zemeckis. *With* Michael
Douglas, Kathleen Turner, and Danny De Vito.
106 min. *PG.* Tape, CED, Laser: CBS/Fox.

Despite superficial resemblances to *Raiders of the Lost
Ark* (resemblances shamelessly, yet successfully, exploited in the print ads), *Romancing the Stone* is a very
different sort of adventure film, with its own peculiar
merits. *Raiders* uses camp humor as a continuously
burning fuse leading from one explosive bit of action to
the next. *Romancing the Stone* has almost the same
outward structure, down to the obligatory climactic
chase scene, but it shifts the emphasis, using suspenseful action mainly to punctuate the central scenes of
comedy and romance. The difference is significant, for it
gives *Romancing the Stone* a warmth and low-key
charm missing from the giddy thrills of *Raiders.*
  Not that this film lacks excitement. The title is a pun
on the occupation of the protagonist, Joan Wilder (Kathleen Turner), a romance writer hopelessly in love with
the larger-than-life men of her silly novels. After her
brother-in-law is murdered in Colombia, Joan receives a
mysterious treasure map in the mail. From then on her
uneventful life runs off the rails into a story of danger
and intrigue suspiciously like one of her own plots. She
even meets a man as impressive (and exasperating) as
those she has invented: Jack T. Colton (Michael
Douglas), an easygoing rogue who scrapes a living out of
peddling rare South American birds. *Romancing the
Stone* is like an updated *African Queen,* with Joan becoming stronger and Jack nobler through the adventures they share. Along the way they tease and infuriate
each other, and finally fall in love.
  The humor is consistent and often uproarious—especially the antics of Danny DeVito and Zack Norman as a
pair of fruitcake gangsters attempting to horn in on the
race for the treasure. Watch for a final scene as clever
and concise as that in Hitchcock's *North By Northwest,*
where a few choice camera angles tie up the story better
than any amount of dialogue.

TARZAN, THE APE MAN

(1932), **B/W,** *Director:* W. S. Van Dyke. *With* Johnny
Weissmuller, Maureen O'Sullivan, C. Aubrey Smith,
Neil Hamilton, and Doris Lloyd. **104 min.** *NR*. Tape:
MGM/UA.

Of all the actors that have played Edgar Rice Bur-
roughs's famous Lord of the Apes, Johnny Weissmuller
remains the best. Lean, powerful, gifted with a strong
screen persona, Weissmuller is as close to being the
definitive Tarzan as Basil Rathbone is to being Sherlock
Holmes.

This 1932 MGM film is the first and finest of Weissmuller's six original outings in the role. Its direct sequel,
Tarzan and His Mate (1934), is also highly recommended.

Both films star the lovely Maureen O'Sullivan as Jane
Porter, Tarzan's paramour. In the first picture (remade a
number of times since, most recently in an abominable
version starring Bo Derek), Jane arrives in the jungle
and sets off with her father on an expedition to find the
legendary Graveyard of the Elephants. The expedition
runs afoul of some savage beasts, of Tarzan himself (who
kidnaps Jane, then lets her go), and of a nasty bunch of
pygmies. Overall, the film contains enough action and
excitement to satisfy any audience. There is even a bit of
humor with Cheetah, the chimpanzee, which is merci-
fully not as broad as it became in the sequels.

The first two MGM Tarzan films were not B pictures,
although they have a back-lot look about them. W. S.
Van Dyke's direction is suspenseful, yet unobtrusive.
The wonderful thing about *Tarzan, the Ape Man* is that
it contains all those ingredients which, since then, have
become clichés: Tarzan swinging from vine to vine; his
famous cry; the "Me Tarzan, you Jane" dialogue;
Cheetah warning Tarzan; the elephants coming to the
rescue . . . Yet, in this film, none appears dated or comical.

Like a fruit, the outer skin of this film may be a bit
wrinkled with age, but the inside has not changed. It
remains as fresh and tasty as it ever was.

TREASURE ISLAND

(1934), B/W, *Director:* Victor Fleming. *With* Wallace
Beery, Jackie Cooper, Lionel Barrymore, Lewis Stone,
Otto Kruger, Nigel Bruce, and Douglass Dumbrille.
102 min. *NR*. Tape, CED: MGM/UA.

This first film adaptation of Robert Louis Stevenson's
well-known pirate story remains the most thrilling of
the lot. Gripping and entertaining, it is one of the best
MGM adventure films of the 1930s.

The tale of young Jim Hawkins and pirate Long John
Silver, and of their search for buried treasure, is one we
carry with us from childhood to old age. It is, in fact,
almost singlehandedly responsible for the creation of the
sub-genre of pirate stories.

The 1934 version is the most faithful of all of the
Stevenson adaptations. Unlike Disney's 1950 version
(which is remarkable in its own right), it retains the
book's original ending. In this film, Jackie Cooper as Jim
Hawkins is teamed with Wallace Beery as Long John
Silver, and the two make an excellent combination.

Cooper, one of the most popular child stars of the
period, gives us a fairly stout-hearted Jim Hawkins,
adequately translating the mixture of innocence and
bravery at the core of the character. Beery is a sheer
delight as Silver. His expressive physique, roguish voice
and boisterous countenance make him such a convincing
embodiment of the one-legged pirate that even the excellent Robert Newton (from the 1950 version) is difficult to
accept in the role. Film buffs will also delight in Lionel
Barrymore's fine performance as Billy Bones.

Victor Fleming, who went on to do *Captains Courageous* (1937) and *The Wizard of Oz* (1939), directs in his
characteristically solid and entertaining style. He
makes excellent use of superior production values and,
as usual, gets marvelous performances out of his actors.

The film is filled with memorable gems such as Billy
Bones taking over the Hawkins's tavern; the ominous
arrival of Blind Pew; Ben Gunn's half-crazed dialogue;
and the hilarious parting monologue delivered by Long
John Silver. Set sail for *Treasure Island,* says I!

THE TREASURE
OF THE SIERRA MADRE

(1948), B/W, *Director:* John Huston. *With* Humphrey
Bogart, Tim Holt, Walter Huston, Bruce Bennett, John
Huston, and Robert Blake. **124 min.** *NR*. Tape: Key;
CED: RCA VideoDisc; Laser: CBS/Fox.

Few adventure films so starkly unveil what lies at the
core of adventure as *The Treasure of the Sierra Madre*.
From *Tarzan, the Ape Man* to *Raiders of the Lost Ark,*
the same motivation holds sway: greed.

In this 1948 Warner film, greed is the true villain of
the piece. It destroys friendships, causes fortunes to be
lost, and even kills. The film follows down-on-their-luck
Americans in Mexico (Humphrey Bogart and Tim Holt)
who decide to become partners with an old prospector
(Walter Huston) and go gold digging in the Sierra Madre
mountains. The trouble starts when they find the gold
that they desire. . . . Will their friendship survive?

In addition to Walter Huston's Oscar-winning performance (Huston is director John Huston's father), as the
cynical but jolly old prospector, the film boasts excellent
acting by Holt and Bogart. The latter gives us a frightening depiction of a man's gradual mental disintegra-
tion, until he falls into the pit of paranoiac insanity.

The film contains some interesting cameos, by John
Huston himself as the American tourist who gives
Bogart money, and by Robert Blake, later of *Baretta*
fame, as the young boy selling chances at a lottery.

The moral of the film is delivered in a strong fashion,
but not as heavy-handedly as B. Traven's original novel.
John Huston's expert direction and script turn our sympathies towards the characters. The film underscores its
message with some very human moments.

The Treasure of the Sierra Madre proved to be a turning point for the pure adventure film. When the old
prospector decides to retire, it is the simpler hero of the
1930s and 1940s that goes with him. The introduction of
a deeper morality into adventure films was about to
change their nature for the next two decades.

20,000 LEAGUES UNDER THE SEA

(1954), C, *Director:* Richard Fleischer. *With* Kirk
Douglas, Peter Lorre, James Mason, Paul Lukas, Robert
J. Wilke, and Carleton Young. **127 min.** *G.* Tape, Laser:
Disney; CED: RCA VideoDisc.

Much has been written—deservedly so—about this
lavish Walt Disney adaptation of Jules Verne's classic
novel. In an age of remakes, it is indeed a fitting tribute
to this film that no one has yet considered doing one of
20,000 Leagues—although Disney's SF epic *The Black
Hole* certainly acknowledged its parentage.

Earl Felton's screenplay manages to out-Verne Verne,
with its wild mixture of rococo science fiction and under-
sea adventure. The movie's plot otherwise remains
basically faithful to that of the novel. Prof. Arronax
(Paul Lukas), his domestic Conseil (Peter Lorre) and
harpooner Ned Land (Kirk Douglas) investigate rumors
of a sea monster, and end up the prisoners of the mysterious Captain Nemo (James Mason), enigmatic in-
ventor and master of the "Nautilus," the world's first
submarine craft. Although the film's ending greatly dif-
fers from that of Verne's, it is properly suspenseful and
satisfying.

20,000 Leagues benefits from outstanding technical
credits, ranging from the "Nautilus's" strikingly brilliant and original design (by Harper Goff), to beautiful
underwater photography. Director Richard Fleischer
embues the whole picture with an epic sense of scale, as
in the battle scene against a giant squid.

The cast uniformly rises to the level of the picture,
giving fine performances, in registers different from
their usual casting. Mason's broody, mercurial Nemo is
the definitive impersonation of the character. Douglas,
as Ned Land, is for once not high-strung. Both Lukas and
Lorre, who played mostly villains, are fine as Arronax
and the comic relief Conseil.

In recognition of its incredible achievements, the film
received two well-deserved Academy Awards. It remains, to this day, one of Disney's best live-action adventure films.

ANIMATED FILMS

Adults should make more of an effort to wrest Animated Films from the tots' domain, for when the quality of animation is high—as it is in these ten titles—the viewing can be rich, entertaining, and very *adult*, indeed. That's not to say that we should scuttle the kids away from the set. Television is *the* format for animation, as most of us came to know cartoons through Saturday morning programming. The general brightness of the colors, the emphasis on character, and the zany plot lines are easily enjoyed within the home. We felt it necessary to strike a balance, to show the range of animation on tape—from the wonders of Disney, to the anarchy of Looney Tunes, to the very adult and controversial *Fritz the Cat*. Remember: Most of these titles were made with two audiences in mind, kids and adults. And, since there's so much great programming available, it's important to consider the also-rans: *Allegro Non Troppo* (adult themes), *Beany & Cecil* (5 volumes and growing), *The Collector's Edition of Betty Boop*, and Disney's *Limited Gold Edition* series (unavailable for sale, but still a rental item).

The Secret of NIMH. *John Carradine provides the voice and embodies the character of the Great Owl.*

THE COLOR
ADVENTURES OF SUPERMAN

(1941–1943), C, *Director:* Max Fleischer. *Animated.*
52 min. *NR*. Tape: Video Yesteryear.

On the short-subject front, although the Popeye cartoons were a huge success for Max Fleischer, the animator longed to do more realistic work. Thus, when the
comic book adventures of Superman began publication
in 1938, he saw them as a means to do a Popeye of "flesh
and blood." The result, the 17 cartoons he produced between 1941 and 1943, are the most exciting, spectacular,
and costly animated shorts in film history.

The seven selections on this tape are *The Mad Scientist,* in which Superman battles a destructive ray; *The
Mechanical Monsters,* about an army of robber-robots;
The Magnetic Telescope, wherein a scientist draws a
comet toward earth for study and loses control of it; *The
Bulleteers,* involving thieves who go where they please,
in an indestructible bullet-plane; *The Japoteurs,* a brilliant propagandistic World War II drama in which
Superman recovers a hijacked bomber; *Jungle Drums,*
about a witch-doctor Nazi; and *The Mummy Strikes,* a
murder mystery with a fantasy twist.

In his Superman cartoons, Fleischer pushed animation to its limits to create adventure films that could
never have been shot using live action. Not only do the
cartoon characters use melodramatic gestures, which
would be ludicrous coming from actors, but the camera
angles and feats of strength could never be duplicated on
a soundstage. Mickey Mouse and company may have
charmed the public, Bugs Bunny and friends elevated
slapstick and sarcasm to new heights, but the Superman
cartoons are animation at its most powerful and exciting.

DUMBO

(1941), C, *Director:* Ben Sharpsteen. *Animated.* **64 min.**
NR. Tape, CED, Laser: Disney.

While other animators have come and gone, Walt Disney survived, in large part because he knew how to satisfy the family market. As a result, his name became synonymous with all that is saccharine in moviemaking —unfairly, since films like *Pinocchio* and *Lady and the Tramp* contain some of the most frightening scenes ever filmed. That which is sweet in a Disney film is *not* necessarily superficial.

If there is a "typical" Disney feature of this kind, it is *Dumbo*. After the stork delivers a baby to circus elephant Mrs. Jumbo, the newborn becomes an outcast among pachyderms because of his big ears. The mistreatment of her son finally gets to her, and Mrs. Jumbo goes on a rampage, forcing the owners to chain and cage her as a mad elephant. Alone, Dumbo is befriended by Timothy the Mouse. One day Dumbo discovers that because of the size of his ears he can fly. The former outcast thus becomes the star of the circus, his mother is returned to him, and both live—yes, happily ever after.

As uncomplicated as the story and characters are in *Dumbo*, there probably isn't a scene in film history that has the power both to evoke tears and warm the spirit as when Mrs. Jumbo, caged, tries to hold her son. Her futile effort to reach him, her frustration, and the eventual compromise she makes, rocking him in her curled trunk, is anything but mindlessly sweet; the sequence distills and captures a parent's love with powerful visual images. Speaking of visuals, after Dumbo accidentally imbibes the champagne, the Disney artists present one of their wildest animation rides ever, in the "Pink Elephants on Parade" number as Dumbo imagines elephants prancing about, melding, inflating, splitting, and turning into various objects.

The shortest of Disney's animated features, *Dumbo* is sugar, not saccharin, served up in a torte of classic taste, texture, and color.

Dumbo. *Timothy the Mouse and Dumbo, the flying circus elephant, make friends. The Disney Studio pioneered the animation of individual body movements and facial expressions which not only created movement, but actually delineated character.*

Fantastic Planet. *French artist Roland Topor collaborated with the director Rene Laloux to create this surreal science fiction animation. The graphic styles of Topor and Laloux, both renowned cartoonists, are reminiscent of 19th century lithographs.*

FANTASTIC PLANET

(1973), C, *Director:* Rene Laloux. *Animated.* **68 min.**
NR. Tape: Video Yesteryear.

In 1973, *Fantastic Planet* became the first full-length
animated film to be honored at the Cannes Film Festival, receiving the Special Critics' Award.

This science fiction parable took director Rene Laloux
and artist Roland Topor three years to create. *La Planete
Sauvage* (the original French title actually translates as
"The Wild Planet") is based on a 1957 science fiction
novel by French writer Stephen Wul.

Fantastic Planet tells the story of the conflict between
the Draags, who are 40-foot-tall, red-eyed, blue-skinned
humanoids, and the Oms (a pun on the French word
"homme," which means man), whom they treat as pests
and pets. A young Om, Terr, causes his people to redis-
cover space travel and get the upper hand over the
Draags. The giants are then forced to acknowledge that
the Oms are their equals, and eventually make peace
with them.

The film's animation, which was done in Czechoslo-
vakia, uses a technique of paper cut-outs. What makes
the film truly remarkable, however, is Topor's out-
rageously bizarre designs, such as a giggling plant that
seems to spend most of its time swatting at little animals! The story may appear simplistic to some, but is
well told and suspenseful. And it takes place against
such an arrestingly weird background that the film's
limitations do not seriously hamper its enjoyment.

FRITZ THE CAT

(1972), C, *Directors:* Ralph Bakshi and Steve Krantz.
Animated. **78 min.** *R.* Tape: Warner.

Fritz the Cat holds the dubious honor of having been
the first X-rated, full-length animated cartoon, which
probably contributed to its commercial success in 1972.
Yet, today, this Ralph Bakshi/Steve Krantz production,
inspired by underground comic artist Robert Crumb, has
become a classic.

In spite of a lawsuit brought by the disillusioned
Crumb, who had sold his character for a flat fee, Bakshi's
film is actually fairly faithful to the strip, using many of
Crumb's scenes and story ideas. Nevertheless, the film is
permeated by Bakshi's politics and vision of the 1960s.
These attitudes were to become further concretized in
the director's next film, *Heavy Traffic* (1973). The odyssey of Fritz, a frolicking and slightly sleazy feline, from
the New York pop culture through the Harlem riots and
the left-wing extremists to the California hippies, appears as a kaleidoscopic vision of life in the 1960s.

Fritz the Cat contains some startlingly imaginative
animation, such as the death scene of a pool player. In
this sequence, the movements of pool balls are used to
mirror the slowing thumps of the player's dying heart.
The transformation of human characters into animals,
i.e., policemen being portrayed as pigs, blacks as crows,
etc., is also singularly effective, even if questionable in
taste.

The characters' and the film's preoccupation with sex
may appear somewhat dated to today's audiences. Yet
Fritz the Cat evokes a deep nostalgia and strikes a personal chord in all those who have lived through the
turbulent times so well depicted in the film.

GULLIVER'S TRAVELS

(1939), C, *Director:* Dave Fleischer. *Animated.* **77 min.**
NR. Tape: NTA. CED, Laser: Vestron.

In the middle 1930s there was some doubt whether an audience would sit still for feature-length cartoons. The question was how to balance realism with caricature and sustain interest across all age groups. Walt Disney went a more cartoonlike route; his chief rival of the era, Max Fleischer—famous for his Popeye and Betty Boop cartoons—opted for a more lifelike product.

In Fleischer's first feature, *Gulliver's Travels,* the ship of English physician Lemuel Gulliver is sunk in a storm and he washes ashore on the island of Lilliput. There, he finds the inches-tall Lilliputians at war with the equally diminutive people of neighboring Blefescu, over the issue of whose national anthem should be played at a wedding of state. Surviving an intricate death-plot hatched by spies from Blefescu, Gulliver ends the war by towing Blefescu's warships aground and suggesting a "harmonious" solution to the problems.

Fleischer gave his film full, textured animation as fine as any the screen has seen. His main character moves with graceful realism and speaks in a sonorous voice, which makes us believe in him. Fleischer also worked wonders with lighting and camera angles, creating a visually dynamic film. Especially effective is the lightning, which gives a nightmarish quality to Gulliver's arrival on the beach and his subsequent discovery by the terrified town crier, Gabby. Narratively, the film is also bold in its attempt to capture both a juvenile and adult market. Like the Jonathan Swift novel on which it was based, *Gulliver's Travels* casts a satiric eye on government, giving it a level of political sophistication to which Disney never aspired.

Fleischer's biggest problem was that while Disney was his own man, he worked for Paramount, hamstrung by the studio's creative and budgetary interference. Had they supported his features with more enthusiasm, it is conceivable that they would have had a library equal if not superior to Disney's.

THE LOONEY TUNES VIDEO SHOW

(1940s–1960s), C, (7 volumes). *Directors:* Chuck Jones, Tex Avery, Bob Clampett, Robert McKimson, Friz Freleng, etc. *Animated.* **38 to 60 min.** *NR*. Tape: Warner.

Although Warner's *Looney Tunes* and *Merrie Melodies* are not a full-length feature, this body of work that spans 20 years is something that no fan of animation can ignore.

Under the direction of such giants as Chuck Jones, Tex Avery, Bob Clampett, Robert McKimson, Friz Freleng, etc., an entire universe was formed. Greed and stupidity are the two nemeses that plague characters like Yosemite Sam, Elmer Fudd, or Wile E. Coyote in their hapless encounters with Daffy Duck, Bugs Bunny, or the Road Runner. Other endearing figures of the Warner Universe include Sylvester, the accident-prone cat, who is forever condemned to lust after the unattainable Tweety Pie; the stuttering Porky Pig; the loquacious Foghorn Leghorn; and the inimitable French lover, Pepe Le Pew.

The best collection available on the market is *The Looney Tunes Video Show* (seven volumes available), which contains unedited cartoons dating from the late 1940s to the late 1960s, put together in a peculiarly haphazard fashion. Many of them are classics, such as *8 Ball Bunny* (Chuck Jones, 1950), in which Humphrey Bogart helps Bugs out of several troublesome spots; or *Two Scents Worth* (Chuck Jones, 1955), where the love-struck Pepe pursues a female cat, which has been painted to resemble a skunk, and is understandably undesirous of his attentions.

The Looney Tunes Video Show is a better package than the so-called feature-length films like *Bugs Bunny's 1001 Rabbit Tales* or *Daffy Duck's Fantastic Island,* which consist of classic cartoons edited together and intercut with new material that does not match the quality of the original animation.

THE SECRET OF NIMH

(1982), C, *Director:* Don Bluth. *Animated.* **83 min.** *G.*
Tape, CED, Laser: MGM/UA.

There have been a number of interesting independent animated feature films, from Ralph Bakshi's X-rated *Fritz the Cat* (1972) to the dark science fiction chiller *Fantastic Planet* (1973). All have their singular merits, yet none quite matches the scope, artistry, characterization, and sheer imaginative power of Don Bluth's *The Secret of NIMH*.

Mrs. Brisby is the widow of a mouse who died under mysterious circumstances. Living with her children in a field, her home is threatened when the spring thaw brings the farmer and his harvesting equipment. Seeking help from fellow creatures, such as Jeremy the crow and the Great Owl, she eventually falls in with a race of super-intelligent rats. They were bred at the National Institute of Mental Health, and freed in a final act of self-sacrifice by none other than her husband. However, Mrs. Brisby seeks the rats' help at a time when there is internal dissention about how to conduct their affairs. In as exciting a climax as any animation *or* live-action film has seen, the rival forces come to blows while trying to move Mrs. Brisby's house—at which point, and from a surprising source, Mrs. Brisby discovers that she has magical powers.

Although *The Secret of NIMH* was a box-office failure, former Disney animator Bluth—who went on to create the video games *Dragon's Lair* and *Space Ace*—proved that even if the public traditionally rejects non-Disney animated features, there's still a lot that can be done with the medium. Bluth's characters, though animals, give restrained, atypically human "performances" and, through them, he creates a rat society of interesting characters and even more interesting politics.

Lying somewhere between the naturalism of Fleischer and the fancy of Disney, *The Secret of NIMH* is a work of rare originality and beauty. One hopes Bluth will return to feature cartoon-making soon.

THE THREE CABALLEROS

(1945), C, *Director:* Norman Ferguson. *Animated.*
70 min. *NR.* Tape: Disney.

Not all of the animated features produced by Walt
Disney were paeans to love and devotion. Many were
experimental and quite bizarre, though none is quite so
off-the-wall and full of life as *The Three Caballeros.* For
all the artistry of films like *Snow White and the Seven
Dwarfs* and *Pinocchio,* this travelogue-cum-history lesson can lay claim to being the most fascinating animated
feature of all time.

For his birthday, Donald Duck is given a movie pro-
jector. After screening a cartoon about a cold-hating
penguin named Pablo and another about a flying don-
key, he opens a package containing his nutty parrot pal,
Joe Carioca. The two tour Mexico—which is shown via
live-action clips and stunning animation—before being
joined by the lunatic, gun-toting rooster, Panchito. After
the trip, the three friends celebrate Donald's birthday in
what has to be the most frenetic and surrealistic animation ever created.

The Three Caballeros is a smorgasbord of artistic
styles and narrative treasures, as likely to hop from a
history of Christmas in Mexico, to a Donald-in-space
"dream sequence," to dancing cacti. Less structured
than *Fantasia,* it is at once more unpredictable and endlessly entertaining. It is also a remarkable *ensemble*
piece, the characters playing off one another with hilarious results. Indeed, the "Three Caballeros" number,
with Donald and Joe trying to prevent Panchito from
singing, is something the Marx Brothers might have
designed had they turned to animation.

Children may prefer the more structured and traditional *Dumbo,* but *The Three Caballeros* is in a class by
itself.

TOM & JERRY CARTOONS

(1940s–1950s), C, (3 volumes). *Directors:* Bill Hanna and
Joseph Barbera. *Animated.* **58 to 60 min.** *NR*. Tape,
CED (except Vol. III): MGM/UA.

Tom and Jerry are, unquestionably, the most famous
cat-and-mouse team in media history. Created in 1939
for MGM by Bill Hanna and Joseph Barbera as a one-
shot gag, Tom and Jerry became immediate hits.

Those familiar with the names of Hanna and Barbera
from the pitiful shadows of animation that adorn Saturday mornings, should not allow themselves to be preju-
diced against Tom and Jerry. Created for theatrical release before parents' groups called for the censoring of
cartoons, these collections are a delight to watch. Their
quality was recognized by the Motion Picture Academy,
which awarded them seven Oscars—more than any
other animated characters.

The frantic pace of the cartoons, the droll ambiance of
the situations, and the actions of the characters create a
feeling of slapstick that is very different from the surrealistic world of Warner Brothers' *Looney Tunes* and
Merrie Melodies. In fact, Tom and Jerry almost seem to
be animated versions of a human comedy team, such as
Laurel and Hardy. They are at their best when the
stories reflect Tom's single-minded pursuit of Jerry, although there are some wonderful moments when the
team is joined by Spike the Bulldog or Little Nibbles, the
ever-hungry baby mouse.

There are three volumes in release so far, which in-
clude some of the Oscar-winning cartoons such as *Cat
Concerto* (1947), where Jerry sabotages Tom's concert of
Liszt's Hungarian Rhapsody No. 2; and *The Little
Orphan* (1949), which has Jerry and Little Nibbles going
to war with Tom over a Thanksgiving dinner.

WATERSHIP DOWN

(1978), C, *Director:* Martin Rosen. *Animated.* **92 min.**
PG. Tape: Warner; CED: RCA VideoDisc.

Richard Adams's best-selling book about a community of rabbits forced to leave their home, and their
ensuing struggle in a hostile world to create a new one,
posed a number of challenges to filmmaker Martin
Rosen. Yet the result is a film that almost miraculously
manages to be both faithful to Adams's semiallegorical
tale and a wonderful animated picture.

Rosen's rabbits have preserved Adams's vision. They
are neither cute, like Disney's, nor zany, like Warners'.
They are only slightly anthropomorphized and retain
their basic animal characteristics. As in Adams's book,
they have a culture of their own, with legends and oral
traditions. Adams's rabbits look at man as man looks at
his Gods, and Rosen has cleverly incorporated this
quasi-mythological aspect of the story in his film
through the use of simplified but beautiful animation.
The story of God's creation of the world, as seen by the
rabbits, is a striking case in point.

The animation, done by a talented crew of British
artists, is vastly different and superior to that usually
found in children's films. The picture contains a unique
sense of depth and detail, with moving shots during
animated sequences (which may well be a first). Even
the backgrounds are beautifully rendered, in a style
reminiscent of fine British watercolors.

Because it is respectful of its source, *Watership Down*
contains much violence. The film does not hide the
cruelty of Nature, and many scenes may be considered
too gory for younger viewers. About the only comic relief
in the film is provided by the character of Keehar, a
loony seagull with Zero Mostel's voice. But the violence
in *Watership Down* is never exploitative or degrading. It
is honest, like the rest of this wonderful film.

Rosen later adapted another, possibly even grimmer,
Adams book, *The Plague Dogs,* but sadly for true fans of
animation, he has not been able to release his film in this
country.

ART FILMS

The films in this chapter are those that are primarily concerned with exploring the artistic possibilities of film —the ones in which filmmakers take chances, often substituting unusual creative techniques for traditional means of storytelling. These films were made to be shown in theaters; much of their subtlety lies hidden at the edges of the screen or within the dense properties of film itself. They may not always translate successfully to a small screen. Although many great actors and actresses appear in these films, they are primarily a director's medium—often mood is more important than characterization, and originality more important than coherency. We chose films for this section that are accessible: They operate quite well as entertainment. They will, however, require a good deal of concentration. Besides the films discussed in this chapter, other fine Art Films available on video are: *The American Friend, Barry Lyndon, Interiors, Manhattan, Picnic at Hanging Rock, Repulsion, Rumble Fish, Saint Jack, The Tenant,* and *Zelig.* Note: Many similar films are discussed in the Foreign Films chapter.

Potemkin. *The Odessa Steps sequence from one of the most praised films of all time. Video allows viewers to study the intricate and intelligent editing of filmmaker Sergei Eisenstein.*

BADLANDS

(1973), C, *Director:* Terence Malick. *With* Martin Sheen, Sissy Spacek, Warren Oates, Ramon Bieri, and Alan Vint. **95 min.** *PG*. Tape, Laser: Warner.

The heroes of director Terence Malick's sleek, stunningly photographed debut picture are a pair of young killers as cold and affectless as Bonnie and Clyde were hot and bothered. Based on the actual killing spree of Charles Starkweather and Caril Ann Fugate in the late 1950s, *Badlands* presents its young killers as heartless crusaders on an abstract, existential quest. These kids don't know where they're going or why they're killing people, and this icy amorality is meant to reflect the amorality of the culture at large; an America that turns killers like Charles Starkweather into glamorous celebrities. Kit Carruthers (Martin Sheen) is a free-spirited rascal who corrals a passive teenager named Holly (Sissy Spacek) into a love affair. He kills her father (Warren Oates), who had tried to put a stop to their affair. The two escape from the law by setting out on a trek through the Badlands of South Dakota, with the trigger-happy Kit blowing away anyone who gets in the way. Sheen doesn't have abundant depth as an actor, but here his surface proficiency fits in perfectly, since Kit himself is a kind of empty vessel who models himself on James Dean. He's a figure at once hollow and romantic, and Malick underlines his ambivalence toward the character through the stark beauty of his images. *Badlands* was one of the key movies of the 1970s.

BLOW–UP

(1966), **B/W,** *Director:* Michelangelo Antonioni. *With*
David Hemmings, Vanessa Redgrave, Sarah Miles, Jill
Kennington, and Verushka. **108 min.** *NR.* Tape:
MGM/UA.

Blow-Up, director Michelangelo Antonioni's meta-
physical whodunit, is that rare philosophical movie
that's as much fun to watch as it is to think about. The
story is a logical puzzle, but the mood is one of stylish
angst. Art film connoisseurs have long admired this
story of a chic London fashion photographer who thinks
he may have photographed a murder. Wandering
through a lush city park one afternoon, the unnamed
photographer (David Hemmings) spots a woman (Vanessa Redgrave) and a man who appears to be her lover.
Being part voyeur and part aesthete, he begins to snap
pictures of them. Moments later, he finds the man dead
on the grass; and when he blows up one of the photos to
huge, grainy proportions, the image seems to reveal a
gunman hidden in the bushes. The photographer becomes obsessed with this photograph as he tries unsuc-
cessfully to decipher just what exactly is in his picture.
The photographer is presented as an amoral man who
sees the world through a camera lens. He's at once a
stand-in for the 1960s generation, with their excessive
appetite for sensation, and a surrogate for Antonioni, in
that he is an artist doomed to a state of frustrated isolation. We may not care much for this photographer as a
human being, but we can appreciate his confusion and
admire his persistence. Antonioni's colorful vision of
"swinging London" is an artfully magnified and exaggerated view of the city. The glistening pace and tele-
scopic visual effects become a perfect metaphor for the
photographer's way of seeing. *Blow-Up* is memorable
not for the profundity of its illusion-and-reality theme,
but because that theme is expressed so eloquently
through the medium of cinema. Also notable: the fine
rock-and-roll score by The Yardbirds.

THE CONVERSATION

(1974), C, *Director:* **Francis Ford Coppola.** *With* **Gene Hackman, John Cazale, Allan Garfield, Frederic Forrest, Cindy Williams, Teri Garr, and Harrison Ford. 113 min.** *PG.* **Tape, Laser: Paramount.**

Trying to tap into the paranoia and surveillance mania of the Watergate era, most directors would have been content with producing a suspense yarn about an undercover operator who finds himself in danger of being "exposed." Director Francis Ford Coppola was inspired to choose as his wiretapping hero a sad, wayward lump of a man; and to show him in conflict not with the government or the press, but with his own quivering psyche. Gene Hackman plays Harry Call, a freelance surveillance whiz who'll spy on anybody for a price. Coppola's brilliant direction puts us at the very center of Harry's whirring high-tech universe. Harry is such a four-square schmoe that he's not the least bit intrigued by the secret tapes he's always delivering to his clients. At least, not until he realizes that one conversation may hold the clues to a murderous conspiracy. For the first time in his career, Harry is forced to take action, but the only thing he can think to do is more wiretapping. This electronic *Heart of Darkness* leads him deeper into his own paranoia and further away from the reality he seeks. Hackman uses his shy grin and chinless middle-aged demeanor to create in Harry a walking blank; a man with such a weak hold on his own identity that listening in on other people's conversations somehow completes him. By now, one can easily see *The Conversation* as an autobiographical statement from a director who has become consumed in the last few years by forays into high technology.

Blow-Up. *Photographer David Hemmings tempts and tortures Vanessa Redgrave with the photographic evidence of what she has done. What has she done? What has he seen? Blow-Up is a mystery in which the understanding is much more important than the answers.*

Don't Look Now. *Donald Sutherland examines the mosaic tiles from the mural he must restore. He will soon discover the dangers inherent in working with only a part of the picture—in his case a part of his future.*

DON'T LOOK NOW

(1973), C, *Director:* Nicolas Roeg. *With* Donald
Sutherland, Julie Christie, Hilary Mason, Clelia
Matania, and Massimo Serato. **110 min.** *R.* Tape, CED,
Laser: Paramount.

Gothic material has probably never received such an
arty, poker-faced treatment as it gets in director Nicolas
Roeg's classic chiller, *Don't Look Now.* Based on a
Daphne du Maurier novel, it is an incredibly elaborate
modern ghost story. John and Laura Baxter (Donald
Sutherland and Julie Christie) are the parents of a little
blonde girl who drowns in a pond in the opening scene.
The couple travels to Venice, where John is directing the
restoration of an ancient cathedral. Once there, they
begin to receive messages—disquieting signs that their
dead daughter is still with them. Laura thinks these
signs may be significant, but John cannot accept this.
John's continuous refusal to acknowledge the possibility
of his daughter's spiritual presence leads him to the
movie's terrifying climax. It's a moment that will haunt
you for weeks to come. Roeg's jarring, fragmentary techniques might seem at odds with a du Maurier tale of the
supernatural, but his hyper-realistic style, with its
jump-cuts and surgical close-ups of crumbling Venetian
ruins, seduces the viewer into this world in a way that
hokey omens (as in *The Haunting*) never could. Sutherland and Christie have a steamy sex scene here (it barely
escaped getting an X rating), yet the characters they
play are often distant towards each other. For Roeg, the
forces that keep sophisticated modern people in their
own emotional space are also those that keep them from
believing in the unseen.

HIROSHIMA, MON AMOUR

(1959), B/W, *Director:* Alain Resnais. *With* Eiji Okada,
Emmanuele Riva, Stella Dassas, and Pierre Barband.
88 min. *NR*. Tape: Budget.

   The same year Francois Truffaut and Jean-Luc
Godard were spearheading the New Wave with films
about adolescence (*The Four Hundred Blows*) and gangsters (*Breathless*), their colleague-in-arms Alain
Resnais was off making . . . a love story. Not that *Hiroshima, Mon Amour* is your everyday boy-meets-girl
saga. It is, rather, a Proustian swirl of memory and
emotion, as Resnais looks at the impassioned affair of a
Japanese architect (Eiji Okada) and a French actress
(Emmanuele Riva) who meet in Hiroshima in 1950. The
actress has come to the island to make a movie about the
1945 bombings—and Resnais' film begins with an un-
settling semi-documentary look at the H-bomb's cata-
strophic effects. At first, you may think the movie is
going to be anti-bomb agitprop, but Resnais is after
something subtler. Though appalled by what happened
to Hiroshima, he's made a movie about the bomb's
haunting effects on the rest of us, a look at how the fear
and dread of living in the nuclear age can seep into the
most precious corners of our lives. Resnais cuts back and
forth in time, setting the hushed intimacies of the
doomed love affair against actual footage of Hiroshima
survivors. To scout the film for facile answers is to miss
the point. Resnais is, above all, a master of mood; and the
dark, desultory atmosphere of *Hiroshima, Mon Amour*
(complemented by a gorgeous Georges Delerue score)
remains the movie's most memorable achievement.

LAST TANGO IN PARIS

(1973), C, *Director:* Bernardo Bertolucci. *With* Marlon
Brando, Maria Schneider, Jean-Pierre Leaud, Darling
Legitimos, Catherine Sola, Mauro Marchetti, and Dan
Diament. **159 min.** *R.* Tape, Laser: CBS/Fox; CED: RCA
VideoDisc.

The movie that launched a thousand butter jokes has
never quite outgrown its reputation as an arty sex film.
That's a shame, since director Bernardo Bertolucci's
story of a haunted expatriate (Marlon Brando) who
spends several days staging his sexual fantasies with a
young Parisian (Maria Schneider) was never meant to
be a "turn on." It is, rather, a look at the gap between
desire and fulfillment, and only when approached as an
enigmatic character study can it truly be enjoyed—or
understood. Brando's performance *is* the movie. His
Paul is a middle-aged drifter whose wife has just committed suicide, and inside the character there are frag-
ments of every seething, cynical brooder that Brando
ever played. In his rambling monologues and the searing, emotionally naked sex scenes with the girl, one
detects the tragic despair of a man who's given up all
hope of finding salvation. Despite its sensationalistic
overtones, the movie's main impression is one of nostalgic melancholy. Bertolucci shoots Paris through a
late-afternoon haze of yellows and oranges, and Gato
Barbieri's score seems drenched in the sadness of half-
submerged memories. What finally makes *Last Tango*
special is that, as Paul spirals toward his self-destruc-
tive end, you feel you're actually watching a man use up
his entire life.

MY DINNER WITH ANDRE

(1981), C, *Director:* Louis Malle. *With* Andre Gregory
and Wallace Shawn. **110 min.** *PG*. Tape: Pacific Arts.

It's the sort of wondrously simple premise that anyone
could have come up with, but no one brought off until *My
Dinner with Andre*: a film about two people talking.
Conversation makes up the entire movie—there is no
plot, action, or drama in the accepted sense of those
words. What could easily have become mundane and
boring is, instead, a fascinating visit to the netherminds
of two very different men.

Avant-garde theater director Andre Gregory and
playwright Wallace Shawn (both playing exaggerated
versions of themselves) meet at a posh French restaurant, order a succulent meal, and talk. Their dinner-
table conversation, though meticulously scripted
(Shawn spent months taping their real dinner conversations, which were distilled into a seamless 90-minute
script) has the spontaneous, natural texture of a documentary. We feel we are eavesdropping on their conversation. Exuberant talkers both, they turn a casual
reunion dinner into the setting for a rangy, high-
powered debate about the meaning of life. Andre, the
dashing, middle-aged charmer, describes at great length
his globe-trotting quests for spiritual enlightenment.
The bald, Yoda-like Wally listens attentively. Finally,
Wally rises up to defend the supreme pleasures of everyday life in the material world. Who's right? That's beside
the point. Anyone who has ever engaged in a late-night
rap session will recognize these two verbal warriors. The
talkfest jumps from Western theater to Eastern mysti-
cism, from New York City to Auschwitz, from the im-
perial joys of scaling Mt. Everest to the cozy comforts of
electric blankets. What's wonderful about *My Dinner
with Andre* is that it celebrates conversation not just as a
vehicle for ideas, but as a way of turning our daily lives
into creative acts. And as a film, it rekindles our wonder
at the dramatic power of "mere" talk.

POTEMKIN

(1925), B/W, *Director:* Sergei Eisenstein. *With*
Alexander Antorov, Vladimir Barsky, Grigori
Alexandrov, and Mikhail Goronorov. **67 min.** *NR*. Tape:
Budget.

If D. W. Griffith was the first director to stitch images
together into a rich, dynamic narrative, then Sergei
Eisenstein was the first to use narrative as a vehicle for
rich, dynamic imagery. *Potemkin,* his silent masterpiece, has the primitive visual power of a propaganda
poster come to life. Reenacting the Russian workers'
uprising aboard the Battleship Potemkin in 1905, Eisenstein uses the screen as a giant canvas. Characters
and events are organized into a Marxist fable that succeeds on a level far grander than that of its rather
simple-minded story. The scenes before the mutiny are
coldly horrifying. The camera has been placed well back
to reveal the entire deck of the ship, where a group of
disobedient soldiers is being herded under a tarpaulin by
brutish superiors and assassinated. In the famous
Odessa Steps sequence, the director uses rapidly juxtaposed images to create a bold cinematic metaphor for the
terrifying chaos that violence provokes. This sequence,
with its scurrying crowds, goose-stepping soldiers, and
the baby carriage that bounds down the stairs like a tiny
runaway caboose, is perhaps the single most celebrated
10 minutes in movie history. Watching it, one feels both
the horror of the events themselves and a ticklish wonder at seeing them miraculously converted into art.

THE SHOUT

(1979), C, *Director:* Jerzy Skolimowski. *With* John Hurt, Susannah York, Alan Bates, Robert Stephens, and Tim Curry. **87 min.** *R.* Tape: RCA/Columbia.

For those who like their psychodrama with a dash of supernaturalism, this fascinating fable from director Jerzy Skolimowski is made to order. It begins, simply enough, as the tale of an adulterous man (John Hurt) deceiving his loving wife (Susannah York), but soon unfolds into an ominous account of the sinister control the mysterious Crossley (Alan Bates) gains over the two. From the second Crossley enters their cozy country lives, flexing his eyebrows and looking like a British Rasputin, it's clear that he's up to no good. Skolimowski's direction invests every cobblestone street and cloud-covered landscape with an ominous life of its own. The three engage in assorted Pinteresque cat-and-mice scenes, but there's something more afoot. During his 18 years in the Australian outback, Crossley has learned some uncanny tricks; foremost among them is the ability to produce a lethal shout. He soon comes to threaten not only this couple's marriage but their lives and souls. His bone-chilling shout (accomplished with the aid of impressive electronic sound effects) is Skolimowski's most precarious idea, and with another actor in the role the movie might have tipped toward contrivance. But Alan Bates has both the physical presence to suggest impending violence and the intelligence to make the character's mystical abilities seem emblems of some otherworldly knowledge beyond our ken. It is ironic that the slightly haughty, quiet-spoken man who tells the entire story is this same Crossley. If there are a few incongruities in the story line, they are of little consequence in a film as compelling and provocative as *The Shout*.

SMASH PALACE

(1981), **C,** *Director:* Roger Donaldson. *With* Bruno
Lawrence, Anna Jemison, Greer Robson, Keith
Aberdein, and Desmond Kelly. **100 min.** *NR*. Tape:
Vestron.

This unheralded domestic drama from New Zealand's
Roger Donaldson (who went on to direct *The Bounty*) is a
portrait of a crumbling marriage that is quietly more
powerful than *Shoot the Moon.* The two films contain
remarkably similar stories that investigate the same
emotional terrain. But in *Smash Palace* (the first made)
the couple under scrutiny are as earthy and natural as
Moon's were chic and Hollywood-theatrical. To an un-
precedented degree you feel you're watching the disinte-
gration of a *real* marriage, with all the passion and
violence that entails; the protective glitter of cinema has
been scraped away. Bald, glowering Bruno Lawrence is
Al, a former race-car driver who spends his days running
a dilapidated wrecking yard and tinkering with his
souped-up autos. Al treats his young daughter like a
princess and his wife like a doormat. One sees both the
product of the love that once sustained this marriage and
the hate that has turned it poisonous. The film's centerpiece is a long, tangled squabble that becomes a brilliantly choreographed sex scene in which the characters
still appear to be wrestling—not just with each other,
but with their own warring emotions. The volcano
erupts, as Al, who's been denied the right to see his
daughter, devises an insanely desperate kidnapping
scheme that is carried out with frightening single-
mindedness. In *Smash Palace,* a man is driven to brutal
actions, yet there's no fake catharsis here, no trumped-
up sense of tragedy. What's wrenching about the movie
is the way the characters try to create resolutions for
themselves where none exist.

COMEDIES

Comedy is often a matter of personal preference—what is funny to one person may be dull to another. More often than not, however, comedy is bound by time—the Comedies of one generation simply don't jell with another. (Remember Ma and Pa Kettle? *Francis, the Talking Mule*?) We chose Comedies for this section that have withstood the test of time, that are as funny today as they were years ago. Comedy Films are ideal for home video; they work wonderfully on the small screen, which appeals more to the mind than to the eye. Although many films within this book are funny, the films in this chapter are Comedies *first:* Their main goal is to get the laughs, regardless of any other point they might have. Other fine Comedies to consider are: *Airplane!, Animal House, Bananas, My Man Godfrey, The Pink Panther, Sleeper, To Be or Not To Be* (both versions), *Tootsie, Young Frankenstein,* and several collections of comedy shorts from W. C. Fields, Charlie Chaplin, Harold Lloyd, and Buster Keaton.

Dr. Strangelove. *The Security Council decides whether to annihilate the world in this darkest of black comedies.*

THE BANK DICK

(1940), B/W, *Director:* Eddie Cline. *With* W.C. Fields,
Franklin Pangborn, Grady Sutton, Shemp Howard,
Cora Witherspoon, Una Merkel, Evelyn Del Rio, and
Jessica Ralph. **74 min.** *NR.* Tape: MCA.

By the age of 61 many film stars are washed up or
relegated to playing bit parts. And there are few things
sadder than a 61-year-old has-been comedian. Yet at
that age, W.C. Fields—never one to play by the rules—
turned out one of the funniest films ever made. *The Bank
Dick* is as close to perfect as a screen comedy can get,
containing a screwball plot, witty dialogue, superb slapstick, top-notch supporting characters, and the Great
Man himself at the peak of his considerable comic powers.

Fields's screenplay (written under the nom de plume
"Mahatma Kane Jeeves") rails against his favorite targets of home, family, and law, while plugging his favorite vices of drinking, smoking, fooling around, and petty
larceny. Such is his satiric gift that he makes this anti-
social position seem not merely palatable but *right.* As
the harried Egbert Souse, Fields accidentally foils a
bank robbery, wins a job as a bank detective, convinces
his future son-in-law to embezzle $500 from the bank,
manages to keep the bank examiner from discovering
the crime, and tangles again with a bank robber. Along
the way he takes over the direction of a picture, chang-
ing the script so that the ingenue becomes a bearded
lady. When she protests, he assures her it's "only a short
beard—a Van Dyke."

"The most hilarious sequence is Fields's attempt to
keep the bank examiner away from the bank. "Has
Michael Finn been in lately?" Fields says meaningfully
to the bartender, Joe. "No, but he will be," Joe replies,
and slips him a drink that keeps him nauseous for three
days. Fields torments him by talking about such deli-
cacies as "steaming hot pork sandwiches garnished with
codfish gravy." Another highlight is the climactic chase
scene, from which almost every succeeding film chase
has borrowed.

BROADWAY DANNY ROSE

(1984), B/W, *Director:* Woody Allen. *With* Allen, Mia
Farrow, and Nick Apollo Forte. **85 min.** *PG*. Tape:
Vestron.

Woody Allen's twelfth feature as writer/director is his
greatest critical and commercial success since *Manhattan*. It has much in common with that work: it's a romantic comedy shot in black and white, it's set in the New
York he loves, and it touches on the show business world
he knows so well.

Allen's Danny Rose is a small-time theatrical agent;
very small-time—his clients include a one-legged tap
dancer, a one-armed juggler, and a penguin who roller-
skates across the stage while dressed as a rabbi. When
Danny does manage to locate an act with real talent,
they don't stay with him for long, because he doesn't
have the clout or the ruthlessness to help them. The
movie is really an extended anecdote about one particularly comic and poignant episode in Danny's career, his
relationship with a has-been crooner named Lou Canova
(Nick Apollo Forte). Danny helps Lou make a comeback,
giving him such sage advice as, "Don't forget to do 'My
Funny Valentine' with the special lyrics about the moon
landing." Then Danny meets Lou's mistress, Tina (wonderfully played by Mia Farrow), a tough Mafia widow
who says of her husband's murder by his associates, "He
had it comin'." Through Tina, Danny gets in trouble
with the mob, and the two of them go on the lam together. Naturally, they fall in love along the way. But as
in the screwball comedies of the 1930s and 1940s,
romance comes somewhat reluctantly and love runs a
distant second to laughter. There's not a dull or dim-
witted moment in the film.

Woody's writing and directing keep getting better,
and it's a special pleasure to see Milton Berle and other
comics playing themselves and having a ball. Attentive
viewers will find traces of Damon Runyon, Charles
Dickens, and Frank Capra in this comedy, but in the end
Broadway Danny Rose is pure Woody Allen. And who
could ask for more?

DR. STRANGELOVE

(1964), B/W, *Director:* Stanley Kubrick. *With* Peter
Sellers, George C. Scott, Sterling Hayden, Slim Pickens,
Keenan Wynn, Peter Bull, and James Earl Jones.
93 min. *NR.* Tape, CED, Laser: RCA/Columbia.

Director/writer Stanley Kubrick is not noted for his
cheery outlook, so it's appropriate that his one comedy
should be a black one lampooning the end of civilization
by a nuclear holocaust. What's amazing is how many
laughs he's able to milk out of a genuinely horrifying
situation without mitigating the horror. *Dr. Strangelove: Or, How I Learned to Stop Worrying and Love the
Bomb* captures the irony and insanity of the nuclear age
as a serious film like, say, *Fail Safe,* can't hope to do.

The plot is precisely that of *Fail Safe* in fact, but
played for laughs: American bombers are accidentally
launched in a preemptive strike against the Soviet
Union. The strike is called by General Jack Ripper
(Sterling Hayden), a paranoid psychotic who believes
the commies are trying to "sap and impurify all of our
precious bodily fluids." After the launching, the President admits to Soviet Premier Kissoff that "One of our
base commanders . . . went and did a silly thing," and
the race is on to recall the planes. Slim Pickens, better
known as a Hollywood cowboy, has a terrific role as
Major Kong, pilot of the plane that can't be stopped.
George C. Scott proves he can play comedy as brilliantly
as drama in his portrayal of General Buck Turgidson, a
hardcore military man.

The film belongs to Peter Sellers, who plays three
hilarious characters: the timid U.S. President who says
things like, "Gentlemen, you can't fight in here, this is
the War Room"; British Colonel Lionel Mandrake, who
tries to halt General Ripper; and the demented Dr.
Strangelove, a not-so-ex-Nazi working as U.S. director
of weapons research who unconsciously calls the President "mein fuhrer." Sellers' work here is arguably the
finest of his career. The subtle yet savagely dark humor
of *Dr. Strangelove* has become more pertinent in the 20
years since its release.

DUCK SOUP

(1933), B/W, *Director:* Leo McCarey. *With* The Marx Brothers (Groucho, Harpo, Chico, Zeppo), Margaret Dumont, Edgar Kennedy, and Edmund Breese. **72 min.** *NR.* Tape: MCA; CED: RCA VideoDisc.

Duck Soup was a commercial flop when it was first released in 1933, which caused Paramount to drop The Marx Brothers (or vice versa). Today it is recognized as their best film and one of the two or three funniest pictures of all time. It is also the last film featuring all four Marxes—Groucho, Harpo, Chico, and Zeppo.

The witty script is by Tin Pan Alley songwriters Bert Kalmar and Harry Ruby. They give Groucho his most supremely ridiculous role as Rufus T. Firefly, unlikely leader of the fictitious land of Freedonia. Groucho starts a war with the neighboring country of Sylvania by insulting the ambassador and everyone else within earshot. Then he refuses any attempt to avoid the war because he's "already paid a month's rent on the battlefield." Most of Groucho's lines still sound fresh more than 50 years later. Harpo and Chico are not left out. They have a series of classic slapstick encounters with an enraged lemonade vendor (Edgar Kennedy) and a number of other comic bits, though for once Harpo doesn't get to play the harp, and Chico doesn't play the piano. Zeppo may be a straight man, but he's the best one his brothers ever had; and their eternal straight woman, Margaret Dumont, is in top form here as well, dutifully enduring such insults as, "Remember, you're fighting for this woman's honor, which is probably more than she ever did."

Even the songs are funny, including a mock spiritual entitled, "All God's Chillun Got Guns." *Duck Soup* also contains the famous "mirror scene" in which Harpo and Chico dress like Groucho and mime his every move. Animal lovers should note the wickedly funny sight gag in which Harpo slips past the censors the suggestion of a ménage à trois between a man, a woman, and a horse.

THE GOLD RUSH

(1925), B/W, *Director:* Charlie Chaplin. *With* Charlie
Chaplin, Georgia Hale, Mack Swain, and Tom Murray.
82 min. *NR.* Tape: Budget.

Charlie Chaplin is the best and most fascinating filmmaker of the silent picture era, and when he goes all out
for laughs he gets as many as anyone before or since.

The Gold Rush showcases both sides of Chaplin—the
irrepressible comic and the serious artist—to full advantage. It contains some of his funniest as well as his most
touching moments, and it is the last of his films to favor
comedy over romance. *The Gold Rush* is about hunger:
for food, for wealth, and for love. Its plot, that old cinema standby of boy-meets-girl, with boy-finds-fortune
thrown in for good measure, is not new. But Chaplin's
unique embellishments as writer, director, and performer set this comedy apart from all others. In one
scene, for example, Charlie and his Alaskan prospecting
buddy, Big Jim (Mack Swain), are so hungry that they
cook and eat one of Charlie's shoes—an idea that has
been used a hundred times since. Yet Chaplin's version
of the gag never palls. Another comic highlight is the
scene in which Big Jim is so hungry that he envisions
Charlie as an immense chicken and chases him around
the cabin with an ax.

Chaplin had a penchant for beautiful leading ladies,
and Georgia Hale is perhaps the most lovely. She plays a
dance hall girl who pretends to return Charlie's affections as a joke, before she really falls for him. Chaplin's
adroitness is at its most breathtaking and heartbreaking when Georgia stands him up on New Year's Eve.
Charlie falls asleep waiting for her, dreaming their date
as it ought to be. He sticks a dinner roll on the end of each
of two forks and uses them as impromptu "legs" to mime
a miniature dance hall girl doing the cancan. Only
Chaplin could pull this off. The video version of *The Gold
Rush* is not the silent original, but the 1942 rerelease
with narration and a lush, moving musical score by
Chaplin himself. Chaplin's last short, *Pay Day,* is also
included as a bonus.

HIS GIRL FRIDAY

(1940), B/W, *Director:* Howard Hawks. *With* Cary
Grant, Rosalind Russell, and Ralph Bellamy. **92 min.**
NR. Tape: Budget.

His Girl Friday is one of the very few remakes that
takes an excellent film and actually improves on it.
Director Howard Hawks starts with Hecht and Mac-
Arthur's *The Front Page,* about the good-natured battle
between a newspaper editor and his favorite reporter,
and gives it more comic twists.

The reporter in Hawks's version is a woman—the
editor's ex-wife—and she's about to marry a chump just
to spite her ex. There's also some complicated nonsense
about a guy down on his luck who goes temporarily
insane and shoots a policeman. With Hawks's legendary
breakneck pace, the result is one of the finest examples of
screwball comedy. Perhaps the acting has a little something to do with it, too; Cary Grant plays the charming
but unscrupulous editor, Walter Burns, and Rosalind
Russell is his star reporter, Hilde Johnson. They get to
trade such romantic lines as, "Divorce makes a fellow
. . . feel he isn't wanted," and, "I am fond of you, you
know; I often wish you weren't such a stinker." Walter
has several goals in his conniving mind: to save the
killer from hanging, to have Hilde cover the case in her
inimitable style, and to keep Hilde from marrying Bruce
Baldwin (Ralph Bellamy), a nice but hopelessly dull
insurance man.

Walter has Bruce framed and sent to jail on several
minor charges, and tricks Hilde into covering just one
more story before her aborted honeymoon.

The ending isn't hard to guess, and anyway, the story
is merely an excuse for Grant and Russell to ham up the
deliciously malicious dialogue. As in all of Hawks's
films, the female lead is strong-willed, sarcastic, and
independent. Don't even try to catch everything the first
time around but listen closely for the comic asides muttered throughout by cynical newspapermen.

MONTY PYTHON'S THE MEANING OF LIFE

(1983), C, *Director:* Terry Jones. *With* Graham
Chapman, John Cleese, Terry Gilliam, Eric Idle, Terry
Jones, and Michael Palin. **107 min.** *R*. Tape, CED,
Laser: MCA.

The Monty Python troupe and Woody Allen are the
only contemporary comedians producing films of lasting
value. Not that the Python's films are flawless. On the
contrary. Like their celebrated BBC television series,
their features are a mixed bag, sometimes awfully funny
and sometimes simply awful. But when they're on target, the Pythons are funnier than anyone.

The Meaning of Life duplicates the free style of their
Flying Circus program, with a much larger budget and
no interference from the censors. *The Meaning of Life* is
willfully outrageous and frequently offensive, but almost always comical. The advantage of watching it on
video is that one can skip over the obnoxious or unfunny
parts and cut right to the brilliant moments, of which
there are many.

The opening sequence is the best—a mini-epic in the
grand fantasy style of Terry Gilliam's *Time Bandits*—
involving a group of doddering insurance clerks who
commandeer their building and "sail" it like a pirate
vessel through the financial district, plundering other
buildings. It's done with wonderful panache and can be
wholeheartedly recommended to children. After this
scene they should be sent to bed. It wouldn't do to have
them see "Part I: The Miracle of Birth," in which John
Cleese and Graham Chapman play doctors in charge of
the Fetus Frightening Room, or "Part II: Growth and
Learning," with Michael Palin as a pastor leading
schoolboys in the hymn, "Oh Lord, Please Don't Burn
Us," or the infamous "Part VI: The Autumn Years,"
wherein director Terry Jones portrays the fattest and
vilest man in the world. What with this and "Part V:
Live Organ Transplants," *The Meaning of Life* is not for
the timid or the prudish. But then neither is Chaucer.

A SHOT IN THE DARK

(1964), C, *Director:* Blake Edwards. *With* Peter Sellers, Herbert Lom, Elke Sommer, George Sanders, and Graham Stark. **103 min.** *NR.* Tape, CED, Laser: CBS/Fox.

If Peter Sellers had done nothing but appear in the Pink Panther films, he would still be remembered as one of the most gifted comic actors ever to face a camera. His Inspector Clouseau ranks with Chaplin's Little Tramp and other cinema immortals as a truly inspired invention. Nowhere is he in better form than in *A Shot in the Dark,* the second in the Panther series. It is with this film that Sellers's characterization really solidifies, revealing the full measure of Clouseau's glorious ineptitude.

A Shot in the Dark introduces those two indispensable foils, Commissioner Dreyfuss (Herbert Lom) and Kato (Bert Kwouk). Here we first see Dreyfuss reduced to a shuddering wreck by Clouseau's hideous and hilarious bungling. This film also begins Kato's honorable tradition of attacking his boss Clouseau when he least suspects it, in order to keep him prepared for anything. Director Blake Edwards is apparently the only modern American filmmaker—aside from Woody Allen—with a serious interest in slapstick. He is the current master of physical comedy, and in combination with the agile Sellers he pulls off some of the best sight gags since the silent era; including a game of billiards played with a bent cue, and the climactic scene in which Sellers artfully stumbles over everything and everyone. Whether he's spraying the ink from a fountain pen onto a suspect, getting his hand caught in a spinning globe, walking into walls, or trying to synchronize a stopped watch, Sellers's Clouseau is a continual delight.

Never mind the plot (in this case a murder mystery with Elke Sommer as the prime suspect). Its only purpose is to provide another impossible case for Clouseau to solve with his invincible incompetence. As Dreyfuss intones, "Give me 10 men like Clouseau and I could destroy the world."

Monty Python's The Meaning of Life. *Terry Jones plays the world's fattest man in the outrageous restaurant sketch. After devouring nearly everything on the menu, he goes just a bit too far.*

Some Like It Hot. *A couple of jazz musicians (Tony Curtis and Jack Lemmon) on the lam from a gangster named "Spats" (George Raft) find themselves at his feet, ear-witnessing his conversation. Among other things, the film slyly spoofs the Hollywood image of the gangster.*

SOME LIKE IT HOT

(1959), B/W, *Director:* Billy Wilder. *With* Tony Curtis,
Jack Lemmon, Marilyn Monroe, Joe E. Brown, George
Raft, and Pat O'Brien. **120 min.** *NR*. Tape, Laser:
CBS/Fox; CED: RCA VideoDisc.

Forget *Tootsie. Some Like It Hot* is the original and
superior article, the father (or rather, mother) of all
succeeding drag comedies. *Tootsie* may be funny, but it
can't hold a training bra to this comic masterpiece,
which boasts a script and direction by the incomparable
Billy Wilder. It stars Tony Curtis, Jack Lemmon, and
Marilyn Monroe in their most laughable roles.

The year is 1929, and Curtis and Lemmon are Chicago
speakeasy musicians looking for work. After accidentally witnessing the St. Valentine's Day Massacre,
they hide from the mob by donning wigs and dresses.
They land jobs with an all-girl band in Florida as
"Josephine" (Curtis) and "Daphne" (Lemmon). The
humor rises out of the tension that develops when they
find themselves surrounded by, but unable to approach,
the beautiful women of the orchestra, including Monroe,
whom each naturally becomes infatuated with. To make
a proper pass at her they'd have to reveal themselves,
but that would mean losing their jobs—and maybe their
lives. So Curtis disguises himself yet again, this time as
a two-bit Cary Grant, in order to impress Monroe; Lemmon consoles himself by getting aging millionaire playboy, Osgood Fielding III (Joe E. Brown), to propose to
him. Lemmon: "I'm engaged." Curtis: "Congratulations.
Who's the lucky girl?" Lemmon: "I am." They make a
perfect pair of cream puffs—Curtis is prissy and pretty,
while Lemmon is garrulous and homely. George Raft is a
convincing gangland bootlegger named Spats, and Monroe sings several torchy songs, including "I Want To Be
Loved by You."

See if you can spot Edward G. Robinson in a bit part,
and note the closing dialogue between Lemmon and
Brown, which contains one of the funniest and most
famous punchlines ever filmed.

WAY OUT WEST

(1936), B/W, *Director:* James W. Horne. *With:* Stan
Laurel, Oliver Hardy, and James Finlayson. **65 min.**
NR. Tape: Nostalgia Merchant.

Chaplin may be more obviously artistic, Keaton more
intriguing, and Lloyd more full of gags; but no one is
funnier, more endearing, or more enduring than Laurel
and Hardy. Stan and Ollie are better known for their
short films (both silent and sound), since most of their
features are a bit uneven. *Way Out West,* however, is a
marvelous exception to that rule, and ranks with their
very best short works—which puts it ahead of practically all contenders in the field of comedy. Two things
set *Way Out West* apart from most of their other features:
the lack of distracting subplots, romantic or otherwise,
and the presence of some unique and delightful musical
numbers.

Stan and Ollie have been sent to the little Western
town of Bushwood Gulch to tell a young girl (Rosina
Lawrence) about her father's death and to deliver her
inheritance, the deed to a goldmine. They are conned by
barkeep Mickey Finn (cross-eyed Laurel-and-Hardy
veteran James Finlayson) into believing that his wife,
Lola, is the girl they're looking for. "Tell me about my
dear, dear daddy," sobs Lola. "Is it true that he's dead?"
"Well, I hope he is," Stan replies. "They buried him."
When they realize they've given the deed to the wrong
girl, Stan says proudly, "That's the first mistake we've
made since that fellow sold us the Brooklyn Bridge."

Among the more memorable routines: Lola getting
the deed from Stan by tickling him until he has an
uncontrollable laughing fit, Ollie trying to lift himself
onto a rooftop with a block and tackle, and Stan using his
flaming thumb as a cigarette lighter. The film also includes their version of the song "The Trail of the Lone-
some Pine," which was a surprise hit in England a few
years ago. (Note: The video edition of *Way Out West*
contains a "bonus," an undistinguished short starring
Thelma Todd and Zasu Pitts.)

COMING-OF-AGE FILMS

This is, for better or worse, *the* film category of the 1980s. And while some Coming-of-Age Films have exploited the process of growing up, others have done a masterful job of exploring the process. The films in this chapter were made for teenagers, although there is something about these specific films that speak to more than one generation—something that gets to the core of the times; that probes the way we live and think about our lives. Since these are movies about characters—adolescents coming to understand their place in the world—the small screen enhances the intimacy that is at the heart of these films. And, lest we forget, these films are about having *fun*— no matter how many barriers have been set up to thwart that fun. There can be no doubt that, as long as girls become women and boys become men, the best is yet to come. Other Coming-of-Age Films to consider are: *Breaking Away, Cooley High, Diner, Fast Times at Ridgemont High, Gregory's Girl, My Bodyguard, Sixteen Candles, To Sir with Love,* and *Valley Girl.*

You're a Big Boy Now. *Bernard (Peter Kastner) enters manhood like a bull enters a china shop. Karen Black is eager to lend a hand.*

AMERICAN GRAFFITI

(1973), C, *Director:* George Lucas. *With* Ron Howard,
Harrison Ford, Paul LeMat, Mackenzie Phillips, Cindy
Williams, Richard Dreyfuss, Charlie Martin Smith,
Candy Clark, Wolfman Jack, Bo Hopkins, Kathy
Quinlan, and Suzanne Somers. **110 min.** *PG.* Tape,
Laser: MCA. CED: RCA VideoDisc.

The second movie directed by George Lucas, *American
Graffiti* is a coming-of-age movie in more ways than one.
Not only does the plot center around a group of kids who
have just graduated from high school in the year 1962,
but the film's tremendous success signaled an auspicious
beginning for Lucas and the many actors seen here:
Harrison Ford, Paul LeMat, Mackenzie Phillips and
Cindy Williams. *Graffiti* is also the movie considered
responsible for making Richard Dreyfuss a star. Ironically, Universal considered the picture a potential failure when it was finished, so it ended up "sitting on the
shelf" for a long time before it was eventually released.

No doubt the major "problem" of the film was its new,
different format for the time. Lucas took several separate stories—the serious kid, the hot-rodder, the dizzy
blonde—and interspersed them throughout the film.
While this cut-and-mesh technique is quite common
today, it showed a bold narrative decision here. Also
widely imitated is Lucas's coda for the movie, which
highlighted each of the main characters and detailed
exactly how their futures had turned out.

Graffiti has a tidy, almost novelistic feel to it, in spite
of the intersecting story lines. The endless driving
around in cars, the eternal quest for action, the restless
dissatisfaction—all of these classic coming-of-age
themes are honed to a fine comic edge. Dreyfuss gives
what is probably the most controlled performance of his
career and LeMat is wonderful and underrated as the
lean, mean guy on the move.

THE GRADUATE

(1967), C, *Director:* **Mike Nichols.** *With* **Dustin Hoffman, Anne Bancroft, Katharine Ross, Murray Hamilton, William Daniels, and Elizabeth Wilson. 106 min.** *NR.* CED: RCA VideoDisc; Laser: CBS/Fox.

A landmark comedy that embodies both the despair and the sarcasm of a certain time and generation, *The Graduate* concerns itself with the search for values. In his first major role, Dustin Hoffman plays Benjamin, a recent college graduate who returns to his parents' home in California. The alienation he feels is reflected in his deadpan face and straight-as-a-pin monotone. He is surrounded by the ridiculous, the overbearing, the absurd. Shortly after this film was released, the punch line of one of its jokes—"plastics"—became a shorthand condemnation of an entire value system.

His quest for redemption takes Benjamin into a sad, grim affair with the seductive Mrs. Robinson, played with a certain lusty, arch reserve by Anne Bancroft. A friend of the family, Bancroft encircles Hoffman until he is confused and dumbfounded almost to the point of becoming an automaton. Then, to liven things up, the Robinson's daughter (Katharine Ross) arrives on the scene. Eventually Hoffman moves into a sincere if baffling relationship with her, and the complications mount.

Director Mike Nichols won an Academy Award for his efforts; screenwriters Buck Henry and Calder Willingham adapted Charles Portis's novel to create a whole range of expressions and characters that found their way into our lives. The soundtrack by Simon and Garfunkel is haunting, lyrical, and—now and again—incredible pop art ("Here's to you, Mrs. Robinson . . .").

To many, the white knight ending was a happy one, but the last, lingering shot of Hoffman and Ross together on the bus suggests otherwise. As the seconds tick by, their smiles falter, their faces droop. The vacant, lost stares return, as if it is finally sinking in that they may have won the battle with their parents only to have lost the war with themselves.

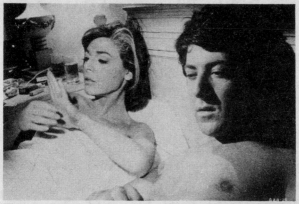

The Graduate. *Benjamin Braddock (Dustin Hoffman) reflects upon his first tryst with a married woman, Mrs. Robinson (Anne Bancroft). Hoffman acutely projects his character's disgust with himself for acclimating to a world that he despises.*

Rebel Without a Cause. *New kid in town Jim Stark (James Dean) doesn't want to fight; he wants to make friends. But he doesn't like being called "chicken" either. He duels leader-of-the-pack Buzz (Corey Allen) with switchblades, a tire iron, and, fatally, a chickie run.*

REBEL WITHOUT A CAUSE

(1955), C, *Director:* Nicholas Ray. *With* James Dean, Natalie Wood, Sal Mineo, Jim Backus, Ann Doran, Corey Allen, Edward Platt, Dennis Hopper, and Nick Adams. **105 min.** *NR.* Tape, Laser: Warner; CED: RCA VideoDisc.

A film too powerful to be contained by the cult mold in which it's often placed, *Rebel Without a Cause* is the only film by director Nicholas Ray to strike and hold the public imagination. Like all of Ray's work, it plays on his usual themes: neurotic insecurity, inner violence, a pervasive feeling of always being on the outside. What made this movie work so well is that Ray placed his themes in the world of the adolescent, where they made a poignant and searing sort of sense. *Rebel* came to speak for the alienation of an entire generation.

As the sensitive, dissatisfied teenager, James Dean gives a seminal performance. He is edgy, aching, in constant pain. As his friends, who provide redemption and salvation, Sal Mineo and Natalie Wood turn in first-rate performances. But the power of the movie can be traced directly to Ray and his overwhelming sense of atmosphere. The claustrophobic atmosphere of the adult, parental world is perfectly detailed; the feeling Dean has about the instability of the universe is elegantly conveyed in the planetarium scene.

The use of color and cinemascope is brilliant, although, unfortunately, the range of the wide screen will be severely curtailed by home video viewing. Nothing, however, can dull the striking color imagery. Dean's red jacket is a perfect emblem of his screaming pain; he is so blatantly hurt that you want to wrap him in bandages.

RISKY BUSINESS

(1983), C, *Director:* Paul Brickman. *With* Tom Cruise and Rebecca deMornay. **99 min.** *R.* Tape, CED, Laser: Warner.

Risky Business comes on—at first—like a typical teenage sex comedy, complete with hot-to-trot suburban boys and cartoonlike parents. But, to his credit, director Paul Brickman takes this formula and twists it to show us its darker side.

Like all rite-of-passage movies, *Risky Business* centers around a teenager, Joel (Tom Cruise), and his loss of innocence. But here his sexual awakening is a metaphor for the bigger, all-encompassing facts of American life; profit motive, competition, free enterprise. In the very beginning, when Joel says, "The dream is always the same," he's not merely talking about an adolescent fantasy, but the American Dream. "Making it" is more than what might happen on a lucky date. It encompasses an Ivy League education, a top starting salary after graduation, what kind of car to drive, what brand of silver to own. The details tell the story here, showing material goods to be the Significant Other in most people's lives.

Joel and his buddies eat this up. They belong to an extracurricular group called Future Enterprisers. They know all about marketing and sales—what they need is a product. The solution, for Joel, is Lana.

A beautiful young prostitute, Lana (Rebecca deMornay) enters the movie in a haunting, lyrical scene. To Joel, she's a dream come true—and like all of his dreams, she brings with her a nightmarish flip side. When she asks Joel, "Are you ready for me?" she's asking about his sense of opportunism as much as sex.

At first, Joel resists her way of operating. He relies instead on upper middle-class manners, plus romance, trust, and honesty. When these values let him down—threaten his future—he turns to the dark side Lana offers. It's a bold coming-of-age move for Joel; in one fell swoop he joins the adult world, secures his future, and becomes the ultimate future enterpriser—a dealer in "human fulfillment."

YOU'RE A BIG BOY NOW

(1966), C, *Director:* **Francis Ford Coppola.** *With* **Peter Kastner, Elizabeth Hartman, Karen Black, Rip Torn, Geraldine Page, Dolph Sweet, Julie Harris, Michael Dunn, and Tony Bill. 96 min.** *NR.* Tape: Warner.

Made in 1966, the screenplay was director Francis Ford Coppola's (he was still using his middle name then) master's thesis at UCLA. The influence of the New Wave is very clear; the editing is jumpy and disconnected in a strikingly offhand manner. At its best, it seems reminiscent of a Richard Lester movie, embodying in the same way a certain hip, free-spiritedness of a particular, short-lived moment of the 1960s.

The plot seems to be a thinly disguised autobiography. Peter Kastner plays an innocent at large, a young man dying to experience the world outside the grasp of his overprotective parents. Zany escapades mount as the film cutting becomes more frenzied. It's best not to try to follow the plot too carefully, but rather to go with the flow. That is exactly what Kastner does when he meets and takes up with a heartless go-go dancer, icily played by Elizabeth Hartman.

As in all coming-of-age films, the lessons the hero learns are not always pleasant ones, and so it goes in *You're a Big Boy Now.* There's a bittersweet edge to the manic activity, a wistfulness and charm amidst the freakiness. Great supporting performances are turned in by Karen Black, Rip Torn, and Geraldine Page. The tough cop, played by Dolph Sweet, is a classic character study. It's hard to compare this flashy, flippy little movie to a steeped-in-doom epic like Coppola's *The Godfather,* but a certain similarly beguiling style is apparent.

CULT FILMS

A Cult Film is a movie with a dedicated, fanatic audience—people who will ritualistically sit through multiple screenings of their particular film. Many Cult Films deal with subject matter that would generally be considered distasteful, anarchic, and vulgar. What makes these films special is the way they handle that subject matter (usually with tongue implanted firmly in cheek). The most famous Cult Film of all time, *The Rocky Horror Picture Show*, is not available on video tape. However, you'll find your share of off-beat, wild, and endearingly unconventional movies right here. Because they are, by definition, audience films, it does little good to watch Cult Films alone. These are the party films, so invite your friends and feel free to gab during the screening. These films will shock you, surprise you, and, happily, entertain you. There's not a dull ten minutes in the entire package. Other Cult Films to consider are: *Beyond the Valley of the Dolls, A Boy and His Dog, Forbidden Zone, Invasion of the Bee Girls, Liquid Sky, Morgan!, Pink Flamingos, Where's Poppa?, The Wicker Man*, and the 16 episodes of *The Prisoner* TV series.

King of Hearts. *British infantrymen surrender to the whimsical inmates of a lunatic asylum.*

LA CAGE AUX FOLLES

(1978), C, *Director:* Edouardo Molinaro. *With* Ugo
Tognazzi, Michel Serrault, Michel Galabru, Claire
Maurier, Remy Laurent, and Benny Luke. **91 min.** *R.*
Tape, CED, Laser: CBS/Fox.

   This delightful hybrid of drag-queen spectacle and
old-fashioned bedroom farce is one of the most entertaining and successful foreign films ever made. The reason
may be that it's one of those rare comedies that can get
you laughing *with* the characters as well as *at* them. The
setting is a ritzy St. Tropez nightclub that specializes in
female impersonation. Ugo Tognazzi plays the proprie-
tor, and Michel Serrault plays his lover, Albin, the club's
irrepressible drag-queen headliner. It's the inspired
camping of these two performers that raises the story
above its formulaic roots.
   Tognazzi is the worldly one, a dignified entrepreneur
who was married once and still tries to keep one foot in
the straight world; Albin (a cross between *Pink
Flamingos'* Divine and *The Odd Couple's* Felix Unger) is
the overgrown cry-baby of the relationship. Jowly and
piggy-eyed, with the body of a diva, Albin cuts a ridiculous figure, but it is an oddly irresistible one. When he
practices presenting a masculine image by trying to
walk like John Wayne, his attempts, while quite funny,
are also very heroic. Serrault's performance is a masterpiece for the empathy it evokes. In the pivotal sequence,
the couple must pass for straight at a dinner party with
some stuffy establishment types, and Albin carries the
evening off by doing an impeccable female impersonation.
   Transvestites have been glitzier and more outrageous than they are in this film, but no movie has ever
made them so endearing.

A CLOCKWORK ORANGE

(1971), C, *Director:* Stanley Kubrick. *With* Malcolm
McDowell, Patrick Magee, Adrienne Corri, Aubrey
Morris, and James Marcus. **137 min.** *R*. Tape, CED,
Laser: Warner.

At the time of its release, many people considered
director Stanley Kubrick's kinky, hypnotic parable
about a future overrun by teenage hoodlums the most
shocking movie of its era. Today the most shocking thing
about it is the gleeful exuberance with which young
audiences greet such legendary encounters as the
"Singin' in the Rain" rape scene. Today's youngsters,
weaned on slasher movies and punk rock, experience *A
Clockwork Orange* as a kick and a turn-on. Perhaps they
understand the movie better than critics did when it
came out.

It was never Kubrick's intention simply to shock the
bourgeoisie. Rather, by creating in Alex (Malcolm Mc-
Dowell) a buoyant and strangely appealing antihero, he
attempts to seduce us right into Alex's brutal, porno-
graphic, anything-goes world. We are meant to experience a faint glimmer of identification with Alex—we
may not be as far removed from him as we'd like to
believe. This does not explain, however, the young
viewers who seem every bit as eager for a (vicarious)
taste of the "old ultra-violence" as are Alex and his
white-clothed, black-derbied gang. Kubrick brings to
the screen with potent visual force a world of plastic
manners, brutal sex, and gratuitous violence—a world
that looks more like our own with every passing year.

A Clockwork Orange. *Young Alex (Malcolm McDowell) is a bolshy bratty who likes the old ultra-violence. Real fears about gang violence and urban decay are magnified into a disturbing look at a future that attacks solutions as harshly as it attacks problems.*

Eating Raoul. *Paul and Mary Bland (Paul Bartel and Mary Woronov) prepare to bop another pervert in the head with a skillet. Again, fears of urban decline and moral laxity are parlayed into a wicked black comedy.*

EATING RAOUL

(1982), C, *Director:* Paul Bartel. *With* Paul Bartel, Mary Woronov, and Ed Begley, Jr. **87 min.** *R.* Tape: CBS/Fox.

As a writer/director, Paul Bartel is somewhat similar to John Waters, creator of *Pink Flamingos.* But while Waters, the king of "gross-out" cinema, shocks his audience into laughter, Bartel makes the murder, perversion, and cannibalism in *Eating Raoul* seem as amusingly quaint as a drawing-room comedy. Even in the cult category, there is no other film quite like this one.

The setting is Los Angeles, where an impossibly priggish couple named Paul and Mary Bland (Bartel and ex-Warhol superstar Mary Woronov) are disgusted by the sleazy goings-on in their swinging apartment complex. Spurred on by their dream of opening a family restaurant, they decide to place an ad in one of the local porno tabloids, lure rich swingers to their home, and murder them for their cash. Joining the operation is a grinning Chicano stud named Raoul, who disposes of the corpses at a dog-food plant, and soon has Mary involved in a little hanky-panky on the side. What the movie's fans love about it is less its outrageousness than its tone of smirky offhandedness. The more bizarre the action gets, the more you can be sure Bartel and company have their tongues planted firmly in their cheeks. Once you get on their wavelength, this irreverent spoof is a delight.

ERASERHEAD

(1978), B/W, *Director:* **David Lynch.** *With* **John Nance, Charlotte Stewart, Allen Joseph, Jeanne Bates, Judith Anna Roberts, Laurel Near, and V. Phipps-Wilson. 90 min.** *NR.* Tape: RCA/Columbia.

Most cult films proudly proclaim their artlessness (even trashiness). This eerie, snail-paced nightmare from director David Lynch (*The Elephant Man*) is a work of intense artistic ambition. It is one of the most authentic dream films ever made—a worthy pop heir to the avant-garde classics of the 1920s and the 1930s. Its followers watch it in a state veering between jokiness and awed silence.

The setting is an unnamed industrial metropolis, where the dust and grime settle like fallout and the roar of clanking machinery fills the air. Through this oppressive atmosphere (photographed in shimmering black and white) scuttles Henry (John Nance), an anxious Everyman with a ragged pillbox hairdo, who fathers a mewling monster-baby. The infant is fabulously grotesque: It looks like a jellied calf's head and emits spine-chilling shrieks and whines (a forerunner to the slimy fetus in *Alien*).

Lynch has more in mind here than turning your stomach, however. *Eraserhead* is a surreal vision of apocalypse, and its most haunting images are those that finally elude analysis: luminous eels falling through the air and squishing to the ground below; Henry's head dropping from his body and the monster-baby's head appearing where Henry's had been (an image worthy of Magritte); the mysterious, doll-faced "Lady in the Radiator," who sings the movie's memorably ironic theme song, "In Heaven, Everything Is Fine." *Eraserhead* seems to have sprung whole from David Lynch's unconscious, and the brilliance of the film is the way it digs straight into ours.

HAROLD AND MAUDE

(1972), C, *Director:* Hal Ashby. *With* Bud Cort, Ruth
Gordon, Vivian Pickles, Cyril Cusack, Charles Tyner,
and Ellen Geer. **91 min.** *PG.* Tape, CED, Laser:
Paramount.

Cult films are, by nature, a counterculture phenomenon (it's no accident they blossomed during the late
1960s). Director Hal Ashby's *Harold and Maude* is probably one of the purest, best-loved examples of the genre.
It celebrates a cadre of lovable lunatics who can't (or
won't) fit into the strictures of the straight world. What's
unique about the movie is the way it tempers its sweetly
idyllic, antiestablishment outlook with a streak of
wicked black comedy.

Harold (Bud Cort), the boyish hero, may be an innocent at heart, but he enjoys staging spectacularly violent
fake suicides. Maude (Ruth Gordon), the eccentric 80-
year-old he hooks up with, may be a cute granny type,
but she's also an ardent free spirit who steals anything
that catches her fancy. She seduces Harold by spouting
hippie-style homilies about daisies and the life force.

As Harold learns Maude's freewheeling ways, Ashby
is indulging his wildest cinematic ideas. He goes from
head-on satire, with a puritanical minister ranting into
the camera, to lyrical long shots of Harold and Maude
picnicking in a cemetery. These devices are fun in themselves, but they also lend this story of two born non-
conformists an integrity it might otherwise lack. *Harold
and Maude* isn't merely funny and touching—it's as
proudly unpredictable as its oddball protagonists.

HIGH SCHOOL CONFIDENTIAL!

(1958), B/W, *Director:* Jack Arnold. *With* Russ Tamblyn, Jan Sterling, John Drew Barrymore, Mamie Van Doren, and Jackie Coogan. **85 min.** *NR.* Tape: NTA.

This riotous exploitation flick about a dope ring at an all-American high school manages to be at once brazenly ahead of its time and absurdly out of touch. The premise was certainly risky for a time when other teen films wouldn't dare mention the word "drugs."

High School Confidential! tells the story of a young undercover agent who poses as a troublemaking hipster in order to bring down a heroin pusher. The dialogue is peppered with so much "cool-cat" slang that the characters seem to be talking in a laughable code. Sample quote: "One swinging day, when Christopher Columbus was sittin' at the beach, goofin', he dug that the world was round!" Solid Jackson! What the movie's followers cherish most is the casting: 1950's sexpot Mamie Van Doren as the hero's incestuously lusty aunt, and persnickety Jackie Coogan as the dope pusher—they might have stepped out of the pages of some cautionary comic book. Best of all is Russ Tamblyn as the hipster agent. Curly-haired and impish, with a bedeviling gleam in his eye, this teenage hellcat, who refers to everyone as "dad," has a Lenny Bruce mind in the body of Eddie Haskell from *Leave It to Beaver.* We do not learn until halfway though the film that he's working for the law, and this twist confirms the movie's own schizoid tone. *High School Confidential!* gets you laughing at its hyped-up version of high-school society and then lets you know that anyone who talks that oddly couldn't possibly be for real.

KING OF HEARTS

(1966), C, *Director:* Phillippe de Broca. *With* Alan Bates,
Genevieve Bujold, Pierre Brasseur, Michel Serrault,
Jean-Claude Brialy, Francoise Christophe, and Adolfo
Celi. **101 min.** *NR.* Tape, CED: CBS/Fox.

Cult films tend to carve out a home of their own—be it
at midnight shows in New York City *(Eraserhead)* or
drive-in theaters in the Midwest *(The Road Warrior)*.
King of Hearts has long been the perennial favorite at
American colleges and universities. It is *the* campus cult
film, a legacy that dates back to the late days of Vietnam, when one of the more fashionable theories going
was that the insane were really the sanest people of all.
Nothing seemed more satisfying then—or more "relevant"—than a movie that made a good antiwar
statement.

King of Hearts has lost some of its relevant sheen since
then, but its story of a French town in World War I that
has been abandoned by everyone except the residents of
the local lunatic asylum remains as enjoyably madcap
as ever. A young, strikingly handsome Alan Bates plays
the Scottish doughboy who wanders into the town and
ends up finding love among the loons (with Genevieve
Bujold). There's a Marx Brothers zaniness around the
edges, as the inmates take over the professions and
attire of the absent townspeople—from barber (played
by *La Cage aux Folle's* Michel Serrault) to duke and
duchess. Director Philippe de Broca also gives this comic
concoction a sweet center, making the movie's rather
naive depiction of psychotics a dreamy, affectionate
conceit rather than any sort of realistic statement. Up
until the very end, the film maintains this sweetly bal-
anced tone. Except for the final lapse, it works.

OUTRAGEOUS!

(1977), C, *Director:* Richard Benner. *With* Craig Russell, Hollis McLaren, Richert Easley, Allan Moyle, and Helen Shaver. **100 min.** *R.* Tape: RCA/Columbia.

No outcast was ever as flamboyantly charismatic (or as wickedly talented) as female impersonator Craig Russell in his role in *Outrageous!* Made in Canada on a shoestring, this terrific little comedy is a fictionalized version of Russell's true-life odyssey to cult stardom.

It opens in Toronto, where Russell, a gay hairdresser, rooms with a fellow outcast, a pregnant schizophrenic played with endearing spaciness by Hollis McLaren. Russell is at once warm and bitchy; the acid wisecracks that keep popping out of his mouth are more than tempered by the affection and generosity he shows toward his poor roomie, whom he's always trying to save from suicide. The movie is about his courage in pulling up stakes, moving to New York City, and trying to make it as a professional drag-queen.

Outrageous! could almost be seen as a camp predecessor to *Fame* and *Flashdance;* it, too, is a pop tale about what it takes to go after your dream. Here, though, the premise is especially fetching, since the female impersonations that are Russell's stock-in-trade are such delicious theatrical revels. This man doesn't merely crave stardom—he *deserves* it. His impressions of Carol Channing, Mae West, Judy Garland, and others are so picture-perfect you'll swear you're watching the real McCoys. The irony is that Russell is never more himself than when he's putting on a show. That's enough to make *Outrageous!* (perhaps more than any other cult film) a triumph of personality.

THE ROAD WARRIOR

(1981), C, *Director:* George Miller. *With* Mel Gibson,
Bruce Spence, Vernon Wells, Emile Minty, Mike
Preston, and Kjell Nilsson. **95 min.** *R.* Tape, CED, Laser:
Warner.

If you measure the impact of a cult movie not just by
the size of its following but by the fanaticism of its
followers, then this is easily the hottest cult movie
around today. It's not just that director George Miller's
sequel to *Mad Max* is faster, meaner, funnier, and more
shockingly violent than any previous action picture; it's
not just that Mel Gibson as the hero, Max, is as tough as
Clint Eastwood, as sexy as Sly Stallone, and a lot
smarter than either. What makes *The Road Warrior*
such a heady, intoxicating fantasy is that it's set in a
futuristic nightmare world assembled from the shards of
the pop-culture past.

The Lord Humungus and his crew of rampaging
bikers are punks, leather boys, kung fu warriors, and
Hell's Angels all rolled into one. These raping-and-
pillaging goons are as menacing as the monsters in a
horror movie, but they also represent the darkest vision
yet of life after a nuclear holocaust. The movie's final
demolition derby is a 20-minute bravura in which Max,
steering a Mack truck, leads a group of peaceful pilgrims
against the evil bikers. No one has ever mingled teem-
ing, Goyaesque imagery and breakneck editing the way
Miller does here. You feel the jolt of every sudden death,
the kick of every acceleration. The climactic blow-out, in
which Humungus and his right-hand thug, the mo-
hawked warrior, Wez, collide head-on, is perhaps the
greatest finish any movie villain has ever had. Move
over, Peckinpah, Hill, and Romero; with *The Road
Warrior,* George Miller takes the cinema of violence to a
new, nihilistic zenith.

THE WARRIORS

(1979), C, *Director:* Walter Hill. *With* Michael Beck,
James Remar, Thomas Waites, Dorsey Wright, Brian
Tyler, and Deborah Van Valkenburgh. **94 min.** *R.* Tape,
Laser: Paramount.

This flashy ghetto fantasy became a cult movie the
week it was released, as crowds of urban teenagers lined
up to cheer the violence and, in some cases, inflict a bit of
their own on theaters showing the film. It's easy to understand their zeal: *The Warriors* is one of the most
kinetic action films of the 1970s. Writer/director Walter
Hill makes youth gangs his jumping-off point for an
inner-city-gothic kung fu picture. Hill casts the story as
a kind of living comic strip; and the thrill of the movie
lies in its dark, hallucinatory color scheme, its jackknife
editing, and its highly stylized evocation of a New York
City nightworld run by furious adolescents.

The plot is, of all things, a reworking of Xenophon's
march to the sea, with the Coney Island Warriors attempting to fight their way across New York and reach
the safety of their home turf. Every familiar face they
meet is a potential predator. Each of the gangs the Warriors goes up against has its own, otherworldly look and
style—from the towering, shaven-headed Grammercy
Riffs to a nightmarish group that sports baseball outfits
and Kiss-style make-up. And though the actors themselves aren't a particularly vivid crew, that hardly
matters in a movie whose action scenes are as brilliantly
choreographed as any ever filmed. In *The Warriors,* the
thrill of the fight is its own reward.

FAMILY FILMS

The Family Film is quickly overtaking the Horror Film in terms of popularity, which tells us something about the new generation of VCR owners. Although there are many children's films on the market, this chapter salutes those films that the *entire* family can enjoy together. All of the films in this chapter are live-action (not animated) films, and many of them are *about* families—their struggles, concerns, and joys. The television is an ideal way for people to watch these films, as the family gathers together and feels free to talk about the film at will (that same experience once provided by drive-in theaters). There are too many superficial family titles on the rental shelves; you should not settle for less than the best. The movies discussed in this chapter are quality films chosen for their honesty and insight. Other Family Films to consider are: *Born Free, Bugsy Malone, Darby O'Gill and the Little People, The Jungle Book* (with Sabu), *The Parent Trap, Ring of Bright Water,* and *White Mane.* Note: Similar films are found in the Animated Films chapter.

Miracle on 34th Street. *John Payne, Maureen O'Hara, Natalie Wood, and Edmund Gwenn make their Christmas wishes.*

ANNA TO THE INFINITE POWER

(1984), C, *Director:* Robert Wiemer. *With* Dina Merrill, Martha Byrne, and Mark Patton. **107 min.** *NR*. Tape: RCA/Columbia.

It's not easy to live up to a title as compelling as *Anna to the Infinite Power,* but this film does just that. A terrific new addition to the genre of family films, the movie addresses some big questions—Are we who we think we are? Why do we think and act the way we do? Can we change?—and still manages to spin a captivating web of mystery that never lets up.

Anna Hart (Martha Byrne) is a "special" child. She attends a school for the brilliant, has a stratospheric I.Q., and plans to be a world-class physicist when she grows up. She also is a chronic liar, a cheater, and a thief. Though her older brother hates her for it, her disturbing behavior is accepted without question by Anna's scientist mother (Dina Merrill), and grudgingly tolerated by her musician father (Jack Ryland). Anna's life and future seem set in concrete. Then one night the girl dreams of being on board a plane in a storm, crying to a stranger as if this unknown woman was her own mother. The next day Anna sees a television news report covering the crash of a small plane. One of the survivors is a girl with Anna's face.

As Anna probes the increasingly entangled mystery of her alter ego, she begins to question her own identity and the life she has been leading. How much of the Anna she seems to be is really her? How much is the result of fulfilling others' expectations? Anna changes, and in so doing the world around her changes also. Therein lies a lesson for kids and adults alike.

THE BAD NEWS BEARS

(1976), C, *Director:* Michael Ritchie. *With* Walter
Matthau, Tatum O'Neal, Vic Morrow, Joyce Van Patten,
Jackie Earle Haley, and Alfred Lutter. **102 min.** *PG*.
Tape, CED, Laser: Paramount.

A very funny reworking of the "little team that could"
sports theme, *The Bad News Bears* boasts a dozen foul-
mouthed suburban brats and a hilarious performance by
Walter Matthau. It addresses the important questions of
winning and losing and how one plays the game.

Morris Buttermaker (Matthau) cleans swimming
pools for a living, but gets hired to manage a team of
misfit youngsters whose parents have successfully sued
the high-powered local Little League for not letting
them play. A cynical boozer and ex-minor-league ball-
player, Buttermaker is only in it for the money. And the
kids are as motley a crew as was ever assembled. According to the team's runt troublemaker, Tanner, nobody
joins the Bears except "Jews, spics, niggers, pansies, or
booger-eating morons." But when the Bears are humili-
ated in their first game and subsequently abused at
school, Buttermaker gets serious. After the addition of
Amanda Whurlizer (Tatum O'Neal), a pitcher with a
powerful throwing arm, and a young hood who swings a
wicked bat, the Bears become a force to be reckoned
with.

The movie works (unlike its unfortunate sequels)
because it manages to have its cake and eat it too—using
the conventions of the genre while subverting them. The
Bears are plucky misfits who make good without losing
the outsider status that gives them such appeal. They
succeed, but on their own happily warped terms.

THE BLACK STALLION

(1979), C, *Director:* Carroll Ballard. *With* Kelly Reno,
Mickey Rooney, Teri Garr, Clarence Muse, Hoyt Axton,
and Michael Higgins. **103 min.** *G.* Tape, Laser:
CBS/Fox; CED: RCA VideoDisc.

Rare is the animal film that isn't fatally awash with
sentimentality and watered-down romanticism. Fewer
still are those that capture the beauty and power of
nature yet maintain a connection to humanity. *The
Black Stallion* is such a film.

In 1945, off the coast of North Africa, a cruise ship goes
down in stormy waters. A young American boy, Alex
Ramsey (Kelly Reno), saves himself by grabbing onto a
fellow passenger—an untamed, black Arabian horse.
Castaway on a deserted island, Alex sees the beautiful
black stallion running wild, all but flying and snorting
fire like the Bucephalus of Greek legend. The horse
becomes Alex's totem, the almost mystical link between
the boy's 20th-century upbringing and the dark, pri-
mordial rawness of his ancient forebears. The pair are
eventually rescued and face new challenges in America,
but the tension between civilization and nature is never
lost, and the stunning cinematography and direction
never quit. In addition to Reno's amazingly sincere performance, Hoyt Axton and Teri Garr shine as his understanding parents.

Under Carroll Ballard's sensitive direction, Alex and
the horse reenact the mutual taming that took place
thousands of years before between their ancestors. In a
marvelous scene, Alex coaxes the stallion into playfully
chasing him into the sea until the water level rises to the
horse's chest, whereupon the boy easily slips onto the
stallion's back. We view much of this exciting scene from
under water. The wordless narrative is as playful and
sly as Alex's taming of the stallion.

IT'S A WONDERFUL LIFE

(1946), B/W, *Director:* Frank Capra. *With* James
Stewart, Donna Reed, Lionel Barrymore, Henry
Travers, Beulah Bondi, Gloria Grahame, and Frank
Faylen. **129 min.** *NR*. Tape: NTA.

Get out your handkerchiefs.

Director Frank Capra may have a reputation for
corniness in some circles, but you'd need a heart of stone
to sit dry-eyed through *It's a Wonderful Life*.

The film opens with small-town man George Bailey
(the role James Stewart seems born to play) at the end of
his tether, agonizing over his "worthless" life. As he
contemplates suicide on an icy bridge, George prays
desperately for relief. His prayers are heard. Up in
Heaven, Clarence (Henry Travers), "Angel Second
Class," gets ready to convince George of the value of his
life. He reviews the man's story on that great VCR in the
sky, and we see why George is in such sad straits.

Bedford Falls is a small, quiet, mid-American town,
where opportunities for "greatness" don't exist. George
wants nothing better than to get out into the world and
do big and wonderful things, but he just can't seem to
break away. After his father dies, he puts off college to
run the family's chronically broke Building and Loan
Company. George's firm puts people over profits, setting
itself in opposition to Mr. Potter (Lionel Barrymore in a
beautifully villainous role), Bedford Falls' rich and
heartless real estate shark. He marries Mary (Donna
Reed) and is soon too old to go to college. When World
War II comes, a childhood ear injury keeps George out of
active service, while his kid brother enlists and wins a
Congressional Medal of Honor. What kind of a life is that?

With the angel's help, George experiences firsthand
how diminished and unhappy Bedford Falls would be
without him. He comes to realize that it's not the grand
accomplishments and peerless feats of courage that ultimately count in Heaven (or on earth). It's friends and
family and the small, quiet sacrifices made for others
that are the essence of a wonderful life.

It's a Wonderful Life. *George and Mary Bailey (James Stewart and Donna Reed) give their honeymoon money to their worried customers during the Depression. One of the most touching movies ever made about the struggles and sacrifices one makes in a lifetime.*

Mary Poppins. *Bert, the chimney sweep (Dick Van Dyke), and Mary Poppins (Julie Andrews) sing and dance with a group of animated ladies in the winner's circle at the racetrack. Walt Disney's most magical live-action (er, mostly live-action) film.*

MARY POPPINS

(1964), C, *Director:* Robert Stevenson. *With* Julie
Andrews, Dick Van Dyke, David Tomlinson, Glynis
Johns, Ed Wynn, Hermione Baddeley, Karen Dotrice,
Matthew Garber, Arthur Treacher, and Reginald Owen.
140 min. *NR*. Tape, CED, Laser: Disney.

A national treasure that set the box office abuzz, this
film made Julie Andrews a huge star and put the nonsense word "supercalifragilisticexpialidocious" into the
English language. *Mary Poppins* may well be the best of
the family musicals.

Certainly it is the best musical account of a family.
The movie is set in Edwardian England, 1910—as prim,
proper, and refined an era as ever there was. George
Banks, Esq. (David Tomlinson), a bank executive
(naturally), is a pillar of stability and practicality. But
the order he strives to maintain is threatened by his
children, Jane (Karen Dotrice) and Michael (Matthew
Garber). They insist on laughing and playing around
and getting into the sort of mischief young children are
wont to get into. They've run six nannies out of the house
in four months, and pater is getting desperate.

In answer to the latest search for a replacement nanny
comes Mary Poppins (Julie Andrews), floating down
from a cloud via an open umbrella, and carrying a car-
petbag. Mary has a slight, superficial gruffness that
can't hide her magical, laughing heart. It soon becomes
clear that Mary's real mission is aimed not at disci-
plining the kids, but at softening Mr. Banks.

Julie Andrews is a glowingly lovely Mary Poppins,
and Dick Van Dyke is her perfect foil and accomplice as
the imaginative chimney sweep, Bert. It's a measure of
the movie's fullness that the large musical numbers are
still in our memories from years ago, as well as many of
the marvelous smaller bits. The film is fresh and joyous
even today.

MIRACLE ON 34TH STREET

(1947), B/W, *Director:* George Seaton. *With* Maureen
O'Hara, John Payne, Edmund Gwenn, Gene Lockhart,
Natalie Wood, Porter Hall, and William Frawley.
96 min. *NR.* Tape: CBS/Fox.

Probably the most beloved Christmas film of all time,
Miracle on 34th Street raises the important question, "Is
Santa dead?" The answer, director George Seaton has us
know, is a resounding, "Not on your life!" Not only is
Santa very much alive, he is well, and living in Man-
hattan.

As the person in charge of Macy's Thanksgiving Day
parade, Doris Walker (Maureen O'Hara) is responsible
for bringing holiday fantasies to life for thousands of
New Yorkers. But at home, where Doris lives with
daughter Susan (a very young Natalie Wood), there are
no fairy tales allowed. Doris has hardened her heart in
order to cope with the pain caused by a husband who
walked out on her long ago. And she has taught her little
girl never to believe in anything that might make her
vulnerable to disappointment or rejection. Into Macy's
and their lives comes a holiday Santa (Edmund Gwenn)
who goes by the name of Kris Kringle and claims to be
the genuine article. Distressed over the loss of true
Christmas spirit ("There are a lot of bad isms floating
around but one of the worst is commercialism"), Kris
decides that if he can get a pair like Doris and Susan to
believe in him, then there's still hope for the rest of the
world.

The high point of the film comes when Kris is put on
trial by those who want him committed. The pained look
on the judge's face (Gene Lockhart) when he realizes he
must rule on whether or not Santa Claus exists is price-
less. Is Kris really Father Christmas? It doesn't matter.
The real miracle, this film tells us, is that despite the
pain of living we can still dream and believe.

THE MUPPET MOVIE

(1979), C, *Director:* James Frawley. *With* Kermit the Frog, Miss Piggy, Fozzie Bear, and the Muppets (Jim Henson, Frank Oz, Jerry Nelson, Richard Hunt, Dave Goelz), Charles Durning, and Austin Pendleton. **94 Min.** *G.* Tape, Laser: CBS/Fox; CED: RCA VideoDisc.

The best children's movies are those that can entertain adults while amusing the kids. Bullwinkle and the Bugs Bunny menagerie consistently pulled this off in their day. The Muppets, Jim Henson's unique puppet-like creations, do it with great success in ours. *The Muppet Movie,* their first feature-length film, has everything: comedy, music, good guys, bad guys, thrills, chills, and spills.

The plot is simple enough. While singing away in his Southeastern swamp, Kermit the Frog is discovered by a vacationing movie agent (Dom DeLuise). The agent gives Kermit his card and says, "Come to Hollywood, we'll make you a star." Kermit hops on his bicycle (the spindly-legged frog on a bike is truly a sight to behold) to find his friend Fozzie Bear. The pair head West in Fozzie's Studebaker, pursued by the evil owner of a fast-food frog legs franchise who wants Kermit for his publicity campaign. En route they meet James Coburn, Madeline Kahn, Telly Savalas, and Elliott Gould in delightful cameos, along with the inevitable Miss Piggy.

When a savage frog-killer armed with a fork-firing spear gun joins the chase, it looks as though Kermit will never accomplish his life's goal "to sing and dance, and make people happy." Not to worry. He does plenty of the former—there are extravagant production numbers at every bend in the road—and by the end of *The Muppet Movie* he has resoundingly accomplished the latter.

THE RED BALLOON

(1956), C, *Director:* Albert Lamorisse. *With* Pascal
Lamorisse. **35 min.** *NR*. Tape: Embassy.

The Red Balloon, a 35-minute French film with no
dialogue, won almost every possible award when it was
originally released in 1956. It's easy to understand why.
A fresh and funny look at childhood, loneliness, and
friendship, *The Red Balloon* is movie magic at its finest.

On the streets of Paris, a young boy (Pascal Lamorisse)
finds a big red balloon caught on a lamppost. In contrast
to the muted greys and dull browns of the city and its
human inhabitants, the redness of the balloon is vibrant
and dazzling. He climbs up, frees it, and heads home,
pulling the floating balloon along by its string. When he
gets there, the balloon is confiscated and pushed out the
upper story window. Instead of shooting up in the air, the
balloon hangs in place outside the building. When the
boy reemerges on the street, the balloon drops down to
meet him as if it has a mind of its own. It moves under
some mysterious propulsion, its string dangling free; it
follows the boy along the cobblestones, chasing after him
when he boards a streetcar and sneaking into his class-
room through a window in the schoolhouse. When the
boy is mistreated by a gang of rowdy youths, the balloon
comes to his rescue.

Given the natural inclination on the part of children
(and many adults) to anthropomorphize inanimate objects, *The Red Balloon* feels warmly familiar, despite its
preposterous premise. It's like watching the fulfillment
of a wish made when the world seemed very, very
young—and balloons could follow us home.

SMALL CHANGE

(1976), C, *Director:* Francois Truffaut. *With* Geory
Desmouceaux, Philippe Goldman, and Laurent
Devlaeminck. **104 min.** *PG*. Tape: Warner.

No modern filmmaker has delved more deeply or com-
passionately into the inner life of children than French
director Francois Truffaut. *Small Change* is the cul-
mination of Truffaut's extraordinary identification with
and understanding of children, which began with his
first film, *The 400 Blows*.

Unlike that earlier work, however, *Small Change* is
not as painfully autobiographical. Without sidestepping
the many sorrows of childhood, it exults fully in the
joys—innocence, wonder, spontaneity, and laughter.
This wise and moving film is all the more remarkable in
that, despite its loosely episodic structure and large cast,
we come to know each of these children intimately, and
to care for them. The seamlessly interwoven ancedotes
take place in and around a grammar school—the closest
thing to a society of children—and the talented cast of
amateurs seem mostly to play themselves, right down to
using their own names. Life for them is a joyful adventure—except when dampened by the deadness or cruelty
of the adult world. What plot there is here concerns a
battered and neglected child (Philippe Goldman), and
the contrasting styles of two of his teachers. One teacher
is severe and judgmental; he never grasps what's happening to the boy at home. The other, whose childlike
point of view establishes a mutual respect and love between him and his students, is much more understanding.

The most hilarious and touching scene involves a little
girl whose parents punish her unjustly by locking her in
the apartment while they go out to eat. With her father's
megaphone, the girl playfully announces to all the
neighbors, "I'm hungry," and they respond as one, sending her a picnic basket via a makeshift pulley fashioned
from a clothesline. This is filmmaking that cuts across
all barriers of age, culture, and language.

SOUNDER

(1972), C, *Director:* Martin Ritt. *With* Cicely Tyson, Paul Winfield, Kevin Hooks, Carmen Mathews, Taj Mahal, James Best, and Janet MacLachlan. **105 min.** *G.* Tape, CED, Laser: Paramount.

Sounder is an immensely satisfying film with potent themes—racism and the importance of family ties—made even more powerful by the understated, heartfelt way in which they are presented.

Rebecca and Nathan Lee Morgan (Cicely Tyson and Paul Winfield) are Black Louisiana sharecroppers who live in a small cabin with their three children. It's the 1930s and the country is in the worst years of the Great Depression, but the Morgans don't seem particularly affected by it. Things have *always* been tough for this family; the worldwide economic trauma is simply a minor variation on a lifelong pattern. To put meat on the table, Nathan Lee must hunt for raccoons at night, but despite the heroic efforts of his hound dog Sounder, the expeditions fail more often than succeed. After one particularly frustrating attempt, Nathan steals some pig bellies from the general store in town. The next day he is hauled off by the sheriff and sentenced to a year of hard labor.

More so than ever before, the Morgans must confront the bitter fruits of the racist society that surrounds them. The agents of this repression are not whip-toting caricatures. They're just good old boys who follow "rules" that, for instance, forbid a Black woman from visiting her husband in jail or finding out the name of his work camp. It's a racism so fundamental and unquestioned that its very existence seems obvious only to its victims. Sounder's message of family love, loyalty, and strength ultimately offers a vision of hope even in this impossible world.

FOREIGN FILMS

The films in this chapter were not only made outside the United States, they are most often thought of in terms of their native land. On one level, these films provide an insight into people of other cultures—the way they dress, where they dwell, and, most importantly, what they think. On another level, they stand as some of the most innovative and important films in the history of cinema. Foreign Films often translate poorly to the small screen. The language barrier creates more problems on video than in the theater because the subtitles are often more difficult to read. Films that are dubbed into English for the home screen are often dubbed poorly. The films in this section were chosen specifically for their successful adaptation to tape. There are many superb Foreign Films on tape. Other Foreign Films to consider include: *Amacord, Bob Le Flambeur, Cries and Whispers, Diva, La Dolce Vita, Everyman for Himself and God Against All, Grand Illusion, Mephisto, Night of the Shooting Stars, Open City, Pixote, Seven Beauties, La Truite, The Umbrellas of Cherbourg,* and *Yojimbo.*

The Seven Samurai. *Kikuchiyo, the thief turned samurai (Toshiro Mifune), laughs at the peasant's cowardice.*

L'ATALANTE

(1934), B/W, *Director:* Jean Vigo. *With* Jean Dasté, Dita
Parlo, and Michel Simon. **82 min.** In French with
English subtitles. *NR.* Tape: Budget.

Jean Vigo made only four films before his death in
1934 at the age of 29. Yet each of these films has gone on
to become a classic of world cinema—particularly his
semisurrealist comedy *Zero for Conduct,* and his last
film, the romantic melodrama *L'Atalante.*

Set on a river barge of the same name, *L'Atalante* tells
the story of Jean, a barge captain (Jean Dasté) and his
young bride Juliette (Dita Parlo). At first happy to set up
housekeeping on the ship, Juliette quickly finds herself
feeling hemmed-in by its squalid confines. The bizarre
knick-knacks (dolls, puppets, body organs pickled in
brine) collected by the ship's first mate Pere Jules
(Michel Simon) terrify, then amuse her, before finally
making her long for the world outside the river. When
the boat stops in Paris, Juliette can't resist wandering
about the town and looking at the store window displays.
Jean, angered by her attitude, has the boat take off
without her. Juliette, desolate and frightened, drifts
about a now-hostile Paris trying to find work. Jean discovers himself drifting perilously close to the edge of
madness for the loss of her. Finally Pere Jules takes
things into his own hands, returns the ship to Paris,
finds Juliette, and restores her to the man she loves.

On paper it's a slight, even sentimental story. But on
screen Vigo's visual poetry transforms *L'Atalante's*
story into something else entirely. The barge—seen
mostly at night—moves through the river mists as if it
were some strange prehistoric beast. Juliette's loneliness and feelings of entrapment are highlighted by a
decidedly poetic emphasis on the found wonder of everyday objects. Vigo's editing precision makes Paris appear
a luminous fairy tale city when Juliette first sees it, then
quickly transforms it into an eerie, desolate wasteland
when she finds herself marooned there. Best of all is the
film's ending in which the reunited lovers fall to the floor
gripped by passion and exhaustion.

BERLIN ALEXANDERPLATZ

(1980), C, *Director:* Rainer Werner Fassbinder. *With* Gunter Lamprecht, Gottfried John, and Barbara Sukowa. **930 min.** In German with English subtitles. *NR.* Tape: MGM/UA (8 tape set).

Rainer Werner Fassbinder's monumental adaptation of Alfred Doblin's novel of big city lowlife in pre-war Berlin is a landmark in film history. Ordinarily novels are condensed and shorn of subsidiary characters and incidents when adapted for motion pictures or television. Fassbinder, taking full advantage of the television mini-series format, doesn't delete any of Doblin's insights for this massive production, first broadcast in Germany, then released to theaters. Skillfully arranging the narrative into 14 self-contained episodes, Fassbinder's 15½-hour-long epic is an emotionally and intellectually overwhelming experience.

Berlin Alexanderplatz follows, in "Pilgrim's Progress" fashion, the ups and downs of one Franz Bieberkopf (Gunter Lamprecht), a small-time pimp recently released from prison. When he vows to change his ways and go straight we have good reason to believe him. But in Berlin's poverty-stricken Alexanderplatz district in the late 1920s, life is bleak and jobs are scarce. Soon Franz finds himself sinking back into his old criminal ways. Then quite suddenly Franz discovers a brief moment of happiness in the arms of a sweetly childlike streetwalker, Mieze (Barbara Sukowa). But Franz's criminal companion Rheinhold (Gottfried John) quickly destroys their blissful romance through an act of unspeakable violence and horror. Pushed far beyond his emotional limits, Franz descends into madness.

Utilizing every dramatic device at his disposal, Fassbinder captures each nuance of Doblin's tale of tragic grandeur amidst society's flotsam and jetsam. The film's enormous cast is astonishing. Gunter Lamprecht gives one of the greatest performances ever. Altogether they make *Berlin Alexanderplatz* a work of almost inexhaustable cinematic pleasure.

Berlin Alexanderplatz. *Eva (Hanna Schygulla) comforts Franz Bieberkopf (Gunter Lamprecht) through one of his many trials. This immense film is able to give a sense of the fullness and complexity of life by concentrating its 15-1/2-hour length on a two-year span in Franz's life.*

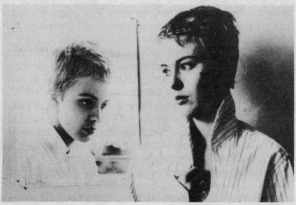

Breathless. *Jean Seberg's Patricia represents an entire generation of American youth. She's restless, smart, and confused. Patricia wants to toy with adventure—without giving up the security of her middle-class existence.*

BREATHLESS

(1961), B/W, *Director:* Jean-Luc Godard. *With* Jean-
Paul Belmondo, Jean Seberg, and Liliane David.
89 min. In French with English subtitles. *R*. Tape:
Festival.

Jean-Luc Godard's first feature, about a French hood-
lum and his equally amoral American girlfriend, has
dazzled and delighted audiences the world over ever
since it premiered. It made a young bit player named
Jean-Paul Belmondo a major star overnight and rescued
the then-sagging fortunes of actress Jean Seberg. As for
writer/director Godard, *Breathless* moved him immediately to the head of the class of the French "New Wave"
—the moniker given to the generation of young filmmakers (among them Francois Truffaut and Claude
Chabrol) whose low-budget shooting methods and icono-
clastic dramatic styles were revolutionizing the staid
French film industry.

Michel Poiccard (Belmondo), a young car thief stopped
for speeding in a stolen vehicle, panics and shoots a
police officer. Instead of making a quick getaway, however, he returns to Paris to continue his new affair with
Patricia (Seberg), an American exchange student.
Michel's plan is to collect on enough past debts from
friends to organize an escape for two. But Patricia, wary
of involvement, hesitates. When she learns of Michel's
crime she helps him for a time, then in a sudden change
of heart turns him over to the police.

On paper this would hardly be the sort of scenario one
would expect for a light romantic comedy, but that—surprising as it may seem—is by and large what *Breathless*
is. The rapid mood swings (embodied in the films nervous "jump-cut" editing style) are perfectly in keeping
with the characters' sensibilities. With their sunglasses,
cigarettes, and continual air of flip nonchalance, Belmondo and Seberg are the embodiment of post-beat cool.
Though many attempts have been made to ape their
style, none has come close to their surefire combination—tough as nails on the outside, sweetly sentimental
at the core.

8½

(1963), C, *Director:* Federico Fellini. *With* Marcello
Mastroianni, Anouk Aimée, Claudia Cardinale, Sandra
Milo, and Barbara Steele. **138 min.** In Italian with
English subtitles. *NR*. Tape: Vestron.

On its release in 1963, Federico Fellini's perceptive
peek into the private life of a world famous film director
instantly became the most talked about motion picture
since *Citizen Kane*. How, many critics wondered at the
time, are viewers supposed to make sense of a story that
moves freely from nostalgic flashback to gaudy fantasy,
before returning to equally unsettled scenes of a dream-
ily disconcerting present? The simple answer is to forget
about all such distinctions and sit back to enjoy the ride.
And with Fellini—here at the height of his powers—
there is always something to savor.

Marcello Mastroianni stars as Guido Anselmi, a celebrated film director (clearly modeled on Fellini himself)
undergoing a creative crisis largely brought on by personal problems. At a luxury spa where he has gone for
his failing health, Guido is making preparations for his
next project—a science fiction epic whose script exists
more in his mind than on paper. Besieged by producers,
critics, assistants, actors, agents, and all manner of
hangers-on, Guido retreats to an interior world of mel-
ancholic reverie and surreal fantasy. But reality keeps
intruding in the figures of his estranged—and very re-
sentful—wife (Anouk Aimée) and exhuberant but
demanding mistress (Sandra Milo).

With one dazzling scene following another, it's almost
impossible to single out a high point in a film as unique
as this one. Guido's recollection of a childhood meeting
with the enormous prostitute Saraghina (Edra Gale) is
outstanding, but then so is the film's famous harem
scene, where Guido gathers together all the women he
ever loved or dreamed about and has them wait on him
hand and foot. Then there's the grand circus parade
finale where past and present, fantasy and reality, inter-
mingle in giddy abandon. *8-1/2* is an unceasing sensual
delight.

IVAN THE TERRIBLE

(1945), *Part II,* **(1946), B/W,** *Director:* Sergei Eisenstein.
With Nikolai Cherkasov, Ludmila Tselikovskaya, and
Serafina Birman. **96 min.** *Part II,* **84 min.** In Russian
with English subtitles. *NR.* Tape: Budget.

   Sergei Eisenstein's awesome two-part historical epic
is in every way the thinking man's blockbuster. Though
unfinished at the time of his death in 1948, this elaborate Soviet superproduction, shot between 1942 and
1945, traces an important chapter in Russian history in
a visually and emotionally extravagant manner that
has never failed to impress viewers. Part I, released in
1945, presented few problems. Ivan, played by famed
Russian actor Nikolai Cherkasov is shown to be a strong,
sympathetic leader, determined to unite his nation—an
action in clear opposition to the wishes of the powerful
Boyar nobility, who desire feudal-style divisions of terri-
tory. After much court intrigue, and a spectacular battle
scene featuring the capture of the city of Kazan by Ivan's
army, the young Tzar achieves his goal.
   Part II (completed in 1945 and ready for release the
following year) was another story. In this segment of the
saga, court intrigue becomes the major feature, with Ivan
plotting to overthrow the Boyar nobles who stood in his
way and wreak vengeance on those responsible for the
death of his wife (a melodramatic high point of Part I).
   What fascinates critics and audiences today about
Ivan the Terrible is less its political ramifications than
its aesthetics. Turning his back on the documentary-like
realism of *Potemkin,* Eisenstein directs his attention
toward all-stops-out expressionist fantasy. Treating his
highly stylized performers like pieces of decor, Eisenstein arranges their actions in the manner of religious
murals and frescos. Giving full vent to his passion for
grand opera and Kabuki theater, he creates a film quite
unlike any other—dense, rich, otherworldly. A meditation on power gone mad, *Ivan the Terrible* is one of the
supreme triumphs of pure style in the history of cinema.

MERRY CHRISTMAS, MR. LAWRENCE

(1983), C, *Director:* Nagisa Oshima. *With* David Bowie, Tom Conti, and Ryuichi Sakamoto. **122 min.** In Japanese with English subtitles. *R.* Tape: MCA.

Directed by famed Japanese filmmaker Nagisa Oshima, *Merry Christmas, Mr. Lawrence* is one of the most challenging and rewarding foreign films of recent years. Set in a Japanese-run prisoner-of-war camp towards the end of World War II, this tale of a head-on collision between Eastern and Western value systems is alternately harrowing and stark, sensual and bizarre. Nevertheless, viewers willing to suspend conventional expectations about the nature and shape of dramatic material will find *Mr. Lawrence* an unforgettable experience.

Based on Sir Laurens Van Der Post's book *The Seed and the Sower,* Oshima's film explores the moral and temperamental conflict that springs up between British prisoners and their Japanese jailers on a small island in Java. Behavior that the Japanese find cowardly (acceptance of their captured state), the British see as being quite without dishonor. Likewise the Japanese obsession with by-the-book protocol (often leading to ritual suicide at a moment's notice) is viewed by the British as simply insane. Only Major Lawrence (Tom Conti), a British officer well-versed in Japanese ways, can manage to keep peace between the two factions—and then just barely. But even Lawrence's skill is tested when the rebellious young Major Celliers (David Bowie) enters the camp. Oshima brings us closer to the mysterious Celliers, detailing through a lengthy and complex flashback a childhood incident that made him the man he is today. The prison's commanding officer (Ryuichi Sakamoto) is clearly attracted to the dashing officer—a fact that Celliers uses to bring the conflict between captors and captives to a crisis point.

MR. HULOT'S HOLIDAY

(1954), B/W, *Director:* Jacques Tati. *With* Jacques Tati,
Nathalie Pascaud, Michelle Rolla, Valentine Camax,
and Louis Perrault. **86 min.** In French with English
subtitles. *NR.* Tape: Video Yesteryear.

Jacques Tati's comedy about a summer vacation at a
seaside resort was an instant international success on its
release, with its lanky writer/director/star acclaimed a
worthy successor to Charlie Chaplin and Buster Keaton.
But what few moviegoers realized at the time was that,
while Tati was following in the footsteps of those silent
comic geniuses, he was beginning to diverge onto a path
of *sound* comedy all his own.

Like Chaplin and Keaton two-reelers, *Mr. Hulot's
Holiday* wins its laughs through broad physical slapstick. Unlike those films, it stops short of absurdity and
extreme exaggeration. Tati is firmly grounded in the
realist tradition. Nothing you see on screen couldn't
(with allowances) happen in everyday life. Every bit of
this virtually plotless film proceeds from hours of observation of ordinary human behavior—the way people
stand, walk, gesture, etc. Through meticulous selection
and emphasis, Tati makes the most banal events—walking through a door, sitting on a sand dune, eating ice
cream—appear hilarious. Though every bit of business
is precisely timed and executed, Tati always tries to
create the impression of life casually passing before our
eyes as we watch the staff and guests of a small seaside
hotel come and go from their rooms to the beach and then
back to the hotel for dinner. Nothing in the conventional
sense "happens"—even in relation to the tall, gawky,
pipe-smoking, invariably polite Mr. Hulot, played by
Tati himself. Again in contrast to his silent comedy
mentors, Tati doesn't distinguish the character he plays
in any radical way. Hulot is no bedraggled "little man,"
but rather very much a part of society. His problem with
an unwieldy canoe (one of the film's funniest scenes) is
the sort of scrape virtually anyone might find themselves in. Tati never reaches for a big vulgar laugh when
a gentler chuckle would serve just as well.

PROVIDENCE

(1977), C, *Director:* Alain Resnais. *With* John Gielgud,
Dirk Bogarde, David Warner, Ellen Burstyn, and Elaine
Stritch. **104 min.** *R*. Tape: RCA/Columbia.

Like all the works of French filmmaker Alain Resnais,
Providence is a film that fairly bristles with visual wit
and a keen intellectual adventurousness. But unlike
such sobersided Resnais productions as *Hiroshima, Mon
Amour* and *La Guerre est Finie, Providence* plumbs
man's soul in a most unusual way: It's a comedy of
bone-dry drawing room brittleness and sophistication.

Scripted by playwright David Mercer (best known to
moviegoers for writing the hit comedy *Morgan!*), *Providence* centers on an emminent aging man of letters,
Clive Langham (John Gielgud in his finest screen performance). Laying wide awake at night in his enormous
mansion (the "Providence" of the film's title), Langham
is slowly but surely expiring from a number of difficult
and painful illnesses. But rather than face death with
stoic resignation, Langham has elected to go out with a
smile on his lips and an antic gleam in his eye. As he gets
himself soused on a succession of bottles of white wine,
the old novelist begins to compose in his head one final
tale that will bring together in fiction the disparate
elements of his actual life. From the film's first moments
Resnais embroils us in these imaginary scenes featuring
Langham's stuffed-shirt of a son Claude (Dirk Bogarde),
his illegitimate offspring Kevin (David Warner), his
slightly mysterious daughter-in-law Sonia (Ellen Burstyn), and his late wife Molly (Elaine Stritch). The characters shuttle about this way and that in a fanciful tale
involving adultery, terrorism, mercy-killing, and were-
wolves. Dawn's early light reveals the reality behind
Langham's often savage imaginings. All the figures of
his fictional universe are revealed in their actual lives at
a party given to celebrate the old man's birthday. But
Resnais has so upset our usual reactions to people,
places, and events that we aren't sure whether we can
take this "reality" at face value or not.

THE RULES OF THE GAME

(1939), B/W, *Director:* Jean Renoir. *With* Roland
Toutain, Nora Gregor, Marcel Dalio, Gaston Modot,
Mila Parely, and Jean Renoir. **110 min.** In French with
English subtitles. *NR.* Tape: Video Yesteryear.

Though considered a classic today, Jean Renoir's com-
edy-drama about the tumultuous love lives of France's
social upper crust was a virtual disaster when it was
released in 1939. The political right attacked the film as
an insult to French national pride. The left dismissed
Renoir's barbs at the bourgeoisie as frivolous and trivial.
Non-aligned audiences found the film's loosely structured plot and rapid-fire action and dialogue downright
confusing. When World War II arrived and France was
occupied by the Germans, *Rules of the Game* was banned
as damaging to moral character. It wasn't until the film's
revival in the mid-1950s that its reputation became
established—by which time moviegoers found no
trouble in appreciating the social satire and technical
innovativeness of this romantic roundelay.

The center of Renoir's game of societal charades is a
young aviator (Roland Toutain) smitten with the Marquis' wife (Nora Gregor). Invited by the Marquis (Marcel
Dalio)—who has adulterous fish of his own to fry—to
spend a weekend at his country estate, the aviator soon
finds himself buffeted about by the whims of a society
playing games of romance for which the rules are con-
tinually being rewritten. He is swallowed up in the lives
of the Marquis' other guests, which are just as romantically complicated as his own.

Audiences today have little difficulty figuring out
what Renoir and his cast of gameplayers are up to. The
society presented in the film, rather than a vision of the
last gasp of the aristocracy, is actually a foretaste of
today's "jet set," where money and surface charm are far
more important than pedigree. Renoir's subtle inter-
weaving of characters and improvised acting is more the
rule today than the exception. Either as a scrupulously
well-observed satire of social mores or as a pure entertainment, *Rules of the Game* is enthralling.

THE SEVEN SAMURAI

(1954), B/W, *Director:* Akira Kurosawa. *With* Toshiro
Mifune, Takashi Shimura, Yoshio Inaba, Isao Kimura,
Seiji Miyaguchi, and Minoru Chiaki. **141 min.** In
Japanese with English subtitles. *NR.* Tape: Embassy.

The biggest and most expensive Japanese film of its
time, Akira Kurosawa's *Seven Samurai* is also one of the
best action adventure films ever made. Breaking with
the reserved, almost painterly, tradition of Japanese
costume films, Kurosawa thrusts us right into the midst
of the action in this tale of a group of poor farmers
defending themselves against an army of rampaging
war lords through the help of a small handful of outcast
samurai warriors. Rapid cutting and slow-motion techniques that were to become fashionable in later years in
the films of Sam Peckinpah and Stanley Kubrick got
their first outing in this 1954 feature. Not a whit of its
zest and exuberance has been lost through the years.

Toshiro Mifune stars, in an uncharacteristically comic
role, as a young thief with ambitions of becoming a
samurai warrior. Tagging along after the farmers as
they search the countryside for samurai fighters to help
defend a seemingly hopeless cause, he is eventually
accepted as part of the fighting band. The film then
settles down to well over an hour's worth of unadulter-
ated action, beautifully staged. Not since Eisenstein's
Alexander Nevsky has there been anything like the
series of skirmishes we see here between well-armed
horsemen and poorly equipped farmers. Overcoming
brute force with clever strategy, the samurai help the
farmers fight back by teaching them how to take the
offensive and split the army's forces apart. The outcome,
as might be expected, finds good triumphing over evil—
but not before much pain, suffering, and loss of life.

Though remade as a Hollywood western, *The Magnificent Seven,* and further imitated by the so-called
"spaghetti westerns" of Sergio Leone (*A Fistful of Dollars, The Good the Bad and the Ugly*), the power of
Kurosawa's imagery and sense of dramatic detail remain unmatched.

GANGSTER FILMS

Often controversial and always violent, the Gangster Film has come into its own as perhaps the most poignant expression of American social drama. These are hard-hitting films, no doubt, and the criticism that they glorify crime has nipped at the heels of their artistic merits. These films, however, contain some of the landmark performances of all time. Action movies play well on the home screen, and the Gangster Films are no exception. Considering the fact that Gangster Films are as much about characters as they are about action, the home screen provides a forum that can rival the big screen in terms of intensity. Within this chapter are bold studies of blind ambition and ruthless drive. Without doubt, the Gangster Film has provided some of the best documentation of 20th century America—and some of the best dialogue to boot. Other Gangster Films to consider include: *Angels With Dirty Faces, Bonnie and Clyde, The Godfather, High Sierra, Little Caesar, The Petrified Forest,* and *The Roaring Twenties.*

Scarface. *Tony Camonte (Paul Muni) goes out in the same blaze of bullets that first brought him to power.*

THE GODFATHER, PART II

(1974), **C**, *Director:* Francis Ford Coppola. *With* Robert De Niro, Al Pacino, Lee Strasberg, Robert Duvall, Diane Keaton, John Cazale, Talia Shire, and Michael V. Gazzo. **200 min.** *R*. Tape, CED, Laser: Paramount.

Made in the wake of *The Godfather* and its record-breaking popularity, *Part II* is that rarity, a sequel that actually improves on the original. Whereas *Part I* seemed rather constricted by a forced fidelity to Mario Puzo's best seller and the overbearing presence of Marlon Brando, *Part II* moves more freely.

Director Francis Ford Coppola jumps back and forth in time, chronicling the humble origins of the late Godfather, first as a child in Sicily, and later as a young man in New York's Little Italy, where he embarks on a career of crime more for justice than profit. This long, detailed turn-of-the-century flashback is arguably Coppola's best work, and Robert De Niro as the soft-spoken, sensual young Vito Corleone delivers a performance that credibly ennobles the character. This romantic view of an immigrant's initiation into crime is juxtaposed with an exposé of the overwhelming power the crime syndicate has in U.S. and foreign politics today. As the mafiosi make their bid for corporate respectability, the film shows them killing in the same old way. In fact, every murderous deed in the movie's second half foretells or echoes another in the first.

The lengendary actor/teacher Lee Strasberg makes his belated film debut as a frail mobster of the old school, the kind of Jewish uncle you don't turn your back on.

THE LONG GOOD FRIDAY

(1979), C, *Director:* John Mackenzie. *With* Bob Hoskins, Helen Mirren, Pierce Brosnan, Eddie Constantine, Dave King, Bryan Marshall, George Coulouris, and Stephen Davies. **114 min.** *R.* Tape: Thorn/EMI.

Rather than merely transporting the American gangster film to the shores of England, director John Mackenzie has created in *The Long Good Friday* a gangster movie with a very English identity. It depicts the passion and agony of a big-time London racketeer during a particularly violent Easter weekend.

Harold (Bob Hoskins) is setting up the biggest shady deal in Europe when several attempts are made on his life. One of his associates is stabbed in the shower of a public pool, and another is crucified. "Who's having a go at me?" wonders Harold, as his prospective American partners start suspecting that Harold may be a bad risk. To protect himself, Harold must resort to force and intimidation after 10 years of near-respectability. Old-school, self-made mobsters like Harold, the film suggests, would do better to keep an eye on more than just the Common Market; they should realize that there are many forms of violence, and those who kill for a cause can be deadlier than those who kill for profit. To reveal more would be unfair to this complex film.

As muscular and violent as its American counterparts, this film also has a nice eye for flashy clothes and fancy cars, as well as barbed, witty dialogue. (A handy lexicon of British underworld slang is provided in the opening credits). Hoskins is a burly actor with the most dangerous-looking set of lower teeth in the business, a sort of demonic Pat O'Brien. Helen Mirren's sympathetic portrayal of Harold's high-class mistress is a welcome exception in this mostly misogynous genre; and Pierce Brosnan, TV's suave Remington Steele, plays a hit man who lures his victims with his good looks.

The Long Good Friday. *Mob boss Harold Shand (Bob Hoskins, center) corrals his suspects and puts them in the proper mood to talk. The ruthlessness of Shand's methods stands in direct opposition to his avowed intention to "go legit."*

The Public Enemy. *An American classic: the stick-up. Tom Powers (James Cagney) relieves a victim of his money in grand fashion.*

THE PUBLIC ENEMY

(1931), B/W, *Director:* William Wellman. *With* James
Cagney, Jean Harlow, Eddie Woods, Beryl Mercer,
Donald Cook, Joan Blondell, and Mae Clarke. **84 min.**
NR. Tape: CBS/Fox; CED: RCA VideoDisc.

Films like *The Public Enemy* may be technically out-
moded, but they tell us how Americans felt about the
important issues of their time. Such early films function
as time capsules, preserving the slang, fashions, and
attitudes of an era. *The Public Enemy* gives us an insider's view of Prohibition and gangsterism as it was in
the 1930s. The sense of immediacy more than compen-
sates for any stylistic deficiency.

This film surely must be the closest Hollywood ever
came to depicting gangsters as they were, with no
punches pulled and no surface gloss. It's very much like a
documentary. James Cagney became an overnight star
after switching roles with Eddie Woods, who had been
assigned the leading role of Tom Powers. Cagney was
born to play Powers. Like Tom, Cagney came from an
Irish working-class family in a tough neighborhood, and
he knew the grit. In the film, he's a bully and a killer,
spitting beer in a bartender's face, shoving half a grape-
fruit in his girl's face, smacking another moll, and
wiping out a rival gang before he collapses from several
gunshot wounds. ("I ain't so tough," Tom utters directly
to the audience, and we can almost hear a packed 1931
house gasp, "But you are! You are!")

The ending, in which Tom's bloodstained body is delivered like a parcel to his mother's doorstep, packs a
gruesome wallop, but what we remember most is Cagney's energy and power. He almost dances the part.

SCARFACE

(1932), B/W, *Director:* Howard Hawks. *With* Paul Muni,
Ann Dvorak, George Raft, Boris Karloff, Karen Morely,
and Vince Barnett. **94 min.** *NR.* Tape: MCA.

As controversial in its time as *Bonnie and Clyde* or
The Godfather in ours, *Scarface* was charged with excessive violence, social irresponsibility, defamation of
minorities, and inevitably, glorification of crime. Kept
out of circulation for decades by producer Howard
Hughes and recently remade (with Al Pacino), the
original *Scarface* remains a throbbing, vitally American
film. It is a gangland opera, full of fedoras and tommy
guns, with more shadows and symbols than a German
silent picture.

In his first major role, Paul Muni is both repellent and
endearing as gangster Tony Camonte (a portrayal based
on Al Capone), a coarse immigrant rising to the top of the
underworld through energy and cunning. What censors
objected to most was that it is neither society nor the law
that bring Camonte down, but rather a fatal, intrinsic
flaw in his own nature. Possessive of his kid sister (Ann
Dvorak) almost to the point of incest, Camonte kills her
suspected lover (George Raft), a man who had been his
best friend. This first emotional killing in his career
shatters Camonte's self-confidence; he becomes careless
and inept. This leads to his downfall.

Scarface can be seen as proof of Hughes's fascination
with the acquisition of power, or as one of Howard
Hawks's most outrageous comedies, or more reasonably,
as a milestone in the genre. When it was first released,
censors forced Hughes to substitute a more "edifying"
ending, but on tape you'll see the original death-in-the-
gutter finale.

WHITE HEAT

(1949), B/W, *Director:* Raoul Walsh. *With* James
Cagney, Margaret Wycherly, Edmond O'Brien, Virginia
Mayo, and Steve Cochran. **114 min.** *NR.* Tape, CED:
CBS/Fox.

In this 1949 picture, James Cagney played his first
gangster role in 10 years. Crime movies had changed
since the 1930s, the angle now being psychological
rather than behavioral—*why* (rather than *how*) a gangster gets to be that way.

Cagney's Cody Jarrett has a touching affection for his
Ma (Margaret Wycherly), a tough old lady who has
taught her boy all he needs to know about heisting and
running a tight mob. His dependence on her is so strong
that when Cody, serving time in the pen, learns that she
has been killed, he goes spectacularly berserk. An undercover agent (Edmond O'Brien) planted in Cody's cell
eventually comes to replace Ma Jarrett in Cody's life.
Betrayed by the agent, Cody blows himself up in the end
atop a gas tank screaming, "Top of the world, Ma!"

At 51, Cagney looks heavy and jowly, and he doesn't
bounce like the Cagney of old; but this is his last great
gangster role and he makes the most of it, paying tribute
where he must to his films of yesteryear (as when he
kicks his moll off a chair) and displaying a much darker,
1940s brand of humor. Director Raoul Walsh, that most
robust of American directors, easily recapitulates every
trend of this period, and then some.

GREAT BOOKS

One of the most difficult propositions a filmmaker ever faces is making a movie from a classic of literature. The films in this chapter are those that have triumphed over the odds: They have taken great works of fiction and made movies that are equal, if not superior, to the source. In many ways, video brings the translation full circle—back to the home where the book was first discovered. Aided with special effects like freeze-frame and rewind, the movie can actually be watched as a book is read—repeating passages that were especially poignant or that were misunderstood the first time around, going slowly through a favorite scene. There are other films in this book that were based on novels, but the films in the Great Books category are based on literary classics. We have chosen films that compare favorably with these works—films that may provoke you to remark that the book was "different," but never that the book was "better." Other book adaptations to consider are: *All the King's Men, A Farewell to Arms, The Great Gatsby, The Hunchback of Notre Dame, Little Women, Ragtime, Sophie's Choice,* and *The Tin Drum.*

A Tale of Two Cities. *The detailed world of Charles Dickens comes extravagantly alive in this MGM production.*

DELIVERANCE

(1972), C, *Director:* John Boorman. *With* Burt Reynolds, John Voight, Ned Beatty, Ronny Cox, Billy McKinney, Herbert "Cowboy" Coward, and James Dickey. **105 min.** *R*. Tape, CED: Warner; Laser: MCA.

A poet writes a novel of adventure in the American south which an English director then brings to the screen with Burt Reynolds. What should be the result? *Deliverance,* one of the finest films of the 1970s, is the gratifying sum of those disparate parts. Both the film itself and director John Boorman were Oscar nominees for this 1972 release.

James Dickey's brilliant story concerns four middle-class men from suburban Atlanta who spend a weekend canoeing down a challenging river in northern Georgia. A large hydroelectric dam is being built that will soon transform the river and all that surrounds it into a series of lakes and reservoirs. The quartet's interaction with the rural inhabitants, the raging river, and themselves makes for an intense adventure.

Deliverance is a unique film in that Dickey stayed very close to the project. He wrote the screenplay with a fidelity to the source material that only he could provide. And he also turns in a flawless performance as the sheriff, whose quiet weariness is an appropriate response to this rambling tale.

This is as physically exhilarating a movie as anyone could imagine. The ensemble acting is riveting, but the main star is the river itself, with its white-water strength and deafening roar. Its rushing rapids that end in pristine, calm waters carry along an ominous atmosphere that clings to the weekend wanderers.

Deliverance also provides what real drama should: hard choices. The actions taken and the decisions made on the river both enliven and repulse us. The characters are credible human beings; we can't be indifferent to their fates. As their journey progresses we want to grab a paddle and help set a steadier course. However, we are tempered by a sobering doubt: Would we really behave any differently?

EAST OF EDEN

(1955), C, *Director:* Elia Kazan. *With* James Dean, Jo
Van Fleet, Julie Harris, Raymond Massey, Burl Ives,
Richard Davalos, and Albert Dekker. **105 min.** *NR*.
Tape, CED: Warner.

James Dean had only three starring roles in his brief
career, and *East of Eden* is his best. This stunning 1955
adaptation of John Steinbeck's novel was a critical and
box-office success whose appeal has not been tarnished
by time.

The movie is a faithful rendering of the novel. It is an
updated Cain and Abel story, and it should be obvious
who carries the mark of Cain. The story is set in 1917 in
Salinas, California, the "lettuce bowl" of the nation. It
shows a divided family trying to adapt to the strains and
challenges of their time, while the spectre of World War I
casts a shadow on all endeavors.

Director Elia Kazan, fresh from his triumphant *On the
Waterfront,* switched coasts and eras to concoct a boisterous stew of American xenophobia and old testament
fear. The movie is beautifully intense, and its strange
power can be traced to the mother of the tale and the
defiant son (Jo Van Fleet and James Dean).

Van Fleet's performance as Dean's mother justly gar-
nered her an Oscar as Best Supporting Actress. It is a
marvelous, guilty pleasure. Her sly, worldweary smile is
only part of her remarkable presence. She easily com-
mands every scene she graces, and that same presence,
so sure and strong, hovers over the rest of the film.

And James Dean is his mother's son. Dean the
brooder. Dean the violent. Dean the misunderstood. He
is now a legend, practically removed from critical inter-
pretation. But if there is any mystery remaining among
viewers as to how a man dead for three decades can be a
cult figure . . . watch this film and the mystery dissolves
as his stature continues to grow.

East of Eden. *Cal (James Dean) registers a look of compressed heartache as he pines for the favor of his father. John Steinbeck's period novel sets the stage for a powerful drama of brother against brother and son against father.*

The Grapes of Wrath. *The Joad family, Rosasharn (Dorris Bowden), Ma (Jane Darwell), and Tom (Henry Fonda), head for California. Historical perspective permeates this tale of dust-bowl migration, but the personal drama is every bit as strong.*

THE GRAPES OF WRATH

(1940), B/W, *Director:* John Ford. *With* Henry Fonda,
John Carradine, Jane Darwell, Charley Grapewin,
Dorris Bowden, Russell Simpson, and John Qualen.
128 min. *NR.* Tape, CED: CBS/Fox.

It has been over 40 years since John Ford filmed *The
Grapes of Wrath,* and it still ranks among the most
popular American films ever made. Ford was given an
Oscar for directing this classic, and it is also Henry
Fonda's most famous role.

This is Steinbeck's saga of the travail of the Joad
family as they search for employment and social justice
in Depression-era America.

As Tom Joad, Henry Fonda is not the stolid, ever-
decent presence we've come to expect. In this movie he
has a bitter edge. Another surprise is John Carradine's
magnetic performance as Casey the Preacher, whose
beliefs have been supplanted by doubts. Perhaps the
greatest irony is that in this 1940 film the federal government is heroic, fair, and compassionate. It is portrayed as a source of hope. Viewing this movie indicates
how far we have traveled from the New Deal.

All of the splendid performances are perfectly framed
by Ford and cinematographer Gregg Toland *(Citizen
Kane).* The black-and-white images are gritty evoca-
tions of tough times and convey the bleak fervor of the
novel. Steinbeck's book has not been fashioned into a
mere polemic extolling proletarian virtues. It does not
ignore noble efforts made by, and on behalf of, poor and
working people.

This is a great film to see and savor if only for the pure
heat and light of Tom Joad's final soliloquy: ". . . a fella
ain't got a soul of his own, just a little piece of one big
soul . . ." and on he speaks of the need for justice and
determination; words that would echo through the same
fields decades later as Cesar Chavez continued the same
work. Films based on principles are like those same field
workers: We need them, and they must not be diminished.

LORD JIM

(1965), C, *Director:* Richard Brooks. *With* Peter O'Toole,
James Mason, Curt Jurgens, Eli Wallach, Jack
Hawkins, Paul Lukas, Daliah Lavi, and Akim Tamiroff.
154 min. *NR.* Tape: RCA/Columbia.

Lord Jim is a marvelous film that successfully com-
presses and highlights the major themes of Joseph Conrad's masterly novel. It is a movie with resonance
because director Richard Brooks matches the conflicts of
the soul with the questions of physical courage that
haunt the man Conrad referred to as "poor Jim." This
film was also important for demonstrating to audiences
enthralled by his performance in *Lawrence of Arabia,*
that Peter O'Toole is indeed an actor of uncommon depth
and range.

The story of the westerner escaping his past only to
meet it head-on, as if Mercator also drew maps of the
moral sphere, is familiar and frequently employed for a
simple reason: It rings true. *Lord Jim* is a westerner who
first loses his sense of honor and then strives to reclaim
it. The story follows Jim's early, promising career, his
failure, and his slow recuperation, and finally brings
him to an ultimate and inevitable test of will.

The film is more of a linear story than the disjointed
novel, which contained several narrative voices.
Brooks's choice is wise, since it presents us with a story
of ongoing suspense laced with a fearful undertone. The
director presents the challenges of the sea with a vis-
ceral, tingling sense of danger. He examines the exotic
islands and their even more exotic inhabitants with an
equally fresh eye for the bizarre and the beautiful. And
young Peter O'Toole with the not-yet-weathered skin
but the same soulful eyes, invests the film with all the
subtlety that Brooks's approach lacks. The merger of
Brooks's boldness and O'Toole's restraint produces a satisfying film of deceptively quiet strength.

Unbelievably, English was Conrad's third language.
But, thanks to the talents of Brooks and O'Toole, he
speaks to us in this film with a clear, timeless voice.

THE MAN WHO WOULD BE KING

(1975), C, *Director:* John Huston. *With* Sean Connery,
Michael Caine, Christopher Plummer, Saeed Jaffrey,
and Shakira Caine. **129 min.** *PG*. Tape: CBS/Fox.

John Huston has made many memorable films (*The
Maltese Falcon, Treasure of the Sierra Madre*), but this
may be his finest. His adaptation is actually an improve-
ment on the Rudyard Kipling short story, and moves
with a dreamlike assurance. It captures the bemuse-
ment of Kipling while winning us with its kinetic action
and colorful locales.

As the film begins, Kipling (Christopher Plummer)
witnesses Peachy (Michael Caine) and Danny's (Sean
Connery) pact to plunder a remote land beyond the
Khyber Pass. The two adventurers intend to make their
fortunes in Asia Minor, in a land far beyond the Empire's
bureaucratic restraints. The story follows their travels,
triumphs, and tragedies.

This movie is blessed with sensational performances.
As their Gurka interpreter Billy Fish, Saeed Jaffrey is
the model of eastern charm mixed with street-smarts
and plateau-platitudes. Plummer's cameo performance
as Kipling is infused with intelligence and wonder. And
the two central characters are certainly a cause for wonder. Playing Peachy, Caine is a colonial con man, replete
with a larcenous smile and a silvery-cockney tongue.
And Connery simply runs rampant in his greatest role.
Connery has had other successes outside of Her Maj-
esty's Secret Service, but it's this astonishing performance that will stand. His portrayal of Danny, the man
who would not only be King but God as well, is flawless.

The film takes us on a great and foolish adventure,
obscene in its daring, bubbling with imperialist ironies
and Victorian charm. Huston displays his sure touch for
action laced with outrageous humor and grand ideas.

Somewhere, behind the laughter, Rudyard Kipling
must be smiling, certain that the world is a better place
since John Huston made *The Man Who Would Be King*.

ONE FLEW OVER
THE CUCKOO'S NEST

(1975), C, *Director:* Milos Forman. *With* Jack Nicholson,
Louise Fletcher, William Redfield, Michael Beryman,
Brad Dourif, Peter Brocco, and Will Sampson. **129 min.**
R. Tape: Thorn/EMI; CED: RCA VideoDisc.

It is odd, but undeniable, that a brilliant Czech director has captured the exuberance and idealism of the
1960s with a truer spirit than any American can hon-
estly claim. This Milos Forman film deservedly swept all
of the major film awards in 1975. Author Ken Kesey and
some fans of the novel thought the film was somehow
disloyal; McMurphy should be bigger, he should have
red hair, it doesn't feel right, the Nurse should be huge,
the Chief should never speak. Forman obviously did not
simply read the book. He climbed inside it. With due
respect and apologies to all, this film surpasses the book
in feeling, intelligence, and power.

The story begins in Oregon in the early 1960s when
R. P. McMurphy (Jack Nicholson) decides to escape the
penal work farm by getting himself committed to a
mental institution. His war with that institution, sym-
bolized by his battles with Nurse Ratched (Louise
Fletcher), is a metaphor for the struggle for individual
freedom and dignity. McMurphy enlists his fellow patients in a crusade: to come back to life!

Producer Michael Douglas made a series of perfect
choices: Haskell Wexler's superb cinematography, Jack
Nietzche's haunting, bucolic score, and a screenplay by
Laurence Hauben and Bo Goldman that perfectly realizes the seminal line from the book—"It's the truth, even
if it didn't happen." This truth is embodied in Forman's
vivid direction. The truth is also present in Fletcher's
portrayal of Nurse Ratched. She's logical, and that quiet
logic is slowly magnified into authoritarian lunacy.

But most of all, *One Flew Over the Cuckoo's Nest*
belongs to Nicholson. His portrayal of McMurphy is the
essence of American vitality, humor, and common decency. He takes the role of a lifetime and gives the
performance of a lifetime. See it!

SLAUGHTERHOUSE FIVE

(1972), C, *Director:* George Roy Hill. *With* Michael Sacks, Ron Leibman, Eugene Roche, Sharon Gans, Valerie Perrine, John Dehner, Holly Near, and Perry King. **104 min.** *R.* Tape: MCA.

For a film that was awarded the 1972 Jury Prize at the Cannes Film Festival, *Slaughterhouse Five* is a well-kept secret. Kurt Vonnegut's novel appeared to fall into the category of magnificent books that defy screen adaptation. But director George Roy Hill was not dissuaded, and he surprised audiences with a cunningly faithful film version of the work.

In the book, Vonnegut's frequent coda is, "So it goes." Well, this is how it goes: Billy Pilgrim has come "unstuck in time," moving between his middle-American domestic life to the planet Tralfamadore, where he is cohabitating with a sexy film star as part of that planet's study of earthlings and finally, back to the senseless Allied bombing of Dresden, Germany, where he is a P.O.W. These jolting shifts in the story convey the author's sense that life is not so much a clear, linear path as a collection of random moments.

The film contains many fine performances, but it is the haunting images that linger, particularly those of the decaying Third Reich. In the book and the film, the fire storm that destroys Dresden is a metaphor for the random insanity that we can't fit into our daily lives. Billy Pilgrim chooses to sublimate. The pieces of his life jam together like jagged ice. In the first chapter of the book, the wife of one of Vonnegut's war buddies reacts harshly to his idea for a book about Dresden:

"You'll pretend you were men instead of babies, and you'll be played in the movies by Frank Sinatra and John Wayne or some of those other glamorous, warloving, dirty old men. And war will look just wonderful, so we'll have a lot more of them . . ." Kurt Vonnegut promised her that would not happen and the film *Slaughterhouse Five,* like the book, is a promise kept.

A TALE OF TWO CITIES

(1935), B/W, *Director:* Jack Conway. *With* Ronald
Colman, Elizabeth Allan, Blanche Yurka, Reginald
Owen, and Basil Rathbone. **128 min.** *NR*. Tape:
MGM/UA; CED: RCA VideoDisc.

"This is no modern best-seller . . . but a book that is
revered by tens of millions of people here and abroad." So
said David O. Selznick, the producer of *A Tale of Two
Cities,* and his respect for great literature permeates this
film. It was a spectacular popular success and was also
nominated for best picture of the year. Almost 50 years
later it is still a captivating example of the grand tradition of Hollywood moviemaking.

The two cities of the title are Paris, where a revolution
is unleashed, and London, where observers can feel the
anger in partisan France and feel their own discomfort
at its intensity. This is the story of an extended family
inevitably thrust into the Parisian fury. It also tells of
British lawyer Sidney Carton's unrequited love and the
manner in which he ultimately establishes the purity of
that love.

As Carton, Ronald Colman is comfortably confident.
The role requires a sardonic touch that is part of his
natural approach. It has been said that Colman, in all
his roles, always played himself. Judging on the basis of
this film, he made the correct choice. Most of the acting
in the film is well above average, but Blanche Yurka
stands out. As Madam Defarge she is a feverish knitter,
a nasty plotter, and a shameless scene-stealer.

There are mammoth scenes in this movie, such as the
storming of the Bastille, that are old Hollywood on a
grand scale. But the guillotine is the recurring metaphor. It is powered by the same gravity that holds all of
the characters in place; pressed to their fates.

"It was the best of times, it was the worst of times, we
had everything before us, we had nothing before us . . .
in short it was a period very like the present." As a
depiction of love, courage, and devotion, this film, like
the works of Charles Dickens, will be with us as long as
those virtues hold our esteem.

TESS

(1979), C, *Director:* Roman Polanski. *With* Nastassia Kinski, Peter Firth, John Bett, and Tom Chadbon. **170 min.** *PG.* Tape, CED, Laser: RCA/Columbia.

Tess, Roman Polanski's adaptation of Thomas Hardy's *Tess of the d'Urbervilles,* marked his triumphant return to filmmaking. *Tess* was a critical success that gained appreciative audiences on two continents.

In Hardy's novel it was not the butler but the Parson who did it. For from the moment Parson Tringham informs old John Durbeyfield that he is descended from nobility, all the Durbeyfields' problems begin. The father pushes his beautiful daughter on to higher social stratas and unknowingly, into moral dilemmas she is unprepared to face. But with each challenge her character grows.

Tess is a sumptuous feast of a movie with images of such stunning clarity that its afterglow is as strong as its heroine's desires. Hardy's novel was first published in 1891 and described an English countryside that was nearly magical. Polanski has faithfully rendered that magic on the screen. The texture and delicate beauty of this film are hypnotic.

But the director also elicits from this story its innate respect for common wisdom; Tess stands up to champion natural, truthful emotions in the face of artificial upper-class manners. And these stiff manners and studied poses appear to exist only to mask corruption and degeneracy. These class conflicts are beautifully embodied in Tess's relationships with men who long to possess her rather than love her.

As *Tess,* Nastassia Kinski (who was 17 at the time of the filming) ranks among the most startlingly beautiful women in the history of the cinema. And her ravishing beauty does not overshadow her fine performance.

The film rights to *Tess* were purchased from the estate of David O. Selznick. This is appropriate since Polanski brought to this project the same appreciation of classic literature that characterized Selznick's productions. *Tess* is an achingly beautiful movie.

THE THREE MUSKETEERS

(1974), C, *Director:* Richard Lester. *With* Michael York,
Oliver Reed, Frank Finlay, Richard Chamberlain,
Charlton Heston, Raquel Welch, Christopher Lee,
Geraldine Chaplin, and Faye Dunaway. **107 min.** *PG*.
Tape: USA; CED: RCA VideoDisc.

In 1974 director Richard Lester created a splendid
rendering of *The Three Musketeers*. Despite stiff competition, it landed on most ten-best lists and was a substan-
tial box-office success.

Alexandre Dumas's classic historical novel depicted
the factional feuding of 17th Century France. The story
hinges on the romance of Queen Anne and the English
Duke of Buckingham during the reign of King Louis
XIV, the insipid "Sun King." The tale is propelled by the
musketeers' determination to protect the honor and happiness of their Queen. Lester methodically strips away
our preconceptions of this period. He retains the love,
valor and devotion, but in place of ostentatious chivalry
and affected camaraderie he inserts joyful loyalty and a
rambunctious zest for life.

Lester's film is so animated that it makes the 1948 film
version look like an oil painting. Also, Lester's casting is
star-studded yet inventive. The musketeers are Oliver
Reed (Athos), Frank Finlay (Porthos), and Richard
Chamberlain (Aramis), with Michael York as the innocently brazen D'Artagnan. As the Queen, Geraldine
Chaplin glows with a soft beauty that is, quite literally
for the musketeers, worth dying for. Charlton Heston
turns in his best performance in years as Cardinal
Richelieu, the sinister power behind the throne. And this
is Raquel Welch's finest performance.

The fight sequences in this film are broadly comical
because the director is enraptured by frenetic movement. These guys even eat and belch with a certain élan.
But with all of the wide-eyed bravado that cascades from
the screen, the movie does not slight our heroes.

So it's all for one and one for all and all for fun in the
service of a superb movie. All honor to the director, cast,
and crew—and Dumas, too.

HISTORICAL EPICS

These are the expensive films, with casts of thousands, detailed sets and costumes, and difficult location shots. Because the nature of Historical Epics is big, they can't help but be dwarfed by the small screen—it is nearly impossible to take in all the color, characters, and detail on a television set. However, the good Epics are more than spectacle. They are first and foremost powerful dramas that are played out in a historical setting of great proportions. Powerful drama was the test for inclusion in this chapter, and there's no doubt you'll feel the power at home. The Historical Epic has been sadly neglected by most modern filmmakers. Fortunately, video has the goods, and what you can't find in the theaters, you can find on the rental shelves. Other Epics to consider: *Becket, Doctor Zhivago, El Cid, The Fall of the Roman Empire, The Longest Day, The Private Life of Henry VIII, Reds, Samson and Delilah, The Ten Commandments,* and *The Wind and the Lion.*

Ben Hur. *Judah Ben Hur (Charlton Heston) and Messala the Tribune (Stephen Boyd) compete head-to-head in the treacherous chariot race.*

ALEXANDER NEVSKY

(1938), B/W, *Director:* Sergei Eisenstein. *With* Nikolai
Cherkassov, Nikolai Okhlopkov, Alexander Abrikossov,
Dmitri Orlov, and Vassily Novikov. **107 min.** *NR.* Tape:
Budget.

Russian director Sergei Eisenstein made a number of
extraordinary films during his career, among them
Potemkin (1925) and *Ivan The Terrible,* Parts 1 & 2
(1945). But his 1938 epic, *Alexander Nevsky,* is arguably
his finest and most fascinating work. Moreover, it had
dramatic political implications, helping to mobilize the
Soviet people against the threat of Nazi Germany
(though Stalin and Hitler were about to sign their ill-
fated Nonaggression Pact).

It is the first half of the 13th century; Teutonic knights
strike at Russia from the west, conquering cities, plundering, burning children, and hanging civic leaders.
Fisherman Alexander Nevsky lays aside his nets to
rally Russian peasants against the German hordes.
With Nevsky at their head, the crudely armed peasants
battle the mounted knights on the frozen Lake Tchoudsk.
Midway through the decisive conflict, the ice breaks and
the German army, weighted by their armor, sinks and
drowns *en masse.*

As spectacles go, *Alexander Nevsky* is one of the biggest, from its breathtaking vistas of ancient cities to the
climactic battle on the ice. The film also boasts a remarkable synergy between the visuals and the music, Eisenstein having worked closely with composer Sergei Pro-
kofiev during production.

In spite of its jingoism, which is irritating to contemporary eyes, *Alexander Nevsky* is rousing entertainment
and an important look at events that helped to form
modern Russia.

BEN HUR

(1959), C, *Director:* William Wyler. *With* Charlton
Heston, Stephen Boyd, Jack Hawkins, Haya Harareet,
Hugh Griffith, Martha Scott, and Sam Jaffe. **217 min.**
NR. Tape, Laser, CED: MGM/UA.

When MGM decided to film General Lew Wallace's
novel, *Ben Hur,* for a second time—having made a silent
version in 1926—the future of the studio was at stake. If
Ben Hur failed, the $12.5 million investment would
bankrupt MGM. To increase the odds of success, they
hired the brilliant William Wyler to direct, signed
Charlton Heston to star, and sent the cast and crew
packing to Egypt and Italy for location shooting. The
result became one of the top-grossing films of all time,
winning a record 11 Academy Awards to boot.

When the Tribune Messala (Stephen Boyd) asks
Judah Ben Hur, a Jewish prince, to reveal which of his
countrymen are unhappy with Roman rule, the lifelong
friends have a bitter falling out. Later, when Judah's
sister accidentally frightens the horse of the parading
Roman governor, Messala retaliates by sending the girl
and her mother to prison and condemning Judah to row
as a galley slave. During a battle four years later, Judah
saves the life of the Roman Commander Quintus Arrius
(Jack Hawkins) and is given his freedom. But on arriv-
ing home he discovers that his mother and sister have
become lepers. Enraged, Judah meets Messala in a
chariot race, which costs the Tribune his life. The race is
11 minutes of the most thunderous action ever put on
film. His anger spent, Judah becomes a follower of Jesus.
When his mother and sister do likewise, they are cured.

While *Ben Hur* is not a true story, the events it portrays are historical; in fact, the empathy that it shows
existed between Jews and Arabs under Roman rule is
particularly interesting, given their current disagreements. Though the picture is long—nearly 4 hours—it is
never ponderous, thanks to the moving characterizations, Heston's Judah and Hugh Griffith's Sheik Ilderim
chief among them. Both actors won Oscars for their
work, as did Wyler; the movie itself won Best Picture.

LAWRENCE OF ARABIA

(1962), C, *Director:* David Lean. *With* Peter O'Toole, Alec Guinness, Omar Sharif, Anthony Quinn, Jack Hawkins, Anthony Quayle, Claude Rains, Arthur Kennedy, and José Ferrer. **221 min.** *NR.* Tape, Laser, CED: RCA/Columbia.

David Lean has directed some of the most successful and extraordinary films in history, among them *Bridge on the River Kwai* (1957) and *Doctor Zhivago* (1965). *Lawrence of Arabia* is his most fascinating work, however, not only because of its historical significance but because of its glorious, tragic, and charismatic central figure. And no film has ever matched *Lawrence of Arabia's* visual splendor, the picture having been filmed in the actual deserts and cities where Lawrence lived and fought.

During its 221 minutes, *Lawrence of Arabia* traces the career of T. E. Lawrence (Peter O'Toole) from British Army Headquarters in Cairo to his appointment as emissary to Prince Feisal (Alec Guinness) to his taking up arms in the cause of Arab liberation—ultimately turning against his own imperialistic countrymen.

After Marlon Brando and Albert Finney turned down the role, the part of Lawrence went to little-known British stage actor O'Toole. The Oscar-nominated O'Toole did a remarkable job humanizing the complex Lawrence, from his messianic highs to his savage lows, receiving excellent support from Guinness, Omar Sharif, Anthony Quinn, Jack Hawkins, Anthony Quayle, and Claude Rains. Rarely have art and history been so expertly merged, making *Lawrence of Arabia* not only the finest historical epic, but one of the greatest motion pictures of all time.

A MAN FOR ALL SEASONS

(1966), C, *Director:* Fred Zinnemann. *With* Paul Scofield, Wendy Hiller, Leo McKern, Robert Shaw, Orson Welles, Susannah York, Nigel Davenport, and Vanessa Redgrave. **120 min.** *NR*. Tape, Laser: RCA/Columbia.

One of the drawbacks to most historical films is that they are overwhelmed by their size. With the rare exception of a *Ben Hur* or *Lawrence of Arabia*, the characters are lost and, as a result, there's no drama. *A Man for All Seasons* is the antithesis of this kind of filmmaking, a movie in which the spectacle is entirely in the background, leaving center stage to the characters.

Sir Thomas More (1478–1535) was an English lawyer, humanist, and author who was also a Member of Parliament and a friend of King Henry VIII. Above all, however, he was a staunch Catholic, and when More refused to take an oath acknowledging the king, not the Pope, as the head of the Church in England, Sir Thomas was taken from his family and imprisoned, tried, and eventually executed.

In the hands of playwright Robert Bolt—who also penned the screenplay for *Lawrence of Arabia*—More's road to martyrdom is somber but uplifting, and also provides fascinating insight into the church and court politics of the time. There are no battles, no castle-storming, not even a DeMillian crowd scene. But there isn't a moment in *A Man for All Seasons* that doesn't crackle with life and emotion.

Paul Scofield, as the contemplative More, won the Academy Award as Best Actor, and the late Robert Shaw, as a robust Henry, was nominated as Best Supporting Actor. The film itself deservedly won Best Picture.

1776

(1972), C, *Director:* Peter H. Hunt. *With* Howard da
Silva, Ken Howard, William Daniels, Donald Madden,
Ron Holgate, David Ford, Blythe Danner, and Virginia
Vestoff. **141 min.** *G.* Tape: RCA/Columbia.

This film version of the Broadway musical hit offers
an endlessly entertaining history lesson and provides a
showcase for splendid performances by the original
Broadway cast.

As *1776* opens, Massachusetts' John Adams is having
a great deal of difficulty selling the idea of American
independence to the Continental Congress. A few repre-
sentatives, such as Benjamin Franklin (Howard da
Silva) and Thomas Jefferson (Ken Howard), share his
indignation over British tyranny, but most of the rep-
resentatives are content to suffer rather than risk a
noose by advocating rebellion. In order to stir them to
action, Adams, Franklin, and Jefferson undertake to
write a Declaration that they hope will state the griev-
ances against the Crown so clearly and passionately that
it cannot help but move the Congress to approve Independence.

The script for *1776* is virtually identical to the stirring, Pulitzer Prize-winning play, and the actors expertly bring to excitable, fanatic, and fallible life the
hitherto iconographic Founding Fathers—what one his-
torian has called "the most principled group of men ever
assembled." The picture also manages to give us a
glimpse of the legendary romance between Adams and
his wife Abigail.

The outcome of the debate is well-known. Then too,
most of the movie's tunes are merely serviceable upon
first hearing, and the action takes place almost entirely
in the confines of Independence Hall, making for a somewhat static, "stagey" look. Yet *1776* is a movie of ideas
and personalities, not cinematic invention, and is a
superb encapsulation of the American spirit.

HORROR FILMS

There are more Horror Films on tape than any other movie category. And whether the titles and packaging convey it or not, there are more *good* horror titles than you may think. Horror is the most schizophrenic of categories, subdividing quite radically between the "thrillers" of old and the "splatter films" in vogue today. Video, too, has a double-edged influence on the Horror Film. Because of the intimacy video offers, it can enhance the film's suspense in a way that a theater can't. But because videotape cannot reproduce the dense black qualities of film, much of the detail in the dark scenes so common in Horror Films is lost. Still, Horror Films work wonderfully on tape and, because of their popularity, many of the obscure titles are available. Several of the titles in this chapter are graphically violent. If you want to veer far from the gore, be sure to read the reviews carefully. Other Horror Films to consider include: *An American Werewolf in London, The Birds, The Bride of Frankenstein, Cat People, The Dead Zone, Dressed to Kill, The Howling, Play Misty for Me, Scanners,* and *The Shining.*

Dracula. *Bela Lugosi as the fabled count, a vampire who needs the blood of the living to survive.*

THE BROOD

(1979), C, *Director:* David Cronenberg. *With* Oliver
Reed, Samantha Eggar, Art Hindle, Cindy Hinds, Nuala
Fitzgerald, and Susan Hogan. **90 min.** *NR.* Tape:
Embassy.

Canadian director David Cronenberg has been referred to as "a man who likes to mortify the flesh." His
pictures (*They Came From Within, Rabid, Videodrome*)
are often a hypochondriac's nightmare. They usually
concern the psyche in revolt against the body. Cronenberg's crowning achievement, *The Brood,* can be viewed
as a modern-psychology update on the traditional werewolf theme.

In this film, a controversial psychotherapist named
Dr. Raglan (Oliver Reed) attempts to bring out his
patients' repressed anger. His most interesting subject is
Nola (Samantha Eggar) who, abused and neglected as a
child, may pose a threat to her own five-year-old daughter. Nola has unsuspected reserves of hostility. Dr. Raglan, as mad scientists of old, eventually liberates more
than he can control. From Nola's hate springs small,
featureless creatures in bright-colored jumpsuits, bent
on destruction.

The Brood borrows from other films of this genre—
there are inventive reworkings on themes from *Forbidden Planet, Don't Look Now,* and *Psycho.* Heavily cut on
its theatrical release, *The Brood* has now been restored
on tape to full length.

DRACULA

(1931), B/W, *Director:* Tod Browning. *With* Bela Lugosi, David Manners, Helen Chandler, Dwight Frye, Edward Van Sloan, Herbert Bunston, and Frances Dade. **75 min.** *NR*. Tape: MCA.

When *Dracula* was released in 1931, American audiences had never seen a film about vampires. Today—over 50 years and hundreds of vampire films later—the original Dracula still holds a singular, majestic power over the audience. Although the terror that a 1931 audience experienced is almost all gone, a new and rich enchantment is apparent in virtually every frame. The wonderful spectacle of Bela Lugosi's Dracula doesn't fade.

At 49, Lugosi, a character actor who had played Dracula on Broadway in 1927, was called to repeat his role for the film version, replacing Lon Chaney, who died before production began. It was Lugosi's big chance and he went at it in the way actors usually play Lear or Hamlet—as a bid for immortality. The gothic evocation of Transylvania, as well as Lugosi's theatrical posturing and sonorous Hungarian accent, have all become part of American pop legend. The role is forever Lugosi's. No one took the Count more seriously than Lugosi himself, who made it his lifetime role. He played Dracula (or variations) in subsequent pictures, revivals of the play, and eventually in vaudeville. Buried in his Dracula cape, he would finally take the role to his grave.

Although *Dracula* is stagebound and misses many of the wonderful Victorian thrills in the original Bram Stoker novel, it would still be worth seeing for Lugosi's inspired truculence and for that eerie sequence early in the picture when Dracula and his wives leave their coffins at dusk to wander through the crypt of his Carpathian castle.

THE EXORCIST

(1973), C, *Director:* William Friedkin. *With* Linda Blair, Jason Miller, Ellen Burstyn, Max Von Sydow, Lee J. Cobb, Kitty Winn, and Jack MacGowran. **120 min.** *R.* Tape, CED, Laser: Warner.

The Exorcist remains the most expensive, controversial, profitable, and foul-mouthed horror film of our generation. It achieved such distinction by rejecting the secular in favor of a straight, fundamentalist Catholic message: The Devil lives! Based on the best-selling novel by William Peter Blatty, the story is compelling, the acting first-rate, the pacing taut, and the shocks original.

The film tells the story of the demonic possession of the body of 12-year-old Regan MacNeil (Linda Blair). Father Merrin (Max Von Sydow) is summoned to exorcise the Demon, and a doubting younger priest (Jason Miller) helps perform the ancient rites. The young priest's crisis of faith gives the film added relevance and complexity. After the free-wheeling, free-loving pantheism of the 1960s, *The Exorcist* offered a black-and-white certitude that audiences could relate to, if only as an excuse for the vicarious thrill of watching Regan spew obscenities and bile, rotate her head 180 degrees, and desecrate a crucifix. All of this takes place in Georgetown, a mere stone's throw from the Nixon White House.

Notable contributions to the lore and technique of the genre were made by make-up artist Dick Smith, who devised a festering appearance for Regan which miraculously retains something impish about it, and by Mercedes McCambridge, who dubbed the Demon's voice and delivers (with relish) profanities hitherto unheard in a commercial movie. Max Von Sydow gives a remarkably convincing performance as the older priest—a performance that, ironically, had to be built up bit by bit and shot again and again, as Von Sydow, an avowed atheist, could not bring himself to believe in a script about a real God and a real Satan. A close viewing of the film reveals how few of his lines actually express belief.

FRANKENSTEIN

(1931), B/W, *Director:* James Whale. *With* Boris Karloff,
Colin Clive, Mae Clarke, John Boles, Edward Van
Sloan, Lionel Belmore, and Dwight Frye. **71 min.** *NR.*
Tape: MCA.

Coming after two silent versions and various stage
adaptations, director James Whale's brilliant *Frankenstein* crackled and popped with the electric effects of 20th
century alchemy. Thus Mary Shelley's 19th century creation was ushered into the age of Rockefeller Center and
the talkies. What was seen in 1931 as revisionism has, in
this day of even madder scientists, receded into clas-
sicism.

This story of a scientist who creates a monster from
grave-robbed parts has a wide number of interpretations, but it is safe to suggest that a central theme is the
impact this creation has on a superstitious and parochial
society. As conceived by Jack Pierce, cosmetician extra-
ordinaire, and brought to life (this time for keeps!) by
Boris Karloff, Frankenstein's monster is a mute brute,
an awkward child-giant rejected by his father/maker
(who refers to him as *it*) and victimized by a sadistic
hunchback (who, in the film's most unexpected moment,
pauses to pull up his socks—Mel Brooks invented very
little). He's a social misfit that must be destroyed: in
short, a monster for all seasons, the world's beloved
bogeyman.

Whale made life miserable for Karloff during the
shooting, but Karloff was rewarded with instant celeb-
rity and some of the most effective close-ups in all
cinema—in fact, the only close-ups in *Frankenstein.*

HALLOWEEN

(1978), C, *Director:* John Carpenter. *With* Donald
Pleasance, Jamie Lee Curtis, Nancy Loomis, P. J. Soles,
Charles Cyphers, and Kyle Richards. **92 min.** *R*. Tape:
Media.

The current teenagers-in-jeopardy trend in horror
movies dates back to director John Carpenter's *Halloween,* a low-budget, high-profit picture. It has since
been surpassed in gruesome mayhem but not in visual
sophistication and suspense.

The film opens with the brutal knifing of a girl on
Halloween night, as seen through the eyes of the masked
killer, her six-year-old brother, Michael. Fifteen years
later, Michael, now grown into a speechless psychopath
of superhuman strength, escapes from a mental institution and heads home for another Halloween night of
carnage. He seeks out teenage girls whose carnal escapades arouse him to murder. Much of the ensuing
action is seen through his eyes once more, as he stalks
his quarry through the streets and into the homes of
Smalltown, U.S.A. Carpenter builds a tempo that keeps
audiences leaping out of their seats. He switches view-
points to keep us in dread that Michael will turn up in
the unlikeliest places, which of course he does. In his
featureless Halloween mask, Michael becomes the
bogeyman that haunted our childhood nightmares.

Among the actual and prospective victims, Jamie Lee
Curtis is wonderful as the spunky "good girl" who is
never caught unaware. Donald Pleasance is very convincing as Michael's psychiatrist and nemesis.

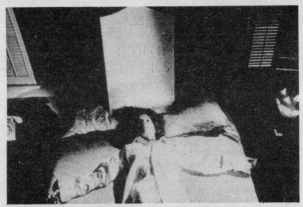

Halloween. *An escaped mental patient kills a young woman and bedecks her dead body with the tombstone of his sister, whom he killed 15 years earlier: a roller-coaster ride of terror for a Halloween night.*

I Walked with a Zombie. *Nurse Betsy (Frances Dee) is awakened by strange sights and sounds during her first night on a Haitian plantation. The filmmakers are able to suggest a plethora of horrors while maintaining a footing in reality.*

I WALKED WITH A ZOMBIE

(1943), B/W, *Director:* Jacques Tourneur. *With* Frances
Dee, Tom Conway, James Ellison, Edith Barrett,
Christine Gordon, Theresa Harris, and James Bell.
69 min. *NR*. Tape: Nostalgia Merchant.

The titles were lurid and the budgets low, but the
ingenious pictures that Val Lewton produced at RKO
Radio in the 1940s represent an early, yet inevitable,
meeting of the horror film and psychoanalysis. Lewton
not only created full-fleshed characters with jobs and
backgrounds; he also endowed them with phobias, ata-
vistic fears, sexual repression, and guilt.

Cleverly transposing Charlotte Brontë's *Jane Eyre* to
the Caribbean, *I Walked with a Zombie* tells of Betsy
(Frances Dee), a young nurse who comes to the island of
St. Sebastian to care for Jessica (Christine Gordon), a
rich planter's wife suffering from a strange malady. The
islanders believe the patient is a zombie, one of the
living dead. Betsy becomes fascinated with the island,
the natives, and their voodoo rituals. The film's major
conflict is the clash between the voodoo of the natives
and the Christian logic of the white man. With low-key
dialogue, off-screen sounds, and dusky, nocturnal
photography, Lewton and Jacques Tourneur, the most
talented of his unit directors, slowly erode our disbelief,
forcing us to admit that voodoo may hold the key to
Jessica's condition.

I Walked with a Zombie scares us with everyday fears:
shadows in the dark, the distant rustling of the wind,
sudden movements, and misunderstood actions. These
are the fears that fuel the supernatural.

NIGHT OF THE LIVING DEAD

(1968), B/W, *Director:* George Romero. *With* Judith O'Dea, Russell Streiner, Duane Jones, Karl Hardman, and Keith Wayne. **90 min.** *NR*. Tape: Media.

Night of the Living Dead marks the watershed of the modern horror film. If you consider it worthless and disgusting, you're not likely to approve of the great horror films made since it appeared. It sets out to shock the viewer out of any notion of good taste or optimism about the final outcome.

The film could be regarded as a masterful variation on the theme of nature murderously reversing its rules, somewhat like *The Birds* and *Jaws*. In both of these films, however, the struggle for survival brought people together and ennobled them. In *Night of the Living Dead,* while zombies are busy randomly killing humans (and vice versa), the film is at work destroying all our comforting and protective notions of the world. Family ties don't matter, courage is not rewarded, logic does not solve; even our familiar notions of plot and horror are thwarted.

The scenes are orchestrated to break taboos one by one—each more disturbing than the last. First we observe an anonymous, partially devoured corpse. Then we see characters that we know and have been led to like ripped apart and devoured, bone by bone, organ by organ. A dead brother tries desperately to kill his living sister. And—the final and most disturbing image—a little dead zombie girl chews mindlessly on the remains of her father. In midnight shows to this day, the young laugh as they shiver.

PSYCHO

(1960), B/W, *Director:* Alfred Hitchcock. *With* Janet
Leigh, Anthony Perkins, Martin Balsam, Vera Miles,
John Gavin, John McIntire, and Patricia Hitchcock.
109 min. *NR.* Tape, Laser: MCA; CED: RCA VideoDisc.

At the premiere engagement of *Psycho* in 1960, director Alfred Hitchcock's voice was heard over a loud-
speaker threatening bodily harm to anyone who gave
away the plot. The master had no reason to worry;
familiarity serves his film as well as surprise. In any
case, the shrill sounds Bernard Herrmann composed for
the murder sequences are themselves enough to shatter
one's disbelief all over again. If *The Birds* was his contribution to science fiction, this is Hitchcock's major
contribution to the horror genre.

Hitchcock pretends to adhere to the conventions of the
old haunted-house pictures, all the better to foil our
expectations. From the beginning of the film we accept
Marion Crane (Janet Leigh) as the heroine of the movie.
We follow her as she leaves her lover and flees the law.
Then Hitchcock dares to have her stabbed to death in a
motel shower. From then on, it's one shock after another.
We switch our identification to Norman Bates (Anthony
Perkins), cleaning up the mess left by his insane mother.
But we're in for a shock here, too, and Hitchcock never
lets us see the truth until the climax. He pulls the strings
mercilessly and we feel the jolt every time.

The camera angles in this film are inspired. The
Olympian viewpoint as Arbogast, the investigator
(Martin Balsam), climbs the stairs of the Bates' house to
meet his doom at the top, helps make the scene chilling.
The lasting power of *Psycho* comes not merely from the
outrageous manipulation of our emotions, but from the
realization that only a consummate filmmaker could
take such chances and still succeed.

ROSEMARY'S BABY

(1968), C, *Director:* Roman Polanski. *With* Mia Farrow,
John Cassavetes, Sidney Blackmer, Ruth Gordon,
Maurice Evans, Ralph Bellamy, Elisha Cook, Jr., and
Patsy Kelly. **137 min.** *R*. Tape, CED, Laser: Paramount.

The first major American film to deal with satanism in
sophisticated terms, *Rosemary's Baby* draws its power
from tight direction and full-fleshed performances.

The naive and waiflike Rosemary (Mia Farrow) moves
into a venerable New York apartment building with her
husband Guy (John Cassavetes). To the delight of her
snoopy neighbors, the Castevets (Sidney Blackmer and
Ruth Gordon), she discovers she is pregnant. As her
pregnancy advances, she suspects her ambitious actor-
husband of making a pact with the Devil to gain Broadway fame, in exchange for which he has allowed Satan to
impregnate her during a witches' Sabbath held in the
building. Clues that at first seem trivial add up: Two
bizarre deaths start looking like murder, and the Castevets fuss suspiciously over Rosemary, giving her strange
potions to drink. The building seems to crawl with
Satanists, and everyone Rosemary turns to for help
seems involved with them.

This darkly humorous, double-edged scenario was reportedly fashioned by director Roman Polanski by past-
ing together the best pages from Ira Levin's novel. While
initially suggesting that Rosemary may be suffering
from anxieties not uncommon to expectant mothers, the
film finally makes clear that a supernatural explanation
is not unfounded. Its offbeat style is no less gripping for
being playful. No dottier Devil worshippers ever appeared on film: They tiptoe into Rosemary's apartment
like fugitives from a Tom & Jerry cartoon, and later
gather by the baby's crib, which is festooned appropri-
ately in black, to offer their best wishes to the mother of
the newborn Antichrist. It is an absurd but chilling
moment in a truly frightening film. Ruth Gordon won an
Academy Award for her supporting role in this film.

THE TEXAS CHAINSAW MASSACRE

(1974), C, *Director:* Tobe Hooper. *With* Gunner Hansen, Marilyn Burns, Ed Neal, Allen Danziger, Paul A. Partain, and William Vail. **86 min.** *R.* Tape: Media; CED, Laser: Vestron.

The Texas Chainsaw Massacre represents regional filmmaking that not only goes beyond the limits of mainstream moviemaking, but rips those structures to pieces. It indulges in uninhibited, crude, comic-book horror in a way Hollywood never dared, skillfully creating tension and suspense in a way Hollywood must envy.

A van-load of youngsters traveling through backwoods Texas stops at a remote farmhouse. One of them reads from a horoscope that "this will be a disturbing and unpredictable day." This is the one understatement in the movie, for in the house dwells a family of degenerates who once operated a slaughterhouse. In their own distorted fashion, they continue to practice their skills. The most vicious member of the family is Leatherface (Gunner Hansen), who goes after the travelers with his trusty chainsaw. The victims are such an obnoxious lot (especially a fat, whining guy in a wheelchair) that their plight awakens a certain relish in the viewer. The one survivor is Sally (Marilyn Burns), who screams for her life—louder, longer, and with better reason, than Fay Wray did at King Kong. The ending leaves you exhausted, with your ears ringing.

Director Tobe Hooper brings suspense and suggestion as well as a certain charnel humor to this film, which may be why *The Texas Chainsaw Massacre* was the best-selling videocassette in America in 1982.

LOVE STORIES

As you scan the list of titles in this chapter, you may question our emphasis on movies about incompatible lovers. But, in a strange twist, the love affairs that make the most compelling drama are those that are rooted in conflict, those in which the lovers have either combative personalities, different economic and ethnic backgrounds, or questionable marital ties. If there were no conflict, there would be no drama—indeed, no movie. And these movies are nothing if not dramatic. They take close aim at the mysteries of the heart and, more often than not, they hit that mark. Love Stories are often told in close-ups. That technique, plus the very intimate nature of the theme, makes TV an ideal vehicle for Love Stories. The movies in this chapter are Love Stories pure and simple. They are not dramatic movies with a love interest, but films that exist solely to explore the quirks and mechanics of love. Other Love Stories to consider are: *It Happened One Night, On Golden Pond, The Quiet Man, Rebecca,* and *Romeo and Juliet.*

An Officer and a Gentleman. *Officer-trainee Zack Mayo (Richard Gere) and his girlfriend Paula (Debra Winger) make sparks fly.*

THE AFRICAN QUEEN

(1951), C, *Director:* John Huston. *With* Katharine
Hepburn, Humphrey Bogart, Robert Morley, Peter Bull,
and Theodore Bikel. **105 min.** *NR.* Tape, Laser:
CBS/Fox; CED: RCA VideoDisc.

A hard-drinking, unshaven riverboat captain and a
skinny, religious old maid would seem unlikely focal
points for a love story. It's a tribute to the acting of
Humphrey Bogart and Katharine Hepburn, as well as to
John Huston's superlative direction, that the combination not only works, but has depth and beauty.

Bogart plays Mr. Allnutt, the boat owner who takes on
spinster Rosie (Hepburn) when her missionary brother
dies. Together they sail through East African waters,
battling malaria, life-threatening rapids, insects,
leeches, and a German battleship—which they conspire
to destroy. They triumph over every obstacle, joyfully
discovering love in the process. Hepburn's Rosie is a
brilliant creation, partly due to director Huston's inspired suggestion that she use Eleanor Roosevelt as her
model for the role. Bogart is tough and uncouth but
thoroughly likable, and Robert Morley has an amusing
cameo as Hepburn's brother. The script, based on a novel
by C. S. Forester, was co-written by James Agee,
Huston, and (uncredited) John Collier. It alternates
beautifully between breezy humor, tenderness, and
heart-stopping suspense. The camaraderie between the
two characters develops slowly and naturally; the
viewer fully accepts and applauds their growing affection.

Bogart's daringly successful attempt to play against
type won him a 1951 Best Actor Oscar, a remarkable
feat considering his competition (Marlon Brando in *A
Streetcar Named Desire*). In 1967 the *Los Angeles Times*
took a poll and found *The African Queen* to be the
favorite movie among their readers. It sparkles today,
its charm and excitement undimmed by time.

ANNIE HALL

(1977), C, *Director:* Woody Allen. *With* Woody Allen, Diane Keaton, Tony Roberts, Paul Simon, Shelley Duvall, Carol Kane, and Colleen Dewhurst. **93 min.** *PG.* Tape, Laser: CBS/Fox; CED: RCA VideoDisc.

Comedies rarely win Oscars for Best Picture, but *Annie Hall* captured this accolade, as well as awards for Best Director (Woody Allen), Best Screenplay (Allen and Marshall Brickman) and Best Actress (Diane Keaton). All were richly deserved, because this film delivers the laughs we expect from a Woody Allen movie, while projecting a deep, memorable humanity.

The story is a semiautobiographical account of Allen's romance with Keaton. He plays Alvy Singer, a nightclub comic who falls for the appealingly awkward Annie. Their differences (Annie orders salami on white with mayonnaise) are amusingly portrayed. In one sequence the two talk to each other while the subtitles below reveal their true feelings. Another scene shows them making love, as a surrealistic image of Annie's spirit leaves her body. These and other innovative devices emphasize the basic incompatibilities between the lovers that eventually lead to their separation.

Allen is still the pessimistic nebbish, but in *Annie Hall* he has a new and surprisingly believable sex appeal, and Keaton's featherheaded dithering has a peculiar strength of its own. Tony Roberts is engaging as Allen's friend, and Paul Simon has a standout cameo as the swinger who announces, "Let's be mellow." Christopher Walken and Shelley Duvall also contribute amusing bits. The chief distinction of *Annie Hall* is the way it combines nonstop hilarity with all-too-human pain. That "if only" feeling that accompanies all powerful film love stories, from *Gone With the Wind* on, is poignantly present when the lovers part at the end.

CASABLANCA

(1942), B/W, *Director:* **Michael Curtiz.** *With* **Humphrey Bogart, Ingrid Bergman, Paul Henreid, Claude Rains, Peter Lorre, Sydney Greenstreet, Conrad Veidt, Dooley Wilson, S. Z. Sakall, and Joy Page. 102 min.** *NR.* **Tape, Laser: CBS/Fox; CED: RCA VideoDisc.**

It seems almost an understatement to refer to *Casablanca* as merely a love story. With its exciting drama, charismatic players, and stream of unforgettable performances, it achieves something magical and incredibly rare. It treats every situation with a sense of humor yet manages to preserve dramatic power and suspense at the same time. And finally, *Casablanca* ranks as the most-quoted picture in film history.

Humphrey Bogart plays the legendary jaded saloon keeper, Rick, who steadfastly avoids political involvement during World War II. Then into his Casablancan cafe comes Ilsa, his lost love (Ingrid Bergman), with her husband, Victor (Paul Henreid), a famous French Resistance leader. Ilsa begs Rick to help Victor escape occupied France and Rick refuses. They rekindle their romance and Rick comes to understand that two people in love "don't amount to a hill of beans" when compared to the importance of winning the war. In the end, Rick puts Ilsa and Victor on a plane, reassuring her that "we'll always have Paris."

It doesn't matter that Bergman actually says, "Play it, Sam," rather than "Play it again, Sam," as often quoted. The moment is unforgettable; so is Dooley Wilson performing "As Time Goes By" (which almost didn't get into the picture). The contrast between Bogart's portrayal of the cynical Rick and Bergman's warm and noble Ilsa creates one-of-a-kind chemistry between the two. Claude Rains, Sidney Greenstreet, Peter Lorre, and Conrad Veidt all have classic moments. But *Casablanca* is, more than anything, one of the greatest love stories ever filmed. No one who has seen it can ever forget the moment when Rick receives Ilsa's letter of goodbye while standing on a railroad platform in the pouring rain.

Casablanca. *Ilsa (Ingrid Bergman) and Rick (Humphrey Bogart) sit in a Parisian cafe and read news of the approaching Nazis. These few brief days of happiness will haunt the lovers for a lifetime. "You must remember this . . ."*

Intermezzo. *The married concert violinist (Leslie Howard) meets secretly with his piano accompanist (Ingrid Bergman). Ingrid Bergman's remarkable ability to convey grand emotion with the slightest gesture made her ideal for romances.*

INTERMEZZO

(1939), B/W, *Director:* Gregory Ratoff. *With* Leslie
Howard, Ingrid Bergman, Edna Best, Cecil Kellaway,
and John Halliday. **70 min.** *NR*. Tape, CED: CBS/Fox.

Intermezzo was Ingrid Bergman's American debut
film. A remake of a Swedish production, it showcased her
talents with such sensitivity that she became an immediate box-office favorite.

Bergman plays a young pianist who falls in love with a
married violinist (Leslie Howard). He reciprocates and
invites her to join him on a concert tour as his accompanist. Their romantic idyll is undermined by mutual
guilt, however, and the violinist finally returns to his
family after his daughter suffers injuries in an auto-
mobile accident.

The plot is simple, sparked to life by the sincerity of
the principals. Howard (who coproduced the picture)
displays that peculiarly individual combination of reserve and intensity that made him a legendary Ashley
Wilkes in *Gone With the Wind.* Bergman is even better.
Her radiance, coupled with complete, unaffected
honesty, puts the audience firmly in her corner throughout. The supporting performances by Ann Todd and
Edna Best, as Howard's daughter and wife, are notable.
Gregory Ratoff directs with quiet grace, and Gregg
Toland (cinematographer on *Wuthering Heights* and
Citizen Kane) contributes gently beautiful images that
enhance the understated charm of the story. The movie's
classical score adds further warmth and tenderness to a
touching and unashamedly romantic film.

NOW, VOYAGER

(1942), B/W, *Director:* Irving Rapper. *With* Bette Davis, Claude Rains, Paul Henreid, Gladys Cooper, Bonita Granville, Janis Wilson, Ilka Chase, John Loder, and Lee Patrick. **117 min.** *NR.* Tape: CBS/Fox.

Now, Voyager falls into several genres—Cinderella story, soap opera, and love story. It's a definitive example of all three.

Bette Davis plays Charlotte Vale, a shy, repressed woman, stifled by her coldly tyrannical mother (Gladys Cooper). On the advice of her sympathetic psychiatrist (Claude Rains), she loses weight, buys some spiffy clothes, and takes a cruise. On board the ship she encounters suave and handsome Jerry (Paul Henreid), who is charmed by her. Although Jerry is married (unhappily), he and Charlotte fall in love and have an affair. Romance makes her feel attractive and self-assured, creating problems when she returns home and begins to defy her domineering mother. She manages to assert herself as a person, though Jerry never leaves his wife. In a finale that could only happen in Hollywood in 1942, she agrees to be his back-street love, rhapsodizing, "Don't ask for the moon ... we have the stars." This sentimental material is transformed by the brilliant treatment it is given. Davis is utterly natural; there are no traces of the stylization that began to afflict her work later in the decade. Henreid perfectly plays the unattainable dream man, and Gladys Cooper is perhaps best of all as Davis's controlling mother. Bonita Granville stands out as a critical niece, and John Loder is stuffy, but human, as a rich suitor Charlotte nearly marries.

Now, Voyager is a prime illustration of plot elements that could become weepy and synthetic but don't. Its saving grace is the conviction and warmth of its cast and the superb directon of Irving Rapper. Davis claims she reworked the script as the picture progressed, adding lines from the original novel by Olive Higgins Prouty. Her "meddling," as she calls it, also enhanced another 1940s classic, *The Great Lie,* and it has the same exhilarating effect here.

AN OFFICER AND A GENTLEMAN

(1982), C, *Director:* Taylor Hackford. *With* Richard
Gere, Debra Winger, Louis Gossett, Jr., David Keith,
and Lisa Blount. **118 min.** *R.* Tape, CED, Laser:
Paramount.

Updating old-fashioned material is a risky proposi-
tion. Director Taylor Hackford succeeds completely with
An Officer and a Gentleman, a reworking of the service
dramas so popular in the 1940s.

Douglas Day Stewart's script follows the hero, Zack
Mayo (Richard Gere), from a bitter childhood to officer
candidate school. Zack is hostile and resistant to discipline until he is pitted against a sergeant (Louis Gossett,
Jr.) who shapes him, brutally when necessary, into a
man. Also helping him to grow is Paula (Debra Winger),
a local girl who dreams of marrying a cadet. Although
Zack and Paula fall in love, Zack isn't ready for com-
mitment. The suicide of his buddy (David Keith), who
has been painfully rejected by the woman he loves, forces
Zack to reevaluate his priorities.

An Officer and a Gentleman is a real audience pleaser.
The sex scenes between Gere and Winger are unusually
sensual; their chemistry gives the film its foundation.
Louis Gossett, Jr. deservedly won a Best Supporting
Oscar for his performance as Sergeant Foley, an impressive blend of power and humanity. David Keith is
exceptionally touching as the doomed cadet, and Lisa
Blount effectively projects selfishness as the gold digger
who deserts him. Hackford keeps the pace hurtling forward. Under his smooth direction, the characters have
such conviction that one never thinks of them as stereotypes. He proves that any subject can be relevant and
affecting for new generations if directed with genuine
passion.

THE PHILADELPHIA STORY

(1940), B/W, *Director:* George Cukor. *With* Cary Grant, Katharine Hepburn, James Stewart, Ruth Hussey, John Howard, Roland Young, Henry Daniel, and Virginia Weidler. **112 min.** *NR*. Tape: MGM/UA.

There have been countless attempts to duplicate the seemingly effortless charm and wit of this film, but there is only one *The Philadelphia Story*—the original screwball love story about a divorced society couple who can't stand each other's faults any more than they can stand to be separated. Philip Barry's original play is very funny, but Donald Ogden Stewart's adaptation is even funnier, without losing the genuinely romantic quality of the stage version. George Cukor's deft direction and an all-star cast complete this impeccable package.

Cary Grant plays C. K. Dexter Haven, the much missed and much despised ex-husband of Tracy Lord (Katharine Hepburn). Tracy seems intent on throwing herself away on a pompous plebian in aristocrat's clothing, one George Kittredge (John Howard). Dexter does everything he can to drive a wedge between Tracy and her boring new beau (which shouldn't be difficult, since it's impossible to imagine any woman preferring John Howard to Cary Grant), but Tracy is intractable. Into the midst of this pops reporter Macauley Connor (James Stewart), sent to cover the upcoming nuptials; suddenly it's a foursome, with Connor falling for Tracy and everyone falling over everyone else as cocktail follows cocktail in grand Noel Coward fashion.

The script includes some of the most endearing sarcasm ever put on film. The moral—that it's better to be loved by someone who knows your faults than to be worshipped by an ignoramus—is still valid, as morals usually are. In the end, Tracy and Dexter are reunited, as we knew they would be, but we are unprepared for the emotional wallop their last-minute remarriage packs. Two classic scenes: the wordless opening, in which Dexter makes as if to sock Tracy but opts for pushing her in the face instead, and a great impersonation of a drunk by James Stewart.

A PLACE IN THE SUN

(1951), B/W, *Director:* George Stevens. *With*
Montgomery Clift, Elizabeth Taylor, Shelley Winters,
Keefe Brasselle, Raymond Burr, and Anne Revere.
122 min. *NR*. Tape, Laser: Paramount.

1951's *A Place in the Sun* demonstrates how truly
erotic love scenes could be in the days before movies
became explicit. It's a reminder that honest feelings are
what create excitement, not nude bodies thrashing
around.

George Stevens's ambitious film, based on Theodore
Dreiser's classic *An American Tragedy,* studies the rise
and fall of George Eastman (Montgomery Clift), a poor
young man with dreams of a better life. While slaving
away in an aimless factory job, Clift becomes involved
with Alice (Shelley Winters), a fellow worker. George
begins to climb the ladder to success and meets wealthy
Sondra (Elizabeth Taylor). All his dreams seem within
his grasp until Alice tells him that she is pregnant by
him. George kills her (though the movie is vaguer on
that point than the novel) and is executed for the crime.

Clift is earnest and sensitive as the young man, who
feels trapped and murders out of panic; Winters's characterization is irritating enough to make audiences sym-
pathize with his desire to pull free of her. Elizabeth
Taylor, at the height of her beauty here, comes across
with strength and passion. She has said that it was the
first time she really gave herself to *acting,* and the effort
to fulfill her potential clearly shows. Anne Revere fur-
nishes a striking cameo as Clift's religious mother, and
the superficial rich are convincingly portrayed by Shep-
perd Strudwick and Keefe Brasselle.

A Place in the Sun is less a portrait of the dichotomy
between rich and poor than a beautifully filmed romance.
When Taylor whispers, "Tell Mama," to a love-drugged
Clift, we are viewing one of the best love scenes ever
committed to film.

SPLENDOR IN THE GRASS

(1961), C, *Director:* Elia Kazan. *With* Natalie Wood, Warren Beatty, Zohra Lampert, Pat Hingle, Audrey Christie, Fred Stewart, Sean Garrison, Sandy Dennis, Phyllis Diller, and Barbara Loden. **124 min.** *NR*. Tape: Warner.

Adults, with smug hindsight, tend to downplay the fervor of young love, dismissing it as "just part of growing up." *Splendor in the Grass* acknowledges the power of teenage passion and the tragic effects its repression can have for years to come.

William Inge's Oscar-winning screenplay focuses on two adolescent lovers, Wilma Dean (Natalie Wood) and Bud (Warren Beatty), who are suffocated by small-town morality and unable to consummate their urgent longings. Bud eventually turns to one of the fast local girls for relief, but Wilma Dean suffers a nervous breakdown. In the end, Bud marries drably devoted Angelina (Zohra Lampert) and Wilma Dean also settles for a second choice. The audience knows all along that they should have remained together. The theatrical direction by Elia Kazan vibrantly conveys the mute needs of the two principals. Sex is the central theme of the story, but lack of communication is also eloquently dramatized. Pat Hingle is commanding as Beatty's hearty, would-be-macho father, who commits suicide after losing his fortune during the Depression; and Audrey Christie is touching as Wood's well-meaning but limited mother. We see them blunder and misunderstand the drives of their children, and we react with frustrated sympathy. Fred Stewart, as Wood's passive father, has a heart-breaking moment at the conclusion of the picture that remains vivid. Wood is beautiful and haunting as the tragic heroine, and Beatty's debut performance is fresher and less mannered than his later work in *Shampoo* and *Reds*.

Splendor in the Grass remains the only American film to treat the pain of adolescent sexuality with dimension and integrity.

THE WAY WE WERE

(1973), C, *Director:* Sydney Pollack. *With* Barbra
Streisand, Robert Redford, Bradford Dillman, Murray
Hamilton, Viveca Lindfors, and Lois Chiles. **118 min.**
PG. Tape, Laser: RCA/Columbia; CED: RCA VideoDisc.

"Opposites attract," the cliché goes, and never has the
screen dramatized this idea more effectively than in *The
Way We Were.*

Arthur Laurents's absorbing script traces the roller-
coaster romance of a political activist (Barbra Streisand)
and an apolitical author (Robert Redford). Streisand
wants Redford to stand up for what's right; he wants to
sidestep conflict. She wants him to write a great novel;
he's content to churn out routine screenplays. They
marry and move to Hollywood. After an idyllic beginning, the McCarthy era invades and Streisand rushes to
Washington to battle for the rights of the Hollywood
Ten. When she returns, their marriage falls apart. Years
later they meet in Manhattan, still in love but achingly
aware that their personality differences can't be sur-
mounted.

The Way We Were develops characters the viewer
cares about intensely. Streisand is brash and tactless,
but vulnerable and realistic. We watch in frustration as
she alienates the man she desperately loves. Redford
convincingly conveys the torment of a husband who
knows he can't live up to his wife's image of him. There
are classic tearjerking moments, such as Streisand sob-
bing on the phone, begging Redford to see her again. The
ending, when the two embrace, silently mourning the
lost years, is unforgettable. Laurents captures the
political confusion and despair of the late 1940s and
early 1950s, and there are fine performances by Bradford Dillman and Lois Chiles. The Oscar-winning title
song also contributes strongly to the emotional impact of
the picture.

MELODRAMAS

When soap operas are endowed with big budgets, fine casts and directors, literary scripts, and a two-hour running time, they're called Melodramas. These are the films of heightened emotions, of unusually complicated situations and characters—films in which the dark past often raises its ugly head. Melodramas have provided some of our great cinematic moments, as a quick glance through our selection will attest. And like the soap operas that dominate daytime and prime-time TV, Melodramas are actually enhanced by the small screen. These are the tearjerkers, the movies where evil characters don deceptively cheery veneers, and where the best of characters are misunderstood, battered, and defeated. If you want to get into somebody's head, or if you want to experience joy and sorrow on a level that is seldom realized in a 75-year life span, then these ten films are for you. Other Melodramas to consider include: *The Elephant Man, On the Waterfront, Ordinary People, Taxi Driver,* and *Winter Kills.*

Mildred Pierce. *Mildred (Joan Crawford) stops at nothing to get what she wants for her spoiled child, Veda (Ann Blyth).*

ALL ABOUT EVE

(1950), B/W, *Director:* Joseph L. Mankiewicz. *With* Bette
Davis, Anne Baxter, Marilyn Monroe, Thelma Ritter,
Celeste Holm, George Sanders, Gary Merrill, and Hugh
Marlowe. **138 min.** *NR.* Tape: CBS/Fox.

All About Eve has often been called a film about "the
theater," but the subtext here is what great melodramas
are made of. Directed and written by Joseph L. Mankiewicz, *Eve* deals in an archetypal way with all kinds of
women—earnest, opportunistic, smart-alecky, naive.

The broadest performance (in all senses of the word) is
given by Bette Davis, who has built her career playing
variations on this role. As Margo Channing, Davis is a
40-year-old actress who, despite a current Broadway
smash, feels old and over the hill. The reason: her
romance with a younger man, played with low-key
charm by Gary Merrill.

As Davis plays it, Margo is riding a seesaw. As her
career options go down (she can't keep playing ingenues
forever), can her chances for love rise?

Balancing the other end is Anne Baxter as Eve, the
"kid" who is Margo's starstruck assistant. There's a distorted, through-the-looking-glass element here. At first
Baxter seems sugar-coated and saintly as opposed to the
wonderfully strident, neurotic Margo. But as the plot
turns, so does Baxter's character. Baxter turns out to be
a mirror image of a younger, more ruthless Margo.

The heart of *All About Eve* is an examination of female
vanity and competition. The plot rolls along with the
intrigues, interpersonal double crosses, and hurt feelings that rise and fall between all the female characters.
The men are marginal figures, the ones who handle the
money, check the coats, and contemplate little flings.
The women get the passion, the drama, and all the best
lines. In a cameo, Marilyn Monroe, as a "graduate from
the school Copa Cabana," is breathtakingly funny.
Thelma Ritter plays a smart old bird with a smart
mouth, and Celeste Holm, the only wife in the story, says
about the men, "They'll do as they're told." You're not
sure she believes it, but the sentiment is right on target.

CITIZEN KANE

(1941), B/W, *Director:* Orson Welles. *With* Orson Welles,
Joseph Cotten, Everett Sloane, Agnes Moorehead,
Dorothy Comingore, Ray Collins, George Coulouris, and
Ruth Warrick. **119 min.** *NR*. Tape: VidAmerica; CED:
RCA VideoDisc.

   Citizen Kane is not merely one of the best melodramas;
it is widely recognized as one of the finest films ever
made, a masterpiece that transcends all categories. It is
the most spectacular debut in film history, featuring the
then-26-year-old Orson Welles as director, star, and co-
author (with Herman J. Mankiewicz).
   The film broke a number of Hollywood rules, and some
social rules as well. Its subject, Charles Foster Kane (a
virtuoso performance by Welles), is a thinly disguised
portrait of newspaper tycoon William Randolph Hearst,
who was alive at the time. Such things simply were not
done—particularly when the portrait was as unflatter-
ing as this. Part of the film's unique appeal is the innovative way it tells the story of Kane's life: as a succession
of blaring newsreels interspersed with private episodes.
The narrative begins in reverse, with Kane's death in
his empty, mist-shrouded mansion. We hear Kane's
dying word, "Rosebud," and the film becomes a reporter's
attempt to unravel this enigma by contrasting Kane's
public life with his private life. What emerges is a
pathetic picture of a potentially great man strangled by
wealth and betrayal.
   The film made a reputation not only for Welles but for
practically everyone who worked on it. Ruth Warrick as
Kane's socialite first wife and Dorothy Comingore as his
working-class second wife are especially outstanding.
Joseph Cotten and Everett Sloane play Kane's loyal
newspaper associates; Agnes Moorehead debuted as his
icy mother; and George Coulouris is the villain (if he can
be called that), Kane's guardian. Much of the credit for
the film's unusual look goes to cinematographer Gregg
Toland, who shot from unheard-of low angles. Don't miss
the final shots or you'll miss the meaning of "Rosebud"
and Alan Ladd in a bit part.

FANNY AND ALEXANDER

(1983), C, *Director:* Ingmar Bergman. *With* Gunn
Wallgren, Allan Edwall, Jarle Kulle, Borje Ahlstedt,
Bertil Guve, Jan Malmsjo, and Ewa Froling. **197 min.** *R.*
Tape, Laser: Embassy.

Let us pause and give thanks that this forty-third film
by Ingmar Bergman is not, as the Swedish director had
prematurely announced, his farewell to movies. It is
rather the capstone of his career thus far, a masterful
and ingenious melodrama on an epic scale, and the winner of a well-deserved Oscar for Best Foreign Film.

Dark and brooding as it often is, *Fanny and Alexander*
is still Bergman's most cheerful work in 20 years. The
title characters (played with amazing precocity by Per-
nilla Allwin and Bertil Guve) are the children of Emilie
Ekdahl (Ewa Froling). The opening scenes reveal the
turn-of-the-century Ekdahl clan to be close, warm,
loving, and bursting with creativity. But when Emilie's
husband dies, she remarries (disastrously) Bishop Vergerus (Jan Malmsjo), a cold-hearted cleric who keeps
them virtual prisoners in his harsh bishopric. Apparently based on Bergman's own upbringing, this "dark
night of the soul" becomes an unbearable ordeal for the
Ekdahls, and they escape. The autobiographical story
helps explain Bergman's lifelong ambivalence toward
God and all things religious. He is repelled yet fascinated. This obsession with the supernatural is also
reflected in a number of breathtaking fantasy sequences,
including one with a beautiful marble statue that
beckons to Alexander. The departed father turns up, as
well—a sad-eyed apparition, looking on helplessly as his
children are tormented in the name of the Lord.

Bergman's script is, as always, a marvel of richness
and concision, and Sven Nykvist's cinematography perfectly captures both the dazzling colors of the Ekdahl
home and the sombre tones of Bishop Vergerus's stone
prison. The videotape is available dubbed into English,
but the subtitled version is far superior, for Bergman is
as careful with his soundtracks as with every other aspect of his art.

GILDA

(1946), B/W, *Director:* Charles Vidor. *With* Rita
Hayworth, Glenn Ford, George Macready, Joseph
Calleia, and Steven Geray. **110 min.** *NR.* Tape, CED:
RCA/Columbia.

This is the movie that defines femme fatale, with Rita
Hayworth in the title role as the gorgeous girl who
makes good by being bad.

The plot doesn't always make sense. Glenn Ford is a
down-on-his-luck gambler who, in some mystical encounter with nightclub owner George Macready, forms
an enduring bond and a new career. All that is threatened when Macready comes back from a trip married to
Hayworth, who, unbeknownst to Macready (or does he
really know all along?), is Ford's ex-lover.

Much of the picture careens off the main beat with
Nazi cartels and a strange, almost campy friendship
between the two men. But the heart and the heat of the
story lie in the physical tension and taunting verbal
exchanges between Ford and Hayworth. She's always
complimenting him in feminine terms. "You're looking
very beautiful," she says one night. And another time,
"How pretty you are." Meanwhile, Ford's disgust for her
behavior (Gilda has the reckless habit of dancing off into
the night with handsome strangers) is so laced with
desire that it threatens to steam up the camera lens.

Throughout, Hayworth is lustrously golden, so radi-
ant that she seems—as her name implies—to be gilded.
This is her quintessential performance. In her famous
mock-strip dance while singing "Put the Blame on
Mame," Hayworth projects a marvelous mix of sensual
abandon and melancholy. With a toss of her head or a
wave of her glove, she shows that she really doesn't want
to be carrying on like this, but what choice do all these
men give her? The time is important here. It's right after
the war, a period of flux when all characters have "no
past and all future." Charles Vidor directed with the
strongest control in his career.

KRAMER VS. KRAMER

(1979), C, *Director:* Robert Benton. *With* Meryl Streep,
Dustin Hoffman, Jane Alexander, Justin Henry,
Howard Duff, and George Coe. **105 min.** *PG*. Tape, CED,
Laser: RCA/Columbia.

This is the classic melodrama: spouse walks out, leaving the other parent to raise the child, readjust, and fend off problems alone. The twist here is that it's the wife, played by Meryl Streep (who won an Oscar for her performance), who leaves hard-working husband Dustin Hoffman.

Male melodrama became a staple of the late 1970s, but *Kramer* probably best exemplifies this subgenre. All the little themes—male bonding, newly discovered sensitivity, career versus caring—are portrayed in full force. *Kramer* tries to focus on the humanization of Hoffman, but often shows him turning into Superdad. Still, audiences found the movie heartwarming and heart-wrenching. The running gag with the French toast (the day after Streep leaves, Hoffman turns the kitchen into a disaster area trying to cook; later he becomes an expert) is cute, effective, and telling; the scenes involving Streep's quest for custody of the child are ruthlessly squeezed for every possible tear. So what if the deck is completely stacked against her and her side of the story? No one ever said melodramas had to be fair.

Robert Benton wrote and directed, although the important, revealing moments of *Kramer* are more completely found in its art direction. Every little detail—the kinds of lamps in the apartment, the books stacked on the floor, the adult toys sitting on the bookshelves—has been carefully thought out and weighed. The art direction carries the message; it speaks more eloquently of the upper-middle-class expectations, ambitions, and longings of the main characters than any of the rather high-blown speeches they end up giving in the courtroom scenes.

MILDRED PIERCE

(1945), B/W, *Director:* Michael Curtiz. *With* Joan Crawford, Zachary Scott, Ann Blyth, Jack Carson, Eve Arden, and Bruce Bennett. **109 min.** *NR.* CED: CBS/Fox.

Mildred Pierce is a strange, arresting mix of film genres. On one level it deals with the classic women's issues of all melodramas: the trials of raising a family, no-account men, ungrateful children, and the struggle to make enough money to buy a good fur coat. Additionally, director Michael Curtiz introduces the elements of *film noir*: doom, uncertainty, destruction. What is unique about *Mildred Pierce* is that it tells a *noir* story from a woman's point of view.

Joan Crawford's Mildred is the shady, tough woman-on-the-make. She's going to get what her family needs, no matter who or what stands in her way. Originally all Pierce wants is a job, but that soon escalates into money, power, and acceptance. The total cost is two husbands (one of whom gets murdered) and the death of her youngest child—the only sweet-tempered, well-meaning person in sight. In the end, Mildred goes bankrupt—no small matter in a movie where money and sex are synonymous with love and marriage.

As the lounge lizard second husband, Zachary Scott is as oily as a bad salad dressing. And the requisite dangerous/destructive woman is, here, Mildred's older daughter Veda. Played with icy, masklike calm by Ann Blyth, Veda is one tough cookie. If she's not gazing lovingly in a mirror, she's busy checking the balance in her mother's bank account.

By making the mother-daughter relationship the catalyst for all the trouble, *Mildred Pierce* adds a new kink to the love-and-be-doomed formula. Men are the pawns in the game played by Mildred and Veda; sex appeal is the weapon. They gain husbands, steal them away, and eventually kill with their wiles. But it's all done because they're only thinking of each other. The background matches the plot, with a dark and steamy hothouse atmosphere throughout.

All About Eve. *Cocktails: battlefield of the urbane. Bill Sampson (Gary Merrill), Margo Channing (Bette Davis), Karen and Lloyd Richards (Celeste Holm and Hugh Marlowe) square off under the guise of friendly conversation.*

Sunset Boulevard. *Norma Desmond (Gloria Swanson) tells her gigolo, Joe Gillis (William Holden), what's what. The dreams of the fading movie star and the failed screenwriter bind them together, but eventually explode.*

SUNSET BOULEVARD

(1950), B/W, *Director:* Billy Wilder. *With* William
Holden, Gloria Swanson, Erich von Stroheim, Buster
Keaton, Cecil B. DeMille, Fred Clark, Jack Webb,
Hedda Hopper, Anna Q. Nilsson, and Nancy Olson.
110 min. *NR.* Tape, CED: Paramount.

In *Sunset Boulevard,* director Billy Wilder starts with
a classic melodramatic premise (an aging star who has
lost her looks and her following) and then gives it a wild,
almost hysterical spin. The result is a black comedy for a
dark, brooding subject; the humor is so disturbingly
macabre that—between laughs—it sets your teeth on
edge.

William Holden is the dead man who tells this tale. A
failed scriptwriter running from the collection agency
and his own tarnished dreams, he stumbles into the
museumlike home of faded silent-screen star Norma
Desmond (Gloria Swanson). With her leopardskin tur-
ban and kohl-rimmed eyes, Swanson is a nightmare of
aging femininity. She tends to look on Holden as her new
pet, which is only natural, since he arrives the night
Swanson's chimpanzee dies. When he lazily slides into
becoming her live-in gigolo, a sexual reversal is played
out: Swanson holds the power and the purse strings
while Holden empties the ashtrays and, eventually,
shares that spooky bed—a cross between a barge on the
Nile and a coffin—with her. Handsome and pampered,
Holden still looks like a golden boy in this role. Swanson
is horrifyingly wonderful. Her manic, choppy gestures
and his downward, slurring delivery convey both crazi-
ness and overly ripe desire.

Superb in his role as Swanson's former director/hus-
band, now butler, is Erich von Stroheim; cameo appearances by Buster Keaton and Cecil B. DeMille add to the
feeling of Hollywood decadence that abounds.

Love, ambition, devotion, failure—these are the
themes that *Sunset Boulevard* explores. It's not a pretty
picture, but it is a compelling one. And Sunset Boulevard isn't a place so much as a disillusioned state of
mind.

TENDER MERCIES

(1983), C, *Director:* Bruce Beresford. *With* Robert
Duvall, Tess Harper, and Betty Buckley. **93 min.** *PG*.
Tape: Thorn/EMI.

Tender Mercies is the result of a near perfect collabor-
ation between director and screenwriter, between subject and visual style. Director Bruce Beresford first made
his mark with the stylistic courtroom drama *Breaker
Morant;* screenwriter Horton Foote is best known for his
graceful, haunting script for *To Kill a Mockingbird.*
Together, they make a tough and grittily wrung-out film
about "real people" (i.e., characters not usually found in
films).

Robert Duvall won a long-awaited Oscar for his portrayal of an alcoholic country-and-western singer. Every
line in his face, every crack in his voice shows that he's
been around the track too many times. He's strung-out,
broken-down, and washed-up. And, as in all melodramas, he happens to walk into one last, redeeming
chance: in this case, in a gas station.

The idea at work here can also be found in *Morant* and
Mockingbird; meaning, and therefore salvation, can be
found in the smallest gestures, the truest-to-life moments. The vitality that Duvall finds with the simple-
speaking, straightforward Tess Harper is in sharp contrast with the lure he feels from drinking and one-night
stands. Following that through, the characters, so terse
and emotionally repressed, also provide high relief
against a simple plot line in which nothing typical of
Hollywood happens. The suspense is strong, but limited
to small, everyday events—just as in most of our lives.

Visually, *Tender Mercies* captures both the southern
landscape and the subtext of emotional bleakness perfectly. At times, the light is harsh and bright; the sun
shines almost too brightly here, revealing too much. In
Beresford's movies, deliverance doesn't come in cheap
talk or dark shadows; you are, instead, blinded by the
light of saving grace. Few films today deal with the
subject of emotional and spiritual healing. Even fewer
do so as believably and movingly as *Tender Mercies.*

TERMS OF ENDEARMENT

(1983), C, *Director:* James Brooks. *With* Shirley
MacLaine, Debra Winger, Jack Nicholson, John
Lithgow, and Jeff Daniels. **130 min.** *PG*. Tape, CED,
Laser: Paramount.

Although melodrama has been out of style lately,
Terms of Endearment became one of the biggest hits of
the last few years precisely because of its successful
handling of the genre. Audiences warmed to this simple
story about people living, loving, and dying.

The core of the film is the uneasy relationship between
a domineering mother, Aurora Greenway, and her all-
accepting daughter, Emma. As the sternly repressed
Aurora, Shirley MacLaine has the movie role of a lifetime. Debra Winger as Emma is fully up to the challenge
of playing opposite the experienced MacLaine. But
neither of them stands a chance against the hilarious
scene-stealing of Jack Nicholson, whose portrayal of
loutish, lecherous Garrett Breedlove, an over-the-hill
ex-astronaut, is the film's high point. Nicholson's character is not in Larry McMurty's original novel, but was
added by writer/director/producer James L. Brooks to
provide a worthy foil to the indomitable Aurora. After
Emma has married and moved away, Garrett makes a
move on Aurora, with laughable results. Emma, meanwhile, has troubles of her own, having found that her
marriage to an unfaithful university professor (Jeff
Daniels) is a long way from paradise. She comforts herself by having an affair with a straight-as-an-arrow
local banker, expertly played by John Lithgow, and
begins to trade schoolgirl confidences with her mother.
At this point the film plunges from light farce to melodramatic tragedy, as Emma develops cancer and, as
surely the entire Western world knows by now, dies.

The point here is not merely that she dies (otherwise
there would be little to separate *Terms of Endearment*
from *Love Story)* but *how* she dies. There are no grand
speeches, no emotional fireworks—just everyday people
trying to come to grips with their feelings and failures in
the face of death.

THE VERDICT

(1982), C, *Director:* Sidney Lumet. *With* Paul Newman,
Charlotte Rampling, Jack Warden, James Mason, Milo
O'Shea, Edward Binns, and Julie Bovasso. **128 min.** *R*.
Tape, CED, Laser: CBS/Fox.

Besides being a great courtroom melodrama on a par
with any other, *The Verdict* is a resounding story of
redemption, of virtue triumphant. It contains Paul Newman's finest screen performance in years, and is perhaps
director Sidney Lumet's best film. As in Lumet's *Twelve
Angry Men* (another outstanding courtroom film) and
Serpico, The Verdict concerns one man's lone struggle to
right a wrong, and the way that struggle transforms
him.

Frank Galvin (Newman) is a has-been, alcoholic shy-
ster who scrapes a living out of offering his card to
bereaved relatives at funerals. Then his one remaining
friend, Mickey (a superb supporting performance by
Jack Warden), finds him the case of a lifetime, a "money-
maker"—if he plays it safe and has his client settle out of
court. But after Galvin visits his client, a girl turned into
a human vegetable by a careless doctor, he is faced with
a difficult moral choice. If he settles out of court, his
client and her family will not receive fair compensation
for this medical negligence, and justice will not be
served. If he takes the case to trial he might lose, and
they will get nothing. In the end he must take that risk
for the sake of his own bruised soul. No one supports him
in his decision—not Mickey, not his new lover (Charlotte
Rampling), not the judge (Milo O'Shea), not the Catholic
Church which owns the hospital where the tragedy oc-
curred, and most certainly not the opposing attorney
(played with all the cold villainy James Mason can
muster).

Playwright David Mamet's screenplay is a marvel of
spare elegance and eloquence (despite being legally
questionable), and Lumet directs with an eye appropri-
ately tuned to sepia tones, shadows, and night. But the
film is Newman's, whose delivery of the summation is
one of his most moving performances.

MUSICALS

These are *big* pictures with large casts, outlandish costumes, and ambitious sets. Unfortunately, Musicals are often hampered by the size and dimension of the small screen. Furthermore, the screen was often meticulously packed to the brim with special details, many of which are lopped off in the transfer to television. There can be no doubt, however, that many of our national treasures are in this chapter—movies that transcend entertainment and approach myth. Musicals are the finest expression of the dreamers and the young-at-heart—and that can never be diminished no matter what size the screen. Other Musicals to consider are: *The Band Wagon, Bye Bye Birdie, Easter Parade, Fiddler on the Roof, 42nd Street, The Gay Divorcee, Showboat, Swing Time, That's Entertainment,* and *Top Hat.* Note: A different kind of musical is discussed in Rock 'n' Roll Movies.

Singin' in the Rain. *One of the most joyous images in all of moviedom: Gene Kelly splashes, sings, and dances out his feelings of love during a downpour.*

AN AMERICAN IN PARIS

(1951), C, *Director:* Vincente Minnelli. *With* Gene Kelly, Nina Foch, Leslie Caron, Georges Guetary, and Oscar Levant. **113 min.** *NR*. Tape, CED, Laser: MGM/UA.

Director Vincente Minnelli, in his biography, *I Remember It Well,* commented about *An American in Paris:* "Though the picture was designed as a highly commercial entertainment, I didn't feel that I should talk down to the audience." The result is an ambitious, innovative, endlessly creative musical that stretches all the talents involved.

The plot centers around an American painter (Gene Kelly). Wealthy patroness Nina Foch sponsors his work with intentions of winning his affections, but he becomes attracted to shopgirl Leslie Caron and Caron is romantically involved with Georges Guetary. Eventually both break free of former entanglements and wind up together.

Alan Jay Lerner's screenplay is full of light humor, but gives a firm foundation to the superb Gershwin score. Kelly is at his best, whether singing "I Got Rhythm" to a group of children, his duet with Oscar Levant, "Tra La La" or, most memorably, dancing along the Seine with Leslie Caron to the haunting strains of "Love Is Here to Stay." This was Caron's debut film, and she proves an enchanting, graceful presence, a true original. Minnelli also devised the art direction based on paintings by Renoir, Lautrec, Utrillo, and Rousseau. Most remarkable, though, is the 17-minute ballet based on Gershwin's "An American in Paris" symphonic suite. John Alton's camerawork and Irene Sharaff's costumes enhance the mood, and the screen spills over with colorful images of men in blazers, can-can girls, flower markets, and rushing policemen. In 1951, MGM worried that the ballet would alienate middle-American audiences. It did just the opposite, proving that culture, properly packaged, can have wide and permanent appeal.

An American in Paris. *In the justifiably famous title ballet, painter Jerry Mulligan (Gene Kelly) dances through the various motifs of the great French painters. Here, he visits Toulouse Lautrec's Moulin Rouge.*

Cabaret. *The stage show at the Kit Kat Club, a seedy little Berlin cabaret in the 1930s. The bawdy and decadent shenanigans are presided over by the goulish MC (Joel Grey, center at top).*

CABARET

(1972), C, *Director:* Bob Fosse. *With* Liza Minnelli, Joel Grey, Michael York, Helmut Griem, Fritz Wepper, and Marisa Berenson. **128 min.** *PG.* Tape, CED, Laser: CBS/Fox.

Most musicals coat their characters and plots with sugar. *Cabaret* broke new ground because it did the opposite. Bisexuality, naked greed, and Nazism are its main ingredients, and Bob Fosse directs with uncompromising realism.

The story (earlier done without music as *I Am a Camera*) focuses on showgirl Sally Bowles (Liza Minnelli), a mediocre singer working in a seedy cabaret presided over by leering master of ceremonies Joel Grey. Minnelli meets author Michael York and they become roommates and lovers. Their romance founders when they unwittingly sleep with the same man (Helmut Griem). In the end, Minnelli and York separate, and she continues her tireless, futile bid for stardom.

Minnelli's Sally Bowles is vulnerable but fundamentally hard-edged, altering the flaky madcap of the original play. Joel Grey's master of ceremonies is a composite of every decadent second-rater in show business history. The numbers project the same repellent fascination as the seedy characters who perform them. They blend effortlessly into the plotline; no one bursts out singing on buses or street corners. Kander and Ebb's sweetly sordid "Tomorrow Belongs to Me" centers on a blond boy with an ingratiating tenor voice, chanting a hymn to the rising Nazi movement. Other tunes, such as "If You Could See Her," "Two Ladies," and "Money, Money," have the same vaguely obscene magnetism.

Cabaret explodes the rule that musicals must have obligatory production numbers, fresh-faced chorus girls, or comedy material. It offers, instead, powerful proof that any subject, no matter how offbeat, can accommodate music if the characters and situations are vital and compelling.

FAME

(1980), C, *Director:* Alan Parker. *With* Irene Cara, Barry Miller, Gene Anthony Ray, Paul McCrane, Anne Meara, Lee Curreri, Eddie Barth, Laura Dean, Maureen Teefy, Antonia Franceschi, Debbie Allen, and Albert Hague. **133 min.** *R*. Tape, CED, Laser: MGM/UA.

Rock musicals in the 1950s were always low-budget embarrassments, mixing guest appearances with a juvenile or nonexistent storyline. *Fame,* from 1980, is one of the first (since *A Hard Day's Night,* anyway) to incorporate powerful rock numbers with a flesh-and-blood plot.

Set in Manhattan's High School of Performing Arts, Christopher Gore's screenplay follows a group of aspiring musicians, dancers, and actors through a grueling four-year course (as a Performing Arts graduate, I can testify to the strict standards portrayed in the film). Most notable in the talented cast are Irene Cara as an aspiring singer; Barry Miller as a Freddie Prinze-type comic; and Gene Anthony Ray as a hell-raising dance major. These and other characters experience hope and heartbreak as they hone their craft and prepare to face the competitive show business world outside.

The title tune, "Fame," won an Oscar, but it's only one of several outstanding numbers. "Out Here On My Own," co-written by Michael Gore and sister Lesley (of "It's My Party" fame), is a haunting ballad which Cara renders superbly. "Red Light," danced with startling animal grace by Ray, is the picture's highlight. There are moments of genuine pathos too, particularly in Paul McCrane's portrait of an overly sensitive homosexual. Anne Meara plays a dedicated teacher with realism and restraint, and Lee Curreri is amusing as a musician who favors electronic sound. *Fame* is significant because it doesn't patronize rock music. Director Alan Parker obviously has a feel for contemporary songs, and he makes each number express the inner life and intensity of the performer. Parker abandons earlier assumptions that rock 'n' roll is for slightly retarded teens, and his respect for the form makes *Fame* a memorable experience.

FUNNY GIRL

(1968), C, *Director:* William Wyler. *With* Barbra
Streisand, Walter Pidgeon, Omar Sharif, Kay Medford,
Anne Francis, Lee Allen, and Gerald Mohr. **155 min.** *G*.
Tape, CED, Laser: RCA/Columbia.

Years ago, reviewing 1952's *The Bad and the Beautiful,* Pauline Kael criticized its depiction of the Hollywood "rat race" as "the softest turf ever." Most movies do
make the leap to fame look easy. Fortunately, *Funny
Girl* has Barbra Streisand (in her first screen role) as
Fanny Brice, and through her stellar performance we
see the incredible drive, determination, and sheer per-
severance needed to attain success.

Streisand portrays the ugly duckling whose dreams of
show business glory are disparaged by family and
friends. Convinced that "I'm the greatest star," she
stubbornly works her way up in the theater, winning
over the man who holds the key to vaudeville stardom,
Flo Ziegfeld (Walter Pidgeon). Romantic problems surface when she falls in love with gambler Nicky Arnstein
(Omar Sharif) and pressures him into marrying her.

Arnstein's luck turns sour while Brice's career soars.
Fanny's mother (Kay Medford, in an Oscar-nominated
role), cautions her, "the man is drowning." Streisand
tries to save the relationship, but in the end Arnstein,
after serving a prison sentence, asks for a divorce.
Streisand sings an explosive, heartbreaking version of
"My Man" when he leaves.

The film's plot is familiar, a thinly disguised reworking of *A Star Is Born.* Yet Streisand's passionate conviction, her power, make every moment credible and
moving. She's in stunning vocal form on the sensitive
"People" and electrifying on "Don't Rain on My Parade."
Herb Ross's choreography is humorous and unobtrusive,
and William Wyler's direction is effectively calculated
to keep the camera on Streisand every second—where it
belongs. She is the lifeblood of the show, a remarkable
performer who can shoot out a wisecrack, wring pathos
from a sad line, and charge any song with freshness and
force.

GIGI

(1959), C, *Director:* Vincente Minnelli. *With* Leslie Caron, Louis Jourdan, Maurice Chevalier, Hermione Gingold, Jacques Bergerac, and Eva Gabor. **116 min.** *NR*. Tape, CED, Laser: MGM/UA.

After 1960, the original screen musical died, giving way to a series of mostly overproduced and unimaginative Broadway adaptations. *Gigi* was the last representative of a glorious tradition, and one of the best.

Based on a novel by Colette, *Gigi* tells of a spirited teenager (Leslie Caron) who rebels against family attempts to train her as a high-priced courtesan. Wealthy playboy Gaston Lachaille (Louis Jourdan) falls in love with her tomboyish ways and finally rescues her from an unwanted fate by marrying her.

Gigi earned nine Academy Awards, including Best Picture, and deserved them all. It includes a witty, ingenious score by Alan Jay Lerner and Frederick Loewe. Such numbers as "I'm Glad I'm Not Young Anymore" (sung with ageless charm by Maurice Chevalier), "I Remember It Well," "It's a Bore" and the incomparable title tune are definitive examples of sophisticated songwriting. Director Vincente Minnelli frames the elegant situations with a vividly colorful, stylized production. Caron, demonstrating a delightful range from gawkiness to glamour, gives the best performance of her career, and supporting players Chevalier and Hermione Gingold also surpass any of their other work.

The movie achieves perfection in every department. It makes the viewer laugh and cry. Every character, within the confines of a fairy-tale framework, is endearingly real. One feels that all hands involved loved the project and put their hearts and souls into it. And that collective joy extends to us.

SEVEN BRIDES
FOR SEVEN BROTHERS

(1954), C, *Director:* Stanley Donen. *With* Jane Powell,
Howard Keel, Russ Tamblyn, Tommy Rall, Matt
Mattox, Jacques D'Amboise, Jeff Richards, Marc Platt,
Virginia Gibson, Julie Newmar, and Ruta Lee. **103 min.**
NR. Tape, CED: MGM/UA.

For roughly an hour, *Seven Brides for Seven Brothers*
coasts delightfully along, buoyed by lively songs and
delightful performances. Then it explodes into the
greatest acrobatic dance ever put on film—a superb
number pitting six brothers against their rivals. The
men challenge one another, competing for the affections
of the town girls, and each movement (conceived by
Michael Kidd) is phenomenally uplifting.

The plot of *Seven Brides,* based on a Stephen Vincent
Benet short story, concerns a young waitress (Jane
Powell) who marries a mountain man (Howard Keel)
and finds she has been tricked into taking care of his six
uncouth, animalistic brothers. She sets her mind to civil-
izing them and marrying them off. Conflicts escalate
when the brothers decide to kidnap their intended
brides, incurring the wrath of the townfolk, but the
ruffians eventually learn how to respect women, and
true love triumphs.

Powell's performance is the centerpiece to *Seven
Brides.* Tiny and fragile looking, she conveys strength
and grit when facing down a houseful of hostile males.
Keel's stature and richly masculine singing voice are
particularly effective on such numbers as "Bless Your
Beautiful Hide." The Johnny Mercer/Saul Chaplin score
is tuneful and rousing, and director Stanley Donen
(fresh from his *Singin' in the Rain* triumph) sustains a
breakneck pace that is consistently exhilarating. Russ
Tamblyn stands out as the youngest brother, Gideon,
although everyone else is properly virile and athletic.
Seven Brides has everything—humor, sentiment, tension, even a tactfully expressed point of view about
women's rights—but most of all, it wins immortality for
its breathtaking dancing.

SINGIN' IN THE RAIN

(1952), C, *Directors:* Gene Kelly and Stanley Donen.
With Gene Kelly, Jean Hagen, Debbie Reynolds, Donald
O'Connor, Cyd Charisse, and Madge Blake. **103 min.**
NR. Tape, CED, Laser: MGM/UA.

When viewers think of most musicals, they generally
recall a number, a dance, a cinematic effect. *Singin' in
the Rain* is that rarity, a musical film with a book as
masterful as the score surrounding it. Writers Betty
Comden and Adolph Green express justifiable pride that
their work is now a part of college cinema courses.

The solidly structured script is a sparkling, incisive
satire of early Hollywood. Gene Kelly plays a 1920s
matinee idol. He becomes identified in the public mind
with leading lady Jean Hagen, whom he loathes. Talkies
add a further problem: Hagen has a high, squeaky voice,
and the team's future looks bleak until Debbie Reynolds
is recruited to dub an acceptable voice for Hagen. Kelly
and Reynolds fall in love, Hagen's inadequacies are exposed, and fans learn which lady is the true talent.

The pre-talkie era is good-naturedly ribbed when
Kelly and his pianist Donald O'Connor receive a musical
elocution lesson through a number, "Moses Supposes"
(written by Comden and Green and Roger Edens).
O'Connor has never been funnier or lighter on his toes,
and his "Make 'em Laugh" is a hilarious and athletic
show-stopper. Kelly's celebrated dance in the rain, singing the title tune, remains a joyously optimistic high
point in film history. Cyd Charisse contributes the
screen's sexiest dance in the Broadway ballet. Debbie
Reynolds, too, is at her best in the sprightly "Good
Mornin'," but *Singin' in the Rain's* greatness—its relevance—rests on the witty, devastatingly accurate
parody of a silent star supplied by Jean Hagen. Though
we laugh, she makes us comprehend what the talkies did
to the industry and its personalities. Legendary stories
—like John Gilbert's career collapse after sound took
over—acquire poignance through Hagen's portrayal.
Singin' in the Rain vibrates with humor, romance,
music, and the re-creation of an exciting era.

THE SOUND OF MUSIC

(1965), C, *Director:* Robert Wise. *With* Julie Andrews, Christopher Plummer, Eleanor Parker, Peggy Wood, and Richard Haydn. **174 min.** *G.* Tape, CED, Laser: CBS/Fox.

Broadway musicals are generally miscast *(South Pacific, Guys and Dolls)*, distorted *(Pal Joey)* or destroyed *(Sweet Charity)* when transferred to film. *The Sound of Music* is a notable exception, a rare instance where the original source material is improved in its screen treatment.

Julie Andrews plays Maria, a nun-to-be who goes to work as governess for seven children belonging to the severe Baron Von Trapp (Christopher Plummer). She finds her charges unruly and rebellious but gradually wins them over—largely with her singing. She softens the rigid baron in the same way, unwittingly attracting him away from a countess (Eleanor Parker). Late in the film they marry and find themselves in jeopardy when the Nazis come to power. Their climactic escape provides a suspenseful and exciting conclusion.

As Maria, Andrews carries this elaborate, 174-minute production. She blends tomboyish energy, drive, discipline, charm, and subtle sexual allure; and her voice is gloriously effective on "My Favorite Things," "Do-Re-Mi," "Something Good," and the majestic title tune. Ted McCord's aerial views of Salzburg are awesome, and the dance routines are simple and appealing. Ernest Lehman's screenplay omits much of the sugar that marred the original stage play, while tightening the drama; and director Robert Wise keeps the staging fluid and alive. The editing on "Do-Re-Mi," in which the children and Maria sing while riding bicycles, is a particular standout. *The Sound of Music* is, in the best sense, good clean fun, and a perfect family picture.

A STAR IS BORN

(1954), C, *Director:* George Cukor. *With* Judy Garland,
James Mason, Jack Carson, Charles Bickford, and Tom
Noonan. **175 min.** *NR.* Tape, CED, Laser: Warner.

When Judy Garland failed to win an Oscar as Best
Actress of 1954, for *A Star Is Born,* Groucho Marx described it as the biggest robbery since Brinks. This judg-
ment is still valid. As the rising star who overshadows
her fading actor husband, Garland gives the finest dramatic performance ever to appear in a musical film.

The story (first filmed in 1932 as *What Price Hollywood?*, and again in 1937 with Frederic March and
Janet Gaynor, and yet again in 1974 with Barbra
Streisand and Kris Kristofferson) chronicles the love
affair between an aspiring singer (Garland) and the
alcoholic movie actor (James Mason) who marries her
and helps her to the top. Garland watches Mason destroy
himself and fights frantically to save him, but in the end
he commits suicide. This offers her that great, climactic
moment when she faces an audience and introduces herself as "Mrs. Norman Maine."

Garland is, in director George Cukor's words, "staggering," whether belting out the superb Harold Arlen/
Ira Gershwin torch song, "The Man That Got Away," or
handling the many musical moods of "Born in a Trunk."
Her spine-chilling high notes make viewers tremble
with excitement. Mason is equally convincing, whether
portraying self-destructiveness, hostility, shame, or
genuine love for his wife. Jack Carson gives his greatest
performance as an embittered press agent, and Charles
Bickford is magnificent as a studio head. Moss Hart's
subtle screenplay supplies a fascinating and colorful
glimpse inside Hollywood.

Forty-five minutes were originally cut from *A Star Is
Born.* The footage has lately been restored, but this issue
(a burning subject among movie buffs) is almost irrele-
vant. What matters is Garland's greatness, and any
version of the film shows why she was considered (and
still remains) the most talented musical female enter-
tainer ever produced by Hollywood.

A Star Is Born. *Vicki Lester (Judy Garland, center)
works her way up the ladder of stardom. This oft-told
Hollywood tale of two stars in love—one on the rise, the
other in decline—is said to be based upon real movie idols
of the late 1920s.*

The Wizard of Oz. *The Tin Man (Jack Haley), Scarecrow
(Ray Bolger), Dorothy (Judy Garland), and the Cowardly Lion (Bert Lahr) look on as the "great and powerful
Wizard of Oz" (Frank Morgan) prepares to helplessly
ascend in his balloon.*

THE WIZARD OF OZ

(1939), C&B/W, *Director:* Victor Fleming. *With:* Judy
Garland, Jack Haley, Ray Bolger, Bert Lahr, Margaret
Hamilton, Billie Burke, and Frank Morgan. **101 min.**
NR. Tape, CED, Laser: MGM/UA.

When Shirley Temple, MGM's first choice for the role
of Dorothy, proved unavailable, producer Arthur Freed
reportedly muttered, "Thank God." We can echo his sen-
timents, because it gave Judy Garland a chance to play
the charming heroine in this musical fairy tale that
seems as fresh today as it did in 1939.

We follow Dorothy down the yellow brick road, as she
encounters a cast of winning characters: Tin Man Jack
Haley, who wants a heart, Scarecrow Ray Bolger, who
longs for a brain, and Cowardly Lion Bert Lahr, who
wants courage. Along the way they encounter the
Wicked Witch of the West (Margaret Hamilton), the
Good Witch (Billie Burke) and finally the Wizard (Frank
Morgan) who proves disappointingly inept at producing
miracles. Other fairy tale favorites include the singing
and dancing Munchkins (delightfully choreographed by
Bobby Connolly). When Dorothy finally returns to Kan-
sas and Auntie Em at the film's conclusion, we feel a
sense of loss, and it's that sense that makes viewers tune
in again and again to see these agelessly entertaining
characters go through their paces.

Victor Fleming's fanciful direction sustains the wonder and magic of L. Frank Baum's beloved *Oz* stories.
Garland (though actually 17) enables one to witness the
whole adventure through pre-adolescent eyes. The im-
mortal score (by Harold Arlen and E. Y. Harburg) perfectly complements the action, and "Over the Rainbow"
(once cut from the finished print and then restored) is
soaringly magical in Garland's hands. Every number
has endured: "Ding Dong, The Witch Is Dead" (which
became a Top 10 smash in the 1960s), "Follow the
Yellow Brick Road," "We're Off to See the Wizard," and
"If I Only Had a Brain." *The Wizard of Oz* is a "fairy tale
for grownups," because it treats juvenile material with
care, honesty, and respect.

MUSIC VIDEO

Perhaps the movies of the future will look something like the modern-day Music Video clip. Called conceptual videos, and popularized by MTV, the new Music Video is hot. It's true that directors like Federico Fellini, Andy Warhol, and John Landis are now experimenting with this new visual form. And for good reason: Music Video is a form without rules or standards. It's becoming an artist's playground as thousands of people try to develop the form. Undoubtedly, these tapes work well on video, for they were *made* for the small screen. We have designed this chapter to appeal to a broad range of tastes. So, hook up your video machine to a hi-fi system, dim the lights low, and turn up the volume. You're about to celebrate the arrival of a new generation. Other Music Video titles to consider are: *The Beast of I.R.S., The Best of Blondie, Cool Cats: The Story of a Sound, Duran, Duran, The Eurythmics: Sweet Dreams, Herbie Hancock and the Rockit Band, The Police Around the World,* and *That Was Rock!*

Girl Groups. *The most famous girl group, the Supremes.*

THE COMPLEAT BEATLES

(1982), B/W & C, *Director:* Patrick Montgomery. *With*
the Beatles, Brian Epstein, and George Martin.
120 min. *NR*. Tape, CED, Laser: MGM/UA.

The Compleat Beatles delves into the Beatles' Liver-
pudlian roots and intricately traces all the phases of the
band's history. The Beatles are shown as a cultural and
musical phenomenon whose group odyssey revolution-
ized pop music and set creative standards that have yet
to be equaled, let alone surpassed.

We witness the slow genesis of the Beatles over eight
years as they emerge from high-school and art-school
groups before finally achieving worldwide fame. We begin
to understand some of the pressures driving them apart
when we realize both how long and tedious their climb to
success was, and how, when they reached America in
1964 (at the pinnacle of their English fame) they were
gobbled up and consumed by young people searching for
sustenance after the assassination of John F. Kennedy.
The tape documents their fateful coupling with manager
Brian Epstein and their unconventional artistic collab-
oration with music producer George Martin. We see the
wearing effects of their fame, their gradual decision to
stop touring, the public's outrage over John's remarks
about Jesus Christ, the aesthetic success of their ground-
breaking "Sergeant Pepper" album, their visits with the
Maharishi, the effect of their marriages on the band's
solidarity (and vice versa), and the gradual dissolution
of the group itself as its members become too individ-
ualized to be contained in a single unit.

This is a fascinating document—eloquently exhaus-
tive in its re-creation of all the elements that produced
and eventually destroyed the Beatles, but not their
music. It's perhaps better suited to the video medium
than to the movie theaters, since most of its footage
comes from old newsclips and TV shows that were originally seen as live events on TV. The story's intimate
point of view mimics the Beatles' love affair with the
public, and works especially well within the one-on-one
relationship of the video medium.

GIRL GROUPS:
THE STORY OF A SOUND

(1983), B/W & C, *Director:* Steve Alpert. *With* Mary
Wells, Diana Ross, Ronnie Spector, Darlene Love, the
Supremes, the Ronettes, and the Shirelles.
65 min. *NR*. Tape, CED: MGM/UA.

Remember the early 1960s and the music at parties
when kids were doing the stroll, snapping their fingers
and swaying to *American Bandstand? Girl Groups:
The Story of a Sound* is a poignant reminder of the
melodic harmonizing of the female groups (many from
Motown) who were then the most bountiful contributors
to pop music. It includes songs by the best groups of the
era, including the Ronettes, the Angels, the Dixie Cups,
Martha and the Vandellas, the Shangri Las, and the
Shirelles.

What makes *Girl Groups* an exceptional music video
is the way director Steve Alpert meshes the roots of this
sound—which reigned before the British Invasion—
with current glimpses of some of these performers. Mary
Wells, Darlene Love, and Ronnie Spector give us a can-
did view of the recording process of the time, which in
many cases revolved around music producer Phil Spector. Phil owned the name and copyright for many of
these groups, and plugged in women singers as he saw
fit. Perhaps the most ironic tale is related by Ronnie
Spector (of the Ronettes) who became *Mrs.* Phil Spector:
"How was I supposed to know that when I married Phil
he'd retire from the music business and that would mean
the end of my singing?"

But when Ronnie Spector sings "Be My Baby" with
that rich, gravelly voice, or the Supremes belt out "Stop,
in the Name of Love," you know that, in spite of being
exploited by Phil Spector and others or effaced by the
British Invasion, these "girl groups" are still popular
musicians with enduring power and range. They pioneered some of the richest rhythm and blues and rock 'n'
roll around.

MAKING MICHAEL JACKSON'S THRILLER

(1983), C, *Directors:* Jerry Kramer and John Landis.
With Michael Jackson. **60 min.** *NR*. Tape: Vestron.

This enormously popular and inventive videotape juxtaposes Michael Jackson's frightening whipcord performance in the "Thriller" music videos against a different Jackson who muses in a soft-spoken way about his profession and goals. This focus on the real person versus his stage persona creates a video that explores the meaning of performing while delivering a marvelous performance. Michael's 35 million admirers get a chance here to see Michael perform, to listen to his thoughts, and to take a guided tour behind the scenes of the "Thriller" segments (a combination no avid fan could resist).

Jackson is so very *good* in his "Thriller" roles as a monstrous cat and a half-human ghoul, that it would be difficult to name an example of the man-to-beast-metamorphosis genre as frightening as this one. The intensity he brings to the roles of eerie schoolboy or horrific monster permeates every tendon of his shaking, dancing body.

The video expertly intertwines the "Thriller" music with the live action. John Landis's epic-style direction is perfect for the dancing-mob mini-horror he creates. Intercut with the "Thriller" material are special effects with a creation theme from recent Jackson brothers' videos. These provide a healthy balance to the ghoulish "Thriller" segments. Also included is old footage of Michael as a pre-adolescent boy wonder singing his heart out on the Ed Sullivan Show. What's so captivating about this videotape is that all these elements work together to give a thorough idea of who Michael Jackson is, what his multifaceted talents are, and why he has so many awestruck fans.

READY STEADY GO!

(1983), B/W, *Directors:* Robert Fleming, Rollo Gamble, Daphne Shadwell, and Michael Lindsay-Hogg. *With* the Beatles, the Animals, Lulu, Gerry and the Pacemakers, Dusty Springfield, Cilla Black, Billy Fury, the Searchers, the Rolling Stones, and the Who. **58 min.** *NR.* Tape: Thorn/EMI.

If you missed history in the making by passing up live performances by the legendary British Invasion groups when they were young and burning with popular energy, *Ready Steady Go!* (Vol. 1) gives you a second chance. It re-creates an exciting and fruitful time in popular music.

All the footage (with the exception of the Dave Clark Five segment) is from the British *Ready Steady Go!* TV show. *RSG* was in some ways an anglicized *American Bandstand.* But there are two major differences between the shows. During the 1960s *RSG* had access to an inexhaustible flow of British musicians who were revolutionizing popular music. And the show was miles ahead of *American Bandstand* in both format and camera work. The result is a series of casual performances (most of which are lip-synched) and interviews during the first half of the program with performers, such as the Beatles, the Animals, Lulu, and Gerry and the Pacemakers. Lip-synching gives the performers (also including Dusty Springfield, Cilla Black, Billy Fury, Them, and the Searchers) the freedom to roam around the set and mix with the crowd. This provides an up-close, personal look at stars we could never get enough of during their heyday.

The music video's second half is perfectly complementary—wild, live, unsynched performances by the Rolling Stones and the Who. The Stones' versions of "Under My Thumb" and "Paint It Black" present us Mick Jagger in his prime, able to incite the women in the audience to pure hysteria. *Ready Steady Go!* gives us everything this era was about, with the passion undiluted after 20 years, and 60 minutes of the best music the 1960s had to offer.

WE'RE ALL DEVO

(1983), C, *Director:* Gerald V. Casale. *With* Devo,
Laraine Newman, and Timothy Leary. **54 min.** *NR*.
Tape: Sony; Laser: Pioneer Artists.

We're All Devo is lush with unique images and rife
with vibrant colors that leap off the screen. Add to this a
dynamic group image that integrates sights and sounds,
and you have a ground-breaking music video.

Devo, a group of "new traditionalists" with a clearly
defined and all-embracing aesthetic, have a wildly unpredictable sense of humor. When Boojie Boy (an
orange-haired doll who is the offspring of General Boy,
Devo's equivalent to a Minister of Propaganda) flies
through the air propelled by an electric shock generated
when he puts his fork into a toaster, we're riveted to the
screen. It's a little like watching the borderline deviant
humor of *Saturday Night Live*. Some of the skits are
undeniably gross and sexist, but when they're performed
in the ironic context of new-wave humor, we can't help
chuckling as we watch.

Although *We're All Devo* is a compilation of 13 separate music videos, interspersed with vignettes featuring
Laraine Newman and Timothy Leary, it works as a
completely integrated unit, as well as a showcase for
such classic Devo tunes as "Are We Not Men?," "Whip
It," and "Working in a Coal Mine." Devo has an instinc-
tive understanding of how to make video. But then what
better tool could there be for their future-oriented
aesthetics than this plastic, easily manipulated medium
of the technological age?

MYSTERIES

It's no coincidence that the best Mysteries were shot in black and white—not to signify good and evil, necessarily, but to make full use of the gray area that falls in between. Mysteries are our most haunting movie form—films that allow us to flirt with the darkest aspects of the soul. When they're working, Mysteries will lead us by the nose, keep us off-guard and cautious, and test our powers of observation and thought. In short, they make us think. And they make us nervous. Mysteries are fine fuel for the home screen. Indeed, their appeal is cerebral, and the brutal realizations that take place in these films come across full-power on the small set. Some of the most memorable performances in films were provided by Mysteries, and some of our finest actors owe their careers to the form. Other Mysteries to consider include: *Body Heat, Detour, D.O.A., I, the Jury, Klute, Rear Window, Sleuth,* and *Vertigo.*

And Then There Were None. *Walter Huston and Roland Young examine a vital clue. The constant shifts in the mood and the direction of suspicion, as well as an impression of claustrophobia, distract the viewer from a cool examination of the clues, a common technique in mysteries.*

AND THEN THERE WERE NONE

(1945), B/W, *Director:* René Clair. *With* Walter Huston,
Roland Young, Barry Fitzgerald, C. Aubrey Smith,
Judith Anderson, Louis Hayward, June Duprez, Mischa
Auer, and Richard Haydn. **98 min.** *NR*. Tape: VCI.

This is the last film of famed French director René
Clair's short-lived Hollywood career, which lasted from
1941–45. The original novel by Agatha Christie was one
of her most popular mysteries, and was later a successful
stage play entitled *Ten Little Indians*. Clair and screenwriter Dudley Nichols take the inexorable logic and
sense of doom inherent in Christie's concept and turn it
into a lighthearted murder mystery, with distinct traces
of black humor. The notion of an unseen killer eliminat-
ing his victims one at a time is a macabre idea; yet the
suspense is somewhat vitiated by the inevitability of the
victim's fate. While eight people are killed in a little over
90 minutes, the filmmakers do not resort to shock tac-
tics, as most of the deaths do not occur on screen.

Eight strangers are invited by a mysterious host for a
weekend at a mansion atop a remote island off the
English coast. The group learns through a special phono-
graph record that their unseen host, one of the eight,
considers them all responsible for the deaths of various
people. The killer has seen to it that all eight will pay for
their unpunished "crimes" by deaths based on the nur-
sery rhyme "Ten Little Indians"—"Ten little Indian
boys going out to dine; One choked his little self and then
there were nine," etc. Soon each person succumbs according to the words in the rhyme. The surviving members become increasingly distrustful of one another,
until only three people are left. Without giving away the
killer's identity, suffice it to say that the conclusion of
the mystery is a victim of the dreaded Hollywood happy-
ending syndrome. However, it's a great pleasure to view
such veteran actors as Walter Huston, Roland Young,
Barry Fitzgerald, C. Aubrey Smith, and Judith Anderson. Their like is rarely seen anymore.

THE BIG HEAT

(1953), B/W, *Director:* Fritz Lang. *With* Glenn Ford,
Jocelyn Brando, Gloria Grahame, Lee Marvin,
Alexander Scourby, Carolyn Jones, and Jeanette Nolan.
90 min. *NR*. Tape: RCA/Columbia.

The notion of the lawless cop personified most recently
in Clint Eastwood's *Dirty Harry* has its genesis in the
rogue cop films of the 1950s, of which *The Big Heat* is a
prime example. As with many of director Fritz Lang's
films, there is a moral ambiguity here that virtually
erases the differences between the avenging cop and the
criminals he pursues.

Police Sergeant Glenn Ford, a member of a police force
controlled by a corrupt city administration, is investi-
gating the suicide of a fellow officer. Ford refuses to heed
warnings from higher-ups to discontinue his investigation, and soon afterwards his wife (Jocelyn Brando—
Marlon's sister) is killed by a car bomb. The rest of this
sordid and violent tale follows Ford's vengeful quest to
track down and bring his wife's murderers to justice.

Much of the violence in *The Big Heat,* which is mainly
directed at women, takes place off camera. We witness
only the results. The most sensational act of this sort is
perpetrated upon Gloria Grahame by her mobster boy-
friend (a very young Lee Marvin). In a jealous rage he
throws a pot of boiling coffee in Grahame's face, but later
in the film she returns the favor. The chief criminal in
the film (Alexander Scourby) is the essence of the 1950s
style gangster—a silky smooth family man/business-
man, while Lee Marvin, Scourby's chief confederate, is
portrayed as a thick-lipped Neanderthal out of the 1940s
school of psychopathic goons. *The Big Heat* is one of Fritz
Lang's best films and also a superior mystery story.

THE BIG SLEEP

(1946), B/W, *Director:* Howard Hawks. *With* Humphrey
Bogart, Lauren Bacall, Dorothy Malone, Martha
Vickers, Elisha Cook, Jr., Peggy Knudsen, and Bob
Steele. **114 min.** *NR*. Tape: CBS/Fox; CED: RCA Video-
Disc.

Not only is Humphrey Bogart the perfect Sam Spade
in *The Maltese Falcon,* but his Philip Marlowe in *The Big
Sleep* is the best-loved evocation of Raymond Chandler's
famous fictional detective. The kind of cynical romanticism that Bogart possesses in *Casablanca* is carried over
into his Marlowe character, a sort of urban knight-in-
shining-armor going down dark, mean streets—a good
man in a corrupt and degrading environment.

Amidst the backdrop of a studio-created, imaginary
Los Angeles circa 1946, Bogart ventures through a
series of incidents that only begin to gain a semblance of
logic toward the film's conclusion. *The Big Sleep* deals
with murder, treachery, and blackmail among gam-
blers, pornographers, nymphomaniacs, and the spoiled
rich. The mystery is so convoluted that, when asked
during the filming, even Raymond Chandler did not
know who killed one of the characters! Atmosphere
always matters more than solutions in a Chandler mystery anyway.

Howard Hawks's direction keeps the film moving at
breakneck speed. The script by William Faulkner, Leigh
Brackett, and Jules Furthman contains some of the
toughest, most amusing, and idiomatic dialogue ever to
grace an American film. Full of subtle sexual innu-
endoes that were able to pass the censors, much of the
dialogue (as the discussion about "horse racing" between
Bogart and Lauren Bacall) by its very suggestiveness is
more erotic than the type of uncensored speech found in
contemporary films. Even more than *The Maltese Falcon,* this film is peopled with a gallery of classic character actors in minor roles, each of whom has at least one
scene in which to shine.

CHINATOWN

(1974), C, *Director:* Roman Polanski. *With* Jack
Nicholson, Faye Dunaway, John Huston, Perry Lopez,
John Hillerman, Darrell Zwerling, and Diane Ladd.
131 min. *R.* Tape, CED, Laser: Paramount.

Chinatown appeared during the era of Watergate and
found a very receptive audience. The Academy Award-
winning story and screenplay by Robert Towne tackles
the subject of public and private corruption. This theme,
combined with a skillful blend of regional history and a
private-eye quest, makes for one of the most effective
mysteries in recent memory.

Los Angeles—1937. Jack Nicholson's sleazy peephole-
snooper of a detective is hired by a female imposter to spy
on her supposedly adulterous husband. When the man's
real wife (Faye Dunaway) later appears, Nicholson finds
himself implicated in a complex plot involving Dunaway's avaricious father (John Huston) and his plan to
divert Los Angeles water for his own private land devel-
opment. Along with this central theme of a big business
conspiracy is the subplot involving Dunaway's family
secret, which she hides from Nicholson. In the end, the
title location becomes the final battleground for the reve-
lation of secrets and schemes alluded to in the preceding
two hours.

Jack Nicholson's J. J. Gittes, unlike other fictional
detectives, such as Sam Spade and Philip Marlowe, is a
sort of crude quasi-jerk, much like Ralph Meeker's Mike
Hammer in *Kiss Me Deadly*. Both men become involved
in events too overwhelming for them to control. Their
meaningless good intentions and the pervasive corruption behind the respectable facade of public leaders are
the two main motifs of the film. Director Roman Polanski has a brief but memorable role as the pint-sized punk
who slices Nicholson's nose with a knife.

THE HOUND
OF THE BASKERVILLES

(1939), B/W, *Director:* Sidney Lanfield. *With* Basil
Rathbone, Nigel Bruce, Lionel Atwill, Richard Greene,
Wendy Barrie, John Carradine, Beryl Mercer, Mary
Gordon, E. E. Clive, Ralph Forbes, and Ivan Simpson.
84 min. *NR.* Tape, CED: CBS/Fox.

This 1939 version of the most commonly filmed of the
Sherlock Holmes tales is notable in a number of respects.
Basil Rathbone, the most renowned interpreter of
Holmes, essays the role here for the first time. Along
with Rathbone, Nigel Bruce's Dr. Watson is definitive.
The Hound of the Baskervilles is the first of 14 films both
men would star in together in this popular series, which
lasted to 1946. Much of the authenticity of the Conan
Doyle story is retained–even Holmes's drug addiction is
mentioned at the conclusion. (20th Century-Fox originally cut this allusion from the 1939 print. It was not
until 1975 that the drug reference was restored in its
entirety.)

A friend (Lionel Atwill) of the Baskerville family
hires Holmes and Watson to protect the heir to the Baskerville fortune. All of the male heirs have met violent
deaths, the last being attacked and killed by a giant
hound in the desolate moors surrounding the family
estate. Holmes disguises himself and ventures into the
moors, where yet another murder occurs. He foils an
attempt on the life of the latest descendant (Richard
Greene) and escapes death in a mine shaft before the
mystery is solved and the killer caught.

Many of the later Holmes films in the Rathbone/Bruce
series take on a contemporary setting. This version has
the Victorian and Edwardian atmosphere of the original
stories, and follows the deductive methods of the classic
mystery. Even on a B-movie budget, 20th Century-Fox
creates a hermetically-sealed England, using a Gothic
mansion and mist-shrouded moors.

LAURA

(1944), B/W, *Director:* Otto Preminger. *With* Clifton
Webb, Dana Andrews, Gene Tierney, Vincent Price,
Judith Anderson, Grant Mitchell, Lane Chandler, and
Dorothy Adams. **88 min.** *NR*. Tape: CBS/Fox; CED:
RCA VideoDisc.

What has become Otto Preminger's most popular film
was begun by director Rouben Mamoulian, with Preminger serving as producer. When disagreements arose
between the two men after a month of shooting, Preminger took over the reins and completed *Laura*. The
crystalline photography for which 20th Century-Fox
was so famous in the 1940s is in full evidence here.

This murder mystery revolves around the obsessive
love of two men for the same woman. One of them is a
fastidious and snobbish radio/newspaper personality
(Clifton Webb), the other a neurotic hard-nosed cop
(Dana Andrews). Both have fallen for Laura Hunt (Gene
Tierney), a young career woman who has apparently
been murdered. However, halfway through the film she
turns up very much alive. In her dark apartment, the
murderer has mistaken a young model for Laura. The
final unmasking of the killer is quite obvious to anyone
following the clues, but along the way we are treated to a
corrosive portrait of the upper classes of New York City.

Prior to *Laura*, Clifton Webb had not appeared in films
since the silent era. He practically steals this picture
with his delivery of the snide, sarcastic witticisms in the
screenplay. Thanks to Webb's Waldo Lydecker, *Laura*
becomes somewhat like *The Big Sleep*, in that we gather
almost as much enjoyment listening as watching. While
Webb's glibness stands out, Dana Andrews's less flam-
boyant portrayal of the love-sick police inspector is the
more complex character study. His investigation of
Laura's apartment, and his questioning of people about
all aspects of her life, moves perilously close to a necro-
philic preoccupation—an odd and disturbing suggestion
for a mystery film.

Laura. *Detective Mark McPherson (Dana Andrews) interrogates the suddenly resurfaced Laura (Gene Tierney). The use of highly exaggerated lighting to express the shadowy nature of the characters was a technique raised to an art form in the mysteries of the 1940s.*

The Maltese Falcon. *The deadly Brigid O'Shaughnessy (Mary Astor) and her detective/lover, Sam Spade (Humphrey Bogart). Spade wavers between his desires and his duty, between the temptation of riches and the moral constraints of his profession.*

THE MALTESE FALCON

(1941), B/W, *Director:* John Huston. *With* Mary Astor,
Humphrey Bogart, Peter Lorre, Sydney Greenstreet,
Elisha Cook, Jr., Gladys George, Barton MacLane, Lee
Patrick, and Jerome Cowan. **101 min.** *NR*. Tape, Laser:
CBS/Fox; CED: RCA VideoDisc.

The Maltese Falcon rejuvenated Mary Astor's sagging
career and firmly established Humphrey Bogart in his
tough screen persona (with all his familiar tics and
grimaces). This study of duplicity, greed, and mysterious
betrayals is an early and unsurpassed example of *film
noir*—a film full of dark images that reflects a dark
mood.

The story concerns the search for a jewel-encrusted
falcon statuette by a group of desperate people eager
enough to kill to obtain their object. The real interest for
the viewer lies not only in the mystery and its downbeat
conclusion, but in the endlessly fascinating array of
characters. The solution is less interesting than the
route we take to reach it. The homosexuality of the three
male villains is surprisingly obvious, considering the
date of the film's release. The main relationship between
Bogart and Astor is filled with ambiguity and tension.
He is attracted to her ("You're good—you're very good"),
but he refuses to help her evade the police because of his
detective's code of honor and his instinct for self-preser-
vation ("You're takin' the fall . . . . I won't play the sap
for you").

This film was John Huston's directorial debut; he also
wrote the screenplay, which keeps Dashiell Hammett's
novel virtually intact. The ensemble acting is of the
highest order. Along with Mary Astor's edgy portrayal of
the treacherous Brigid O'Shaughnessy and Bogart's
cynical but duty-bound Sam Spade, we have three letter-
perfect character roles: the obese crook, Kasper Gutman,
played by Sydney Greenstreet (his film debut); Peter
Lorre's perfumed and epicene human punching bag, Joel
Cairo; and Elisha Cook's Wilmer, who gives new meaning to the term "small-time loser."

MURDER, MY SWEET

(1944), B/W, *Director:* **Edward Dmytryk.** *With* **Dick Powell, Mike Mazurki, Claire Trevor, Ann Shirley, and Otto Kruger. 95 min.** *NR*. Tape: Nostalgia Merchant.

Dick Powell, the boy crooner of 1930s musicals, changed his screen persona in this film. After his unsuccessful attempt to land the lead role in *Double Indemnity,* Powell convinced the director of *Murder, My Sweet,* Edward Dmytryk, to let him star as detective Philip Marlowe. While some may prefer Bogart's hard-boiled Marlowe in *The Big Sleep,* author Raymond Chandler felt that Powell came the closest to capturing the essence of his character in his portrayal of Marlowe. Regardless, it is fascinating to see both actors so convincingly portray the famous detective, with completely different nuances. With the soft, rounded features of an aging choirboy gone to seed, Powell combines an interesting mixture of wisecracking toughness and adolescent bravado.

Told by Powell in the first person, *Murder, My Sweet* is one long, extended flashback as he relates to the police the details of the mystery. From the second scene, in Marlowe's darkened office, in which he is being hired by a thug (Mike Mazurki) to trace his long-lost girlfriend, to an expressionistic drug-induced dream sequence, to the final confrontation in a beach house at night, the film is a highly evocative demonstration of the light-and-shadow play of the 1940s *film noir*. No mystery film has a more appropriate atmosphere.

While looking for Mazurki's girlfriend, Powell becomes involved in a search for a stolen necklace, as well as in a murder. Throughout, we are entertained by Powell's caustic comments about some of the more outlandish members of the Los Angeles community. Three of them in particular—Mazurki, Esther Howard, and Dewey Robinson—have such bizarre countenances that the gargoyles atop French cathedrals pale by comparison.

OUT OF THE PAST

(1947), B/W, *Director:* Jacques Tourneur. *With* Robert
Mitchum, Jane Greer, Kirk Douglas, Richard Webb,
Rhonda Fleming, Dickie Moore, and Steve Brodie.
97 min. *NR*. Tape: Nostalgia Merchant.

When this film first appeared in 1947, it was treated
by critics and audiences alike as just another in the long
line of RKO's competently made murder mysteries. It
was not until the 1970s, with a resurgence of interest in
American *film noir,* that *Out of the Past* gained its present cult status. At the same time, the star of the film,
Robert Mitchum, has become a cultural icon almost on a
par with Bogart. Along with *The Night of the Hunter,*
this is certainly one of Mitchum's finest roles. If the eyes
are indeed the windows of the soul, then Mitchum's eyes
in *Out of the Past* reflect all the world-weariness and
fatalism that permeates the soul of this film.

The plot revolves around a central theme of *film noir*—
the downfall of a more or less decent man by his obsession with an amoral woman (as in *Criss Cross* and *Scarlet
Street*). Mitchum, a former private detective, is attempting to lead a new life, but his past intrudes upon him.
The baroque story relates how his love for the mistress
(Jane Greer) of a gambler (Kirk Douglas) leads to his
being the "fall guy" in an elaborate murder plot engineered by Douglas.

Small nuances are picked up with each viewing of *Out
of the Past.* Most memorable is a scene with Mitchum
drinking a beer and dozing off in the darkness of a
Mexican cantina on a sultry Acapulco afternoon. Suddenly Jane Greer appears in the bright sunlight dressed
all in white—the quintessential *film noir* villainess
dressed for the "kill."

THE THIRD MAN

(1949), B/W, *Director:* Carol Reed. *With* Joseph Cotten,
Orson Welles, Valli, Trevor Howard, and Wilfrid Hyde-
White. **105 min.** *NR*. Tape: Media.

After World War II, director Carol Reed made a trilogy of films set in bleak European cities—*Odd Man Out*
(Belfast), *The Man Between* (Berlin), and *The Third
Man*, set in Vienna. This is not the Vienna of the Haps-
burg Empire or the Strauss waltzes, but a war-ravaged
city filled with bomb-damaged baroque buildings and
psychologically scarred people. The use of chiaroscuro
photographic effects in the nearly deserted streets, and
Anton Karas's haunting zither music add a feeling of
desolation and alien mystery to the film.

A writer (Joseph Cotten) of pulp Western novels comes
to Vienna when a friend of his, Harry Lime (Orson
Welles), offers him a job. The military authorities inform
him that Welles, a notorious black-market profiteer, has
just been killed in an auto accident. Cotten, refusing to
leave Vienna and accept the worst about his friend,
questions a number of Welles's acquaintances about his
business dealings, and gradually unravels a sordid mystery. When he learns that Welles is very much alive,
Cotten must decide between doing his duty and betray-
ing a friend, between public and personal loyalty. The
final confrontation between the two men takes place in
the sewers of Vienna.

Screenwriter Graham Greene makes the Cotten character a naive American on a detective quest in a city
whose citizens exhibit a cynicism and despair foreign to
the American ethic. His foolish posturing makes us un-
comfortable, since he is supposedly the subject of audience identification. The Welles character, also an
American, has accommodated himself to the moral am-
biguities of Europe. While his black marketeering leads
to reprehensible results, he is nonetheless a charming
and amusing rogue.

PRISON/ESCAPE FILMS

Put a man behind bars and you've created a monster—or so goes the logic behind the most versatile of action films, the Prison/Escape Film. Whereas other action-oriented themes (such as films dealing with revenge) wear thin on ideas quickly, the prison situation has consistently provided a powerful context for action. Perhaps it's because there are so many types of prisons— and so many reasons for being locked up in the first place. Or perhaps it's because the claustrophobic situation provides a metaphor for everyday situations. Whatever the reasons, the Prison/Escape Film plays extremely well on the small screen. In fact, the confinement of the characters mirrors the average viewing situation at home. The Prison/Escape Film can be unconsciously exploited, but it has appealed to some talented filmmakers—people who have found in the prisons a powerful forum for social drama. Other Prison/Escape titles include: *The Dirty Dozen, Escape from Alcatraz, The Great Escape, Stalag 17,* and *You Only Live Once.*

The Bridge on the River Kwai. *Colonel Nicholson (Alec Guinness) is released from the hot box—beaten but unbowed.*

BAD BOYS

(1983), C, *Director:* Richard Rosenthal. *With* Sean Penn,
Reni Santoni, Jim Moldy, Esai Morales, and Eric Gurry.
123 min. *R.* Tape: Thorn/EMI.

A hard-edged treatment of wayward teens, *Bad Boys*
offers one of the least romanticized visions of youth in
trouble. But by so doing its ultimate glimpse of hope is
all the more powerful.

The bad boys in question are Mick (Sean Penn) and
Paco (Esai Morales), rival members of loosely knit gangs
in contemporary Chicago. Unlike the adolescent
troublemakers in *The Outsiders* or *West Side Story,* or
any number of similar movies, Mick, Paco, and company
aren't misunderstood kids with hearts of gold beneath a
rough exterior. They're bad and mean, plain and simple.

Mick attempts to rip off Paco's gang, and his play
misfires—Mick's friend is shot to death, and Mick accidentally runs down and kills Paco's kid brother. He is
sent to a juvenile correction facility filled with equally
bad kids from all over the state. To get even, Paco rapes
the 16-year-old girlfriend Mick left behind, and ends up
in the same facility, ready to face Mick and avenge his
brother's death.

Penn gives a moody depth and intelligence to Mick. As
he enters the facility and proceeds to first understand
and then brutally fight his way to the top of the internal
pecking order, it becomes clear that this is how he's
always dealt with life—in his neighborhood, his school,
and in the outside world. Only after hearing of his girlfriend's rape, and escaping to visit her for a moment
before being hauled back in, does something else appear
in Mick. It is a momentary flash of compassion that
surfaces again when Mick must finally choose between
life and death. He's still bad. But even in people whom
society brands as the worst, there lies the capacity for
human decency.

BIRDMAN OF ALCATRAZ

(1962), B/W, *Director:* John Frankenheimer. *With* Burt Lancaster, Karl Malden, Thelma Ritter, Betty Field, Neville Brand, Edmond O'Brien, and Hugh Marlowe. **143 min.** *NR.* Tape, CED: CBS/Fox.

Birdman of Alcatraz is based on the remarkable true story of Robert Stroud, a man with a third-grade education who, during 43 years of solitary prison confinement, became one of the world's leading authorities on bird diseases and anatomy. It is also the moving exploration of an individual's unique worth in the face of an environment that demands conformity.

Sent to prison in 1909 for killing a man who beat up a prostitute, Stroud (Burt Lancaster) stabs a prison guard to death during a mess-hall fight and is condemned to spend the balance of his life in solitary confinement.

With nothing on the agenda but death or old age (and the madness of isolation), Stroud takes in an orphaned baby sparrow and nurses it to health and adulthood. Other prisoners start asking relatives for their own "baby boids," and before long solitary is ringing with canary song. When an epidemic starts killing off the bird population, Stroud becomes obsessed with finding a cure —an obsession that leads to a full-time career behind bars.

Despite the lack of "action"—the film rarely leaves the cell block—*Birdman of Alcatraz* is always compelling; its microcosm pulses with its own rhythms and moods. In one of the finest sequences, Telly Savalas as Feto Gomez, the hardened con in the cell next door, waits nervously as Stroud helps his egg-laying canary. The montage perfectly parodies the classic maternity-ward scene in the outside world, of which these cons can never again be a part. Gomez puffs on a huge cigar like a proud papa when the first baby cheep is heard. New life has entered the prison.

THE BRIDGE ON THE RIVER KWAI

(1957), C, *Director:* David Lean. *With* William Holden, Alec Guinness, Jack Hawkins, Sessue Hayakawa, Geoffrey Horne, and James Donald. **161 min.** *NR*. Tape, CED, Laser: RCA/Columbia.

The Bridge on the River Kwai takes a traditional story of forced labor and places it in the context of World War II. What results is an archetypal battle of wits and resolve between Japanese captor and captive Englishman. Honor, the rules of war, and the meaning of life are at stake.

As the British Colonel Nicholson, Alec Guinness is the very essence of the stiff upper lip. His antagonist, the Japanese Colonel Saito (Sessue Hayakawa) is a would-be Samurai who spurns the Geneva convention for the code of the Bushido warrior. The trouble with the British, he claims, is that they "are defeated but have no shame." Forced by the Japanese to build a strategic railroad bridge over the river Kwai in Indochina, Nicholson will do it only under his terms, but will do the best job in his power, despite its value to his enemy. "One day," he says, "the war will be over, and the bridge will still be standing, and people will be using it and will know who built it, when they built it, and why."

But the immediate needs of war produce quite a different agenda. Without Nicholson's knowledge, an Allied commando team is working its way towards the Kwai, intent on destroying the bridge and disrupting the Japanese supply line. As Nicholson's moral code to get the job done clashes with his larger role as a fighting soldier, he in turn confronts the even larger issue of responsibility towards posterity, and war is revealed as a strange game where the rules are never completely known until it's too late.

COOL HAND LUKE

(1967), C, *Director:* Stuart Rosenberg. *With* Paul
Newman, George Kennedy, J. D. Cannon, Lou Antonio,
Robert Drivas, Strother Martin, Jo Van Fleet, Wayne
Rogers, Anthony Zerbe, Ralph Waite, Harry Dean
Stanton, Dennis Hopper, Richard Davalos, Warren
Finnerty, Morgan Woodward, Clifton James, and Joe
Don Baker. **126 min.** *NR.* Tape, Laser: Warner.

Cool Hand Luke opens in an empty urban parking lot,
late at night. Luke (Paul Newman) is happily knocking
the heads off of parking meters with a sledge hammer.
Maybe he's had a few too many drinks, maybe he just
gets his kicks this way. No matter—Luke's character is
immediately clear. This man revels in stubborn, joyous
defiance of the social order.

Given two years hard labor on a Southern chain gang
for his nocturnal antics, Luke refuses to accept the ar-
bitrary rules of behavior established by penal authorities and prisoners alike. Refusing to give up even though
completely whipped during a bloody boxing match, and
pulling off a gutsy bluff at the dormitory poker table,
Luke is soon something of a mascot for the prisoners. In
one of the most memorable scenes, Luke—completely
out of the blue—claims simply, "I can eat 50 eggs." The
furious betting that goes on as he hilariously tries to
make good the boast would rival a cockfight.

But when Luke starts openly defying the prison bosses
and stubbornly, hopelessly trying to escape, he becomes
more than just a mascot. Luke becomes a rallying symbol of freedom—an almost mythic figure about which
stories will be told down through the years on the chain
gang. He's given them something bigger to live for than
their own petty rules. In the warden's classic words,
"What we have here is a failure to communicate." Not at
all. Luke communicates loud and clear. But the warden
just doesn't like what he's hearing.

Cool Hand Luke. *Luke (Paul Newman) receives coaching from Dragline (George Kennedy) on the fine art of eating eggs. The need for such diversions to break up the monotony of prison life is central to the film.*

Midnight Express. *Billy Hayes (Brad Davis) is held back by fellow prison inmates to prevent him from unleashing his anger—and worsening his situation. The Turkish prison saps the life from its charges, churning their rage, yet preventing them from working it out.*

MIDNIGHT EXPRESS

(1978), C, *Director:* Alan Parker. *With* Brad Davis, Irene Miracle, Bo Hopkins, Randy Quaid, John Hurt, Mike Kellin, and Paul Smith. **121 min.** *R.* Tape, CED, Laser: RCA/Columbia.

Midnight Express portrays the plight of a young American trapped in a Turkish prison. It pushes to the limit the traditional prison-film theme of the social outcast. Not only is the protagonist an alien in Turkish society, he's an alien in the prison subculture as well—an outcast among the outcasts.

In 1970, with hijackers blowing up planes like clockwork and U.S./Turkish relations at an all time low, college boy William Hayes (Brad Davis) tries to stroll through the Istanbul airport with two kilos of hashish taped to his body. In the terrifically tense opening sequence we follow Hayes, doomed to arrest less by his obvious nervousness than by an inexcusable—but characteristic—ignorance of the geopolitical situation.

Seeking to make an example of him, Turkish authorities toss Hayes in a prison that makes Alcatraz look like an afternoon at Knott's Berry Farm. A brutal pig-like warden administers horrible beatings and torture for minor infractions. Between the prisoners themselves, violence follows its own bizarre guidelines. Stabbing or shooting a fellow inmate in the chest, abdomen, or head is attempted murder and thus punishable by prison officials. But anything goes below the belt—a knife in the thigh or buttocks is a perfectly acceptable way to end an argument or get even for an imagined slight.

Hayes meets up with his fellow travelers in this nightmare—a tall, handsome Swede; a moronic, violent American; and an English junkie. "The Midnight Express" is their train metaphor for escape. "It doesn't stop around here," explains the Englishman. It does, Hayes discovers, but the fare is steep, and the ride anything but smooth. Though the film's ending departs from the true-life story of Hayes's book, Hayes himself has endorsed its stark rendering of prison conditions in Turkey.

ROCK 'N' ROLL MOVIES

What started as a vehicle to exploit the frenetic appetites and odd tastes of 1960s teenagers has become a durable movie form—as rich with possibilities as any teenage genre. Rock 'n' roll has meant rebellion from the start, and the movies within this chapter consistently echo an alternative to the existing way of doing things. These movies do more than buck traditional values, however. Many of them are quite experimental in nature, as if the film community itself was getting a kick in the pants. These films do best with an audience, and a few of them may require screaming adolescents to best simulate the theater situation. The music is not going to come across on the home screen as it should, but these movies are primarily about *energy*, and that translates quite well to the television set. Other Rock 'n' Roll titles to consider are: *Rude Boy, Get Crazy, Hair, Magical Mystery Tour, Rock 'n' Roll High School,* and *Tommy.*

A Hard Day's Night. *The Beatles (John, Paul, George, and Ringo) prove themselves to be totally charming and natural performers in their first motion picture.*

A HARD DAY'S NIGHT

(1964), B/W, *Director:* Richard Lester. *With* John
Lennon, Paul McCartney, George Harrison, Ringo
Starr, Wilfred Brambell, Victor Spinetti, and Anna
Quayle. **90 min.** *NR*. Tape, CED, Laser: Maljack.

After a scant six months on the top of the English
charts, fresh from the Sullivan show, the media darlings
of two continents, the Beatles were on a roll and
barely into their 20s. The year was 1964. From the first chord of
the title track, *A Hard Day's Night* recalls the seemingly
guileless charm of the Fab Four, and the unique hysteria
they ignited in their young fans. Allowed to play themselves, John, Paul, George, and Ringo display all the
boundless wit, energy, and talent that were the hall-
marks of the early Beatles.

Pursued everywhere they go by a mob of 14-year-olds,
they board a provincial train en route to a fictional TV
concert at London's Scala Theatre. Paul introduces his
wily grandfather (Wilfred Brambell) and the boys are
called on endlessly to restrain the reckless, womanizing
old man. " 'E's very clean," deadpans Paul. This repeated
reference to his troublemaking grandfather also neatly
satirizes the public's opinion of the Beatles at that time.
The entire film, in fact, is a refreshing exercise in self-
parody.

The rapid-paced editing, along with the brisk screenplay, projects a playful spontaneity reminiscent of the
Marx Brothers. Each of the Beatles is allowed his
moment, and they respond with surprisingly natural
performances—especially Ringo, in his solo scene at the
end, cut to the poignant melody of "This Boy."

Seven bouncy Beatles songs are introduced—reper-
toire beyond reproach—and the Beatles' delivery is as
fresh as Lester's camera angles. *A Hard Day's Night* is
still a gentle spoof of Beatlemania, and 20 years later it
is also delightful nostalgia. Their records made them
famous, but this film established the Beatles' funny and
fun-loving, innocent public image, which they never
quite lost.

JAILHOUSE ROCK

(1957), B/W, *Director:* Richard Thorpe. *With* Elvis
Presley, Judy Tyler, Vaughn Taylor, Dean Jones, and
Mickey Shaughnessy. **96 min.** *NR.* Tape, CED:
MGM/UA.

In *Jailhouse Rock,* one of Elvis Presley's best movies,
Elvis plays Vince Everett, an ex-con fresh from the peni-
tentiary, where the warden has been withholding his fan
mail. As if the manslaughter rap he was framed with
wasn't enough, his cell mate taught him hillbilly riffs
ten years out of date. Once he's released, a guitar-smash-
ing audition in a local nightclub does nothing to improve
either his prospects or his disposition. But there he
meets Peggy, a jukebox exploitation expert, who helps
him cut his first single. All this, of course, is fairly
standard stuff for a Hollywood musical—even one featuring the king of rock 'n' roll.

But *Jailhouse Rock,* made in 1957, is a showcase for
the churlish rebel-without-a-cause image Elvis temporarily inherited from the recently fallen James Dean.
With a curl of the lip and a shake of the hip, Presley
personified a rock-'n'-roll-inspired moral decay that concerned serious-minded parents of the Eisenhower era.
The way the film plays on this misunderstanding delighted many first generation rockers, and is still
intriguing today.

Elvis's portrayal of the fast-rising Hollywood hipster
is not totally convincing (Elvis, after all, was a singer,
not an actor), but the combination of his swagger, jive-
talk, and up-turned collar is the essence of cool. The
soundtrack could use a few more songs, but all of those
used are first-rate, and the title-track performance is
Presley's finest onscreen moment, as well as his personal
favorite. Ultimately, *Jailhouse Rock* is the best remedy
for the legions of Elvis imitators and the Graceland
relics, which sometimes seem to be all that's left. This
film, remember, is where Elvis first said, "Let's rock!"

PERFORMANCE

(1970), C, *Directors:* Nicolas Roeg, and Donald
Cammell. *With* Mick Jagger, Anita Pallenberg, Michele
Breton, James Fox, Ann Sidney, and John Burdon.
105 min. *R.* Tape, Laser: Warner.

Performance is perhaps the most subtle and personal
rock-'n'-roll film ever made. Rather than being about
manic rock-'n'-roll performers or their fans, it explores
how rock music permeates and dictates the lifestyles of
people intimately involved with it. It does this by
examining the life of an ultimate 1960s symbol, the
former pop insider, Turner (Mick Jagger), who has
dropped out of both the rock-'n'-roll subculture and the
larger society of which it's a part.

The film mostly takes place in the cocoon of Turner's
London pad—the backdrop for a multilayered psyche-
delic experience of some of the main subjects of contemporary pop music: androgyny, the search for identity, the quest for fulfillment, and the meaning of death.
Anita Pallenberg is Pherba, Turner's probing live-in
mate; Michele Breton plays Lucy, an androgynous
French drop-out, crashing at Turner's; and James Fox is
Chas, a brutal petty gangster who, through an ironic
twist, rents a room from Turner which he then uses as a
hideout from his gangster pals.

Directors Nicolas Roeg and Donald Cammell create a
narrative like a child's set of toy boxes—as each box is
opened, there's always a smaller box inside containing
yet another, tinier box, with more answers and more
questions. Compelling music by The Last Poets, Ry
Cooder, Randy Newman, and Mick Jagger punctuates
these themes. Jagger performs one of the first and best
"music videos" ever produced when he sings Turner's
theme song, "Memo from Turner," in a tightly choreographed, conceptually integrated number, which is a
sophisticated precursor of the music video trend. *Performance* is a must for anyone interested in the evolution
of popular music and mores.

PINK FLOYD THE WALL

(1982), C, *Director:* Alan Parker. *With* Bob Geldof.
95 min. *R*. Tape, CED, Laser: MGM/UA.

Pink Floyd The Wall is an excruciatingly heavy film;
it is painful to watch and filled with lingering images of
war, death, and martyrdom. Band member Roger
Waters wrote the screenplay and most of the music, and
the film is said to be somewhat autobiographical. If so,
one can't help but wonder how anyone could survive
when plagued by such nightmarish fantasies.

This is the inarticulate story of Pink (Bob Geldof), a
British pop star in the throes of a deep, drug-ridden
alienation that pushes him into self-mutilation and
attempted suicide. The story is mainly told with mute
live action that spills into frightening animation (by
Gerald Scarfe) when Pink's feelings explode with private paranoia too extreme to be expressed by live actors.
The roles are interpreted visually, for the most part,
without dialogue. Pink Floyd's music supplies the narrative. The music is excellent and the lyrics express
quite well the layers of anguish that have built the wall
separating Pink from everything. There is an equilib-
rium between the lyrics and the visuals, although the
lyrics deal with the intense alienation and pain in a
softer way than director Alan Parker's surreal images,
which are extremely harsh and gory. This perilous balance mirrors Pink's inner state. We are privy to his
waking nightmare.

The Wall is an ambitious film made in the Pink Floyd
tradition of cult extravaganzas. Bob Geldof (of the Boom-
town Rats) does an excellent job as Pink, a role he conveys almost exclusively with his pain-ridden face. Pink's
life is not his own; he is possessed by the horrors surrounding him, which drag him, lifeless or enraged,
through each day.

QUADROPHENIA

(1979), C, *Director:* Franc Roddam. *With* Phil Daniels, Mark Wingett, Philip Davis, Leslie Ash, and Gary Cooper. **115 min.** *R.* Tape: RCA/Columbia.

Quadrophenia is an adaptation of the classic Who album (loosely based on band member Pete Townshend's life) about a boy's troubled journey through the murky peer-ridden waters of Mod adolescence. The Mods were stylishly angry young British men who tended to use amphetamines (ever wonder how Townshend had the energy to smash all those guitars?) and who worked in dull office jobs to finance their slick motor scooters and elaborate wardrobes. They also tended toward violent clashes with the Rockers, their natural enemies. While the Mods liked Motown rhythm and blues, the Rockers liked hard-core 1950s rock 'n' roll. Picture a kid in a slick gray suit and polished boots astride a bright scooter covered with mirrors, versus a biker in black leather, and you've got the external conflict.

But this film is really about an *internal* battle. The protagonist, Jim (Phil Daniels), is a displaced adolescent losing contact with his environment as he struggles to define himself. He suffers from "quadrophenia"—double schizophrenia—because he is cut off in four ways: from family, work, girlfriend, and peer group (the Mods). Amphetamines help nurture the disordered feelings, thoughts, and conduct that eventually lead to his complete isolation.

The Mods symbolize what Jim wants for himself: to be a modern seer on a new frontier, creating a new order. But when Jim realizes the Mod lifestyle holds only the most superficial answers to his mounting personal conflicts, his struggle for self-definition leads to anarchy. To the rousing strains of The Who's "Love, Reign o'er Me," Jim takes a wild scooter ride to the brink of disaster—and self-acceptance. Franc Roddam's gritty, personal direction perfectly complements the anthem-like soundtrack and the portrayal of Jim's youthful angst.

SCIENCE FICTION FILMS

The story lines and characters may appear to be the product of an overactive imagination, but the best of Science Fiction Films are firmly anchored in the possibilities of science fact. The home television set has trouble containing the Science Fiction Film—especially the ones that use the realms of outer space as their canvas. And considering the importance of sound to modern Science Fiction (usually a deep, almost tangible effect—Dolby equipped, pumped out of 16 or more loudspeakers), the small screen can seriously diminish a movie's impact. But don't despair! The ten films in this chapter are the absolute classics—films that have, in their time, singlehandedly changed the look of movies in general. It's entertainment at its best. Other Science Fiction Films to consider are: *I Married a Monster from Outer Space, Invaders from Mars, On the Beach, Planet of the Apes, Silent Running, Star Trek II: The Wrath of Khan, Strange Invaders, THX-1138, War of the Worlds,* and *Wavelength.*

2001: A Space Odyssey. *Astronaut Dave (Keir Dullea) reenters the spaceship* Discovery. *The size of the photograph conforms to the shape of the Super Panavision screen.*

ALIEN

(1979), C, *Director:* Ridley Scott. *With* Sigourney
Weaver, Tom Skerritt, John Hurt, Ian Holm, Harry
Dean Stanton, Yaphet Kotto, and Veronica Cartwright.
116 min. *R.* Tape, CED, Laser: CBS/Fox.

Alien is, at heart, the outer space version of the
"there's a monster in the house" horror genre. But under
Ridley Scott's direction, the twist proves deadly. A more
horrifying science fiction film may never hit the screen.

The story opens on the interstellar freighter *Nostromo,* flying back home with its seven crew members
and innumerable tons of mineral ore. Under mysterious
directions from corporate headquarters on Earth, the
workers interrupt their journey to investigate a wrecked
spaceship on a planet along the way.

Over the objections of Sigourney Weaver (playing a
refreshingly strong role in a genre that rarely goes beyond the hysterical female), one of the crew brings the
Alien on board in its embryonic form. The creature soon
proves to be the ultimate galactic predator, rapidly
metamorphosing into a more awful and deadly form at
each stage of its bizarre, metallic-organic life cycle, brutally dismembering the crew one by one. Watch for the
ever-popular "here kitty, kitty" scene, where the audience is all but compelled to shout, "Forget the damn
cat—run, you idiot!"

Unlike the often prissy crews of other cinematic spaceships, the workers of the *Nostromo* are recognizable and
sympathetic—just a bunch of mechanics and foremen
out on a job. And the freighter itself is as dank and gritty
as any Lake Superior coal boat. This strangely familiar
environment allows director Ridley Scott to play to the
hilt the terrifying otherness of the Alien. They don't
make them like this too often. Thank God.

BLADE RUNNER

(1982), C, *Director:* Ridley Scott. *With* Harrison Ford,
Rutger Hauer, Sean Young, Edward James Olmos,
William Sanderson, Daryl Hannah, and Joe Turkel.
117 min. *R.* Tape, CED, Laser: Embassy.

   With an astonishing attention to detail, *Blade Runner*
is unmatched in its creation of a consistently believable
future world. Weird as it might be, director Ridley
Scott's Los Angeles of 2019 seems entirely plausible—
and it supports the story at all levels.
   Based loosely on Philip K. Dick's *Do Androids Dream
of Electric Sheep?, Blade Runner* is the tale of four gen-
etically engineered androids—called replicants—who
have violently escaped from their asteroid work stations
and returned to Earth seeking vengeance and a longer
life span (to lessen their chances for rebellion, they were
designed to die after four years) from the corporation
that manufactured them. Though sick of the bloody business, ace "blade runner" Deckard (Harrison Ford), the
21st century equivalent of a bounty killer, goes after
them.
   Los Angeles, and the Earth as a whole, has been abandoned by everybody who's anybody. What's left is a
bizarre-like neon universe of dilapidated 20th-century
structures and high-tech advertising blimps, exotic
ethnic subgroups, and social misfits. The humans in
Blade Runner have been made soulless by a technological society that values production above all else.
Only the products of that technology—the replicants—
seem capable of questioning and finally transcending
those values.
   Marred by an unnecessary Raymond Chandleresque
voice-over narration, a falsely happy ending, and
(reportedly) massive cuts by the studio, *Blade Runner*
isn't the perfect masterpiece it might have been. But it is
nonetheless a shining example of what science fiction
can do at its best: establish an imaginative realm the
better to examine some fundamental aspects of the
modern human experience.

CLOSE ENCOUNTERS
OF THE THIRD KIND

(1977), C, *Director:* Steven Spielberg. *With* Richard
Dreyfuss, Francois Truffaut, Teri Garr, Melinda Dillon,
Cary Guffey, and Bob Balaban. **152 min.** (Reissued at
132 min.) *PG.* Tape, CED, Laser: RCA/Columbia.

If few science fiction films go beyond captivating the
intellect to reach the emotions, fewer still touch a deep
chord in the human spirit—the longing for a universe
with meaning. *Close Encounters of the Third Kind* does
all three. Director Steven Spielberg unabashedly delivers the sweetest of valentines to all who have looked
into the heavens with the wonder and vulnerability of a
child.

The story opens with a series of inexplicable events:
perfectly preserved World War II fighter planes appearing in the desert, strange radar blips on defense moni-
tors, sightings of Unidentified Flying Objects. Those
individuals who have experienced the latter—a middle-
American electrical worker named Roy (Richard Dreyfuss), a woman and her young son, and an assortment of
social misfits, eccentrics, and artists—all become obsessed with finding the source of these "close encounters." Following the more mundane promptings of their
electronic instruments, an international scientific team
chases the same elusive goal.

The meeting, when it comes, is one of the most spectacular events in the history of science fiction—and of
film. The immense, glitteringly beautiful mother ship
from the stars is awesome in the truest meaning of the
word—sending chills up the spine. And the famous five-
note tone dialogue between the ship and the scientists'
giant synthesizer (supervised by French director Francois
Truffaut in a delightful cameo) is as funny as it is
moving. *Close Encounters of the Third Kind* presents the
loving antithesis of the cold, indifferent cosmos common
to most science fiction films.

THE DAY THE EARTH STOOD STILL

(1951), B/W, *Director:* Robert Wise. *With* Michael Rennie, Patricia Neal, Hugh Marlowe, and Sam Jaffe. **92 min.** *NR*. Tape: CBS/Fox.

Klaatu barada nikto!
Rare is the science fiction afficionado who doesn't know the name of the movie during which that line was uttered. A classic sci-fi film, *The Day the Earth Stood Still* produced one of the genre's most enduring archetypes: the benign but misunderstood alien. And it did so at a time when anything politically or culturally foreign to postwar America was viewed with profound distrust.

The film opens with a large, saucer-shaped craft landing in Washington, D.C. The military goes bananas, throwing a cordon around the area and aiming as much firepower as possible at the ship. Out steps Klaatu, apparently a man, and an eight-foot-tall robot called Gort. A trigger-happy soldier wounds Klaatu, who is subsequently taken captive. He recovers, escapes, and spends the rest of the movie trying to talk sense to these Earthlings, who, with their atomic weapons, are unknowingly posing a threat to the galactic order. If you don't get your act together, suggests Klaatu, somebody else will get it together for you. And he has the robot to back him up. (Interestingly, in the original story on which the film was based, the robot is in charge and Klaatu is his subordinate.)

The message to the audience is clear. A world of suspicion—where to be different is to be branded an alien and persecuted, where megadeath is just a button away —is not a world that can last. This theme makes the film every bit as timely now as it was over 30 years ago.

The Day the Earth Stood Still. *Extraterrestial Michael Rennie warns earthling Patricia Neal of the dangers to her planet. To the left is Gort, Rennie's protective robot.*

Forbidden Planet. *In five years, science fiction robots had progressed to the talking-computer stage. Here, Robby the Robot returns a crew member to Commander Adams (Leslie Nielsen) and Altaira (Anne Francis).*

FORBIDDEN PLANET

(1956), C, *Director:* Fred McLeod Wilcox. *With* Walter Pidgeon, Anne Francis, Leslie Nielsen, Warren Stevens, and Earl Holliman. **98 min.** *NR.* Tape, CED, Laser: MGM/UA.

The best interstellar adventure film from the 1950s, *Forbidden Planet* borrowed heavily from the literary past, and has significantly influenced succeeding efforts in the genre, from *Star Trek* to *Star Wars.* The plot is lifted from Shakespeare's *The Tempest,* with a dash of Freud, but *Forbidden Planet's* starship, with its heroic captain, dedicated first officer, avuncular doctor, and Mr. Fixit engineer, looks suspiciously like an earlier incarnation of the indomitable *Star Trek* gang.

Islandlike in its isolation, the forbidden planet is Altair IV, occupied not by the magician Prospero, but by the scientist Dr. Morbius and his beautiful Mirandaesque daughter, Altaira. The part of Ariel the Sprite goes to Robby the Robot, a forerunner of R2-D2. The mission from Earth finds Morbius and his daughter the only survivors of a scientific expedition that landed on the planet 20 years before. Morbius impresses the crew with a tour of the technological wonders of the planet's long-dead race, the highly advanced Krell. They are also impressed by Altaira, a lovely, miniskirted naif who tries to kiss anything that moves. Morbius says, it's been nice, thanks for coming, but if you don't leave soon something very bad will happen. They don't, and it does.

Peril comes in the form of the "Id-monster," an invisible but destructively tangible manifestation of the terrors that dwell in the depths of the psyche. *Forbidden Planet's* high technology, as embodied by the impossibly powerful yet gentle Robby the Robot, is without exception benign. But the "Id-monster" suggests that even the most advanced beings must sooner or later face their own inner demons. And all the Robbies in the world won't prevent that inevitable confrontation. Note especially the haunting electronic mood music, which was years ahead of its time.

INVASION OF THE BODY SNATCHERS

(1956), B/W, *Director:* Don Siegel. *With* Kevin McCarthy, Dana Wynter, Larry Gates, King Donovan, and Carolyn Jones. **80 min.** *NR.* Tape: NTA.

Released during an era of cold wars and commie scares, the original *Invasion of the Body Snatchers,* coolly directed by Don Siegel, is a vision of paranoia unbound. Nearly three decades later the film retains a creepy deliciousness that justifies its continued popularity on the revival circuit.

Kevin McCarthy plays a small-town family doctor who is suddenly swamped by patients claiming that their loved ones aren't their loved ones anymore—they're emotionless imposters. McCarthy is dubious—it looks like a job for the town shrink. In the film's only reference to the uneasy international politics of the day, the psychiatrist explains it away as a contagious hysteria caused by "worry about what's going on in the world." But gradually the evidence begins to pile up, and McCarthy must face the awful truth: The townsfolk are being taken over by alien pods. The police, the psychiatrist, neighbors of 30 years, closest friends, and dearest relatives—all are being transformed, rendered soulless by an inhuman, outside force.

The red-under-every-bed mentality of the times goes a long way toward explaining the high anxiety level in *Invasion of the Body Snatchers.* But beyond the obvious, the film champions the vision of the loner in any society —the individual whose personal encounter with moral truth is ignored by the established order. The most memorable scene occurs near the end of the film, when McCarthy has escaped from his town and is trying to warn motorists on a nearby highway. His anguished cry of "Won't anybody listen to me?" touches the outsider in each of us. Though the special effects of this low-budget black-and-white picture are not as glamorous as those in the 1979 remake, the earlier film is by far the scarier and more thought-provoking version.

THE MAN WHO FELL TO EARTH

(1976), C, *Director:* Nicolas Roeg. *With* David Bowie, Rip Torn, Candy Clark, Buck Henry, and Jackson D. Kane. **118 min.** *R*. Tape, Laser: RCA/Columbia.

A disturbing meditation on innocence and corruption, *The Man Who Fell to Earth* may well be science fiction's only true art film (with the exception of *2001*). Under Nicolas Roeg's direction, the universal theme is open to any number of specific interpretations. This is a richly layered film that always surprises and always demands our attention.

Rock star David Bowie is superb in the title role as an alien from a drought-plagued planet whose inhabitants have long been picking up television images from the water-abundant Earth. Hoping to return home with relief for those he left behind, Bowie plunges into the cutthroat world of the multinational economic system, trying to create enough wealth and power to build the ship he needs for the trip back. He soon heads a wildly successful high-tech consumer electronics firm, but he realizes too late that to play the game, one inevitably becomes like all the other players.

In one of the most striking scenes, Bowie sits in a quiet dinner theater, watching two Japanese mimes go through a delicate, silent duel that looks almost like a loving dance. At the same time, far away, a college professor engages in violent sex with an 18-year-old student, while they play with one of Bowie's instantly developing electronic cameras. Their animalistic grunting overlaps the silent movements of the Japanese dancers, and Bowie seems somehow aware of and disturbed by the violence that is being captured by his camera. Rationalize as we might, the scene suggests, we are never absolved of responsibility for the products of our imaginations.

METROPOLIS

(1926), B/W, *Director:* Fritz Lang. *With* Brigitte Helm,
Alfred Abel, Gustav Froelich, Rudolf Klein-Rogge, and
Fritz Rasp. **120 min.** *NR*. Tape: Budget.

Metropolis was to 1927 audiences what *2001* and *Star
Wars* were some 50 years later. Inspired by his first
encounter with the Manhattan skyline, German filmmaker Fritz Lang created a special effects blockbuster
the likes of which had never before been seen.

The plot, simple in its morality, is nonetheless byzan-
tine in execution. In the year 2000 A.D., the city of
Metropolis, ruled by the benevolent John Masterman,
seems a bustling utopia, with every citizen an aristocrat.
But all is not as it appears. The standard of living is high
because Masterman and his associates maintain a huge
population of slaves who live and work deep in the
bowels of the city. Revolution is in the air, however. The
slaves have a leader, Maria, whom they all but worship.
Masterman, disturbed by the Maria cult, gets his mad
scientist, Rotwang (great name, that!), to build a robot
duplicate of the young woman with which to mislead the
slaves.

All of which is really beside the point. The city itself is
a marvel, still impressive after half a century. *Metropolis* is an art deco wonder of stepped building facades and
curved walls, domed chambers and ornate passageways.
The immense clocklike machinery and the antlike
masses of slaves are still effective—mindless labor depicted on an epic scale. Even the opening credit sequence,
with the word "Metropolis" burned into the screen, is a
terrific bit of animation that still gets applause today.

And despite decades of Gorts and Robbies and C3POs,
Rotwang's disturbingly erotic Maria robot is without
equal. It remains the embodiment of all that is terrifying
and seductive about technology.

Metropolis. *The above-ground city, a vision painstak-ingly created by director Fritz Lang and designers Otto Hunte, Erich Kettelhut, and Karl Vollbrecht. The future that is depicted has been viewed as both optimistic and dictatorial.*

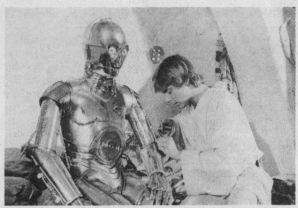

Star Wars. *Luke Skywalker (Mark Hamill) repairs the arm of droid C3PO. Lots of state-of-the-art special effects, but the science never gets in the way of the fiction.*

STAR WARS

(1977), C, *Director:* George Lucas. *With* Mark Hamill, Harrison Ford, Carrie Fisher, Peter Cushing, Alec Guinness, Anthony Daniels, Kenny Baker, and the voice of James Earl Jones. **121 min.** *PG.* Tape, CED, Laser: CBS/Fox.

Then came *Star Wars*. Creator George Lucas fulfilled the promise of earlier space films, taking special effects to undreamed of visual and aural heights. He satisfied an audience that cut across all barriers of age and class. He gave science fiction movies and Hollywood itself a boost that can still be felt and seen today. And he practically redefined the term "blockbuster."

Star Wars is the successful marriage of two very different genres. The setting is pure science fiction: a galaxy full of spaceships and blaster rays, alien worlds, and bizarre beings. The characters are straight out of heroic fantasy: evil lords and beautiful princesses, boy heroes and old wizards.

The plot reflects the Arthurian legends and other tales. A nasty Empire rules the galaxy, opposed by a hearty but rag-tag band of rebels. The Empire's Lord Darth Vader kidnaps rebel Princess Leia and takes her aboard the Death Star, a planet-sized weapon of vast destructive power. Young Luke Skywalker, under the tutelage of the mystical warrior Obi-wan Kenobi, and in the company of dashing mercenary Han Solo, must rescue the Princess and destroy the Death Star.

Lucas's brilliance is reflected in the appeal of his characters, and in the believability of the entire concoction. By adding small touches of wit and idiosyncratic detail whenever possible, his otherwise stock characters assume a three-dimensional depth that absolutely demands affection. By making its advanced technology well-worn—both prone to occasional malfunctions and completely familiar to those who use it—*Star Wars,* its elements of fantasy notwithstanding, achieves a realistic look that eludes most of its science fiction predecessors.

2001: A SPACE ODYSSEY

(1968), C, *Director:* Stanley Kubrick. *With* Keir Dullea,
William Sylvester, Gary Lockwood, and Daniel Richter.
141 min. *G.* Tape, CED, Laser: MGM/UA.

Stanley Kubrick's *2001: A Space Odyssey* marks the
end of one era and the beginning of another. It is the last
major science fiction film to get away with depicting a
"Futurama" world in which (almost) every technological
endeavor functions in pristine flawlessness. But the execution of that vision set a new benchmark in special
effects against which all subsequent efforts would be
judged.

2001 spans nothing less than the history of the human
race, from its proto-hominid beginnings to its destiny
"beyond the stars." The film opens on the African
savannas, where a small band of our apelike ancestors
are having a tough go of it. Along comes the infamous
2001 obelisk—a large, black, rectangular something-or-
other—and the gang gets some bright ideas, such as how
to use a bone as a tool.

Flash forward a few million years, by means of the
most famous cross-cut in film history (the bone-into-
spaceship image). The now tool-happy human race has
discovered an obelisk on the moon (identical to the one
which appeared to our ancestors). It beams a signal
towards the planet Jupiter, and a spaceship carrying
HAL, the infamous onboard computer, journeys to check
it out.

What it all means has been a matter of some dispute.
But that's part of the film's endless appeal. The psyche-
delic "stargate" sequence is still gorgeous, whether it's
interpreted as a metaphorical depiction of the human
soul's ascent into the empyrean or as an interstellar
autobahn. The "starchild"—a very big baby who goes
into orbit around the Earth at the End of the Beginning—is still awe-inspiring, even if you haven't the fog-
giest. No matter. *2001*—from the African dawn to the
pirouetting space stations, to the alien landscapes—
remains an uncannily beautiful achievement, unique in
concept and execution.

SPORTS FILMS

The boxing movie is by far the best cinematic sports form. Through boxing, filmmakers can document the struggles of an individual as he literally fights his way to the top. Other sports have had their day on film but, with few exceptions, have never succeeded in capturing the excitement of the sport itself. Only three sports are represented in this chapter: boxing, football, and track. Although there have been good films made about other sports, the thrust of those dramas have taken place outside the stadium. In the Sports Films included here, the sport is all-important. All of these films are superb home movies. The television set has become *the* vehicle for sports coverage, and all of these films rely heavily on the dramatic techniques that television helped develop. Other Sports Films to consider include: . . . *All the Marbles, Body and Soul, The Bingo Long Traveling All-Stars and Motor Kings, The Champion, Golden Boy, The Pride of the Yankees, Raging Bull,* and *The Set-Up.*

Chariots of Fire. *A highly motivated Jewish student from Cambridge, Harold Abrahams (Ben Cross), trains hard for the 1924 Olympics.*

BRIAN'S SONG

(1970), C, *Director:* Buzz Kulik. *With* Billy Dee
Williams, James Caan, Shelley Fabares, Judy Pace, and
Jack Warden. **73 min.** *N R.* Tape, CED: RCA/Columbia.

For the most part, films that overtly manipulate the
audience's emotions come across as excessively smarmy.
Occasionally, however, a film that sidesteps the brain
and targets the heart hits so squarely that nothing else
matters. *Brian's Song* is such a film, sailing over all the
potential pitfalls thanks to its performances, and superb
musical score (Michel Legrand)—and its truth.

Based on *I Am Third,* the autobiography of Chicago
Bears football great Gale Sayers, this made-for-TV
movie chronicles the on-the-field rivalry and after-hours
friendship of Sayers (Billy Dee Williams) and teammate
Brian Piccolo (James Caan). Although there is much
football action in the film—including authentic footage
of Sayers—this is peripheral to the real story, which is
about "Pick's" losing battle with cancer, and the lessons
in courage Sayers learns from his friend.

When originally aired, this film made stars of new-
comers Williams and Caan, who are superb. Traditionally underrated, however, has been the contribution of
Shelley Fabares as Joy Piccolo, and Judy Pace as Linda
Sayers. Together, the four of them create a tight, caring
little world which, when it loses Pick, creates a void that
each struggles to fill for the other.

Predictable as it may be, *Brian's Song* demonstrates
that in both sports and life, it is courage more than skill
that makes a winner.

CHARIOTS OF FIRE

(1981), C, *Director:* Hugh Hudson. *With* Ian Charleson,
Ben Cross, Nigel Havers, Nick Farrell, Alice Krige,
Cheryl Campbell, Ian Holm, John Gielgud, Lindsay
Anderson, Patrick Magee, Nigel Davenport, Dennis
Christopher, and Brad Davis. **123 min.** *PG.* Tape, CED,
Laser: Warner.

Chariots of Fire won the Best Picture Oscar not just for
its overall excellence, but for its men-with-backbone
theme. Like *Rocky,* the viewer is invited to root for the
underdog-of-his-choice. Unlike Rocky, this story of the
1924 Olympics is set in the halls of Oxford and the
parlors of Paris. There, it seems, is where some of the
really dirty deals in life are conceived.

The heroes in *Chariots of Fire* are Scottish missionary
Eric Liddell (Ian Charleson) and Jewish student Harold
Abrahams (Ben Cross). They are driven to compete for
different reasons, Liddell partly to glorify God, partly
because he likes to win, Abrahams mostly to overcome
anti-Semitic belittlement and alienation. The film de-
votes most of its first half to Abrahams as he struggles to
increase his speed; in the second half, Liddell, a natural
athlete, takes center stage as he refuses to race because
his match is scheduled for a Sunday and he won't compete on the Sabbath. The problem is solved when another member of the British team switches events with
Liddell, who is forced to make an heroic eleventh-hour
adjustment in his racing style.

It has to be said: *Chariots of Fire* distorts history.
Liddell knew six months before the games about the
scheduling and had ample time to prepare. As for Abrahams, he was struggling less against prejudice than to
overcome the long shadows of his two older brothers,
both Olympic competitors. However, this doesn't detract
from the film as *drama.* The strength of one man's drive
and another's convictions are what the picture is really
about. As such, it is powerful filmmaking and superb
entertainment.

GENTLEMAN JIM

(1942), B/W, *Director:* Raoul Walsh. *With* Errol Flynn, Alexis Smith, Jack Carson, Alan Hale, Minor Watson, Ward Bond, and Arthur Shields. **104 min.** *NR*. CED: RCA VideoDisc.

By 1942, Errol Flynn was one of the most popular actors in film, a reputation he had earned almost entirely in period swashbucklers like *The Adventures of Robin Hood* (1938) and *The Sea Hawk* (1940). Anxious to do a contemporary film, he jumped at the chance to play heavyweight boxer Jim Corbett in *Gentleman Jim.* Not only did the film give Flynn one of his best roles, it spotlights a most unusual champion—"Gentleman Jim," so-called because of his uncharacteristically high intellect, exquisite manners, and reliance on "scientific" boxing: fancy footwork and elusive maneuvers combined with a solid, straight left.

The film opens in 1887, with Corbett working as a bank clerk in San Francisco. Happening to attend an illegal bout, he becomes intrigued with the sport, becoming an amateur, then a professional fighter. The picture follows him around the country as he slugs his way to the top, culminating in a 21-round title bout in 1892 with John L. Sullivan (Ward Bond), "The Boston Strong Boy."

Although the boxing scenes aren't as gritty as those in films like *Body and Soul* (1947) or *Champion* (1949), Flynn brilliantly captures Corbett's grace, athletic skill, and boyish enthusiasm. In addition to the star's vigor and panache, what makes *Gentleman Jim* a classic is the time it spends examining the personalities of Corbett and Sullivan. The boxers realize that champions share one thing in common: One day they're going to be beaten. This is movingly demonstrated when the proud loser comes to Corbett's black-tie victory celebration to present him with the champion's belt. Corbett realizes that he will one day have to do the same.

There's no corruption, no contrived heroics in *Gentleman Jim.* It's simply an exciting, uplifting story of one fighter's rise, another's fall, and the emotional risks of competition.

THE LONGEST YARD

(1974), C, *Director:* Robert Aldrich. *With* Burt Reynolds,
Eddie Albert, Ed Lauter, Michael Conrad, Jim
Hampson, and Bernadette Peters. **121 min.** *R*. Tape,
CED, Laser: Paramount.

Both in and out of the sports genre, "good guys vs. bad
guys" has been what most of Burt Reynolds's career has
been about. But he's never been better at rallying audiences than in the football film *The Longest Yard*. In fact,
with the possible exception of the *Rocky* films, this may
be the most rousing "underdog" picture of them all.

Although tearjerkers are a staple of the sports film
genre, the "big game" theme is more popular still. Never
mind that there are yard after yard of clichés, and a
benchful of stereotypes. It's an eternal formula because
it taps the essence of drama: getting the audience solidly
behind an underdog, solidly against the antagonist, then
letting them cheer and boo as the two go at it tooth and
nail. *The Longest Yard* plays this formula to the hilt, and
very skillfully, too.

Reynolds stars as a pro quarterback who earns a jail
sentence for throwing a gridiron game. Inspired by this
talented new jailbird, tyrannical warden Eddie Albert
looks to break the spirit of his inmates by organizing a
match between them and his brutish guards and invit-
ing the public. When the score comes closer than expected, Albert orders Reynolds to throw the game; the
quarterback complies until the sight of the other
prisoners giving their all turns him around. The game,
of course, goes down to the wire—and in tortuous, bone-
crunching slow motion, Reynolds alone must face "the
longest yard."

This is one of those films that critics detest for its
transparent manipulation of the emotions—and that
audiences love for exactly that reason. Both are entirely
right. Like a football game in a thunderstorm, *The
Longest Yard* may not be art. But as entertainment goes,
right down to genuinely hissable villains, dying chums,
and winning one "for the Gipper," Hollywood doesn't
make them any better than this.

ROCKY

(1976), C, *Director:* John G. Avildsen. *With* Sylvester
Stallone, Talia Shire, Carl Weathers, Burt Young,
Burgess Meredith, and Thayer David. **121 min.** *PG*.
Tape, CED, Laser: CBS/Fox.

Everyone has their favorite among the Rocky films.
Purists love *Rocky* because it was the first, jocks cheer
Rocky II (1979) because the boxer wins, and cynics
applaud *Rocky III* (1982) because the hero is corrupted.
Each film in the series has its merits, but neither of the
sequels can match the honesty, impact, and drama of the
first. If it isn't the greatest sports film ever made, *Rocky*
certainly has the most endearing hero.

It begins with heavyweight world champion Apollo
Creed (Carl Weathers) deciding it would be a great publicity gimmick to give a no-name fighter a shot at the
crown. He selects hulking, go-nowhere Rocky Balboa
(Sylvester Stallone), who takes the bout to heart and
works out like a demon. Rocky's goal is not so much to
win but to give Creed a fight—which he does in spectacular fashion. Though he loses, Rocky goes the distance
and thus emerges a true winner. *Rocky II* rematches the
pair, this time giving Balboa the title; in *Rocky III*,
Rocky is decked by Clubber Lang (Mr. T) and must get
back in shape for the climactic rematch.

Rocky, which won the Best Picture Oscar, is the kind
of rags-to-riches film Hollywood stopped making because the story had become so trite. But Stallone, who
also wrote the script, transcends convention by refusing
to give Rocky a neat, unlikely win. He also sends
glamour to the showers and focuses on real people moving through an unforgiving world—an Everyman scenario with which viewers identify. So deeply did Stallone believe in his story, that he refused to sell the script
unless he could star in the picture.

Though Stallone managed to vary the theme in the
second and third films, *Rocky,* like a first love, is the one
we'll always cherish.

SPY FILMS

The Spy Film has a strange and bewildering history. There have not been very many Spy Films made, and many of those that were sank quickly into oblivion. But when a Spy Film hits big—as with 007, James Bond— there are few films that can compete with it in terms of sheer action-oriented entertainment. Spy Films are generally quite complicated; as conspiracies are introduced, characters and their loyalties are slowly revealed, and plots get thick with double-crosses and twists. In many ways, this makes home video a better Spy Film format than the theater, because you can control the action or clear up any confusion with a quick pass on the rewind switch. There are three Alfred Hitchcock films represented in this chapter, which may signal the important role a director plays in the success of a Spy Film. Other Spy Films to consider are: *Dr. No, The Looking Glass War, The Osterman Weekend, Thunderball,* and *You Only Live Twice.*

North By Northwest. *Advertising man Roger Thornhill (Cary Grant) suddenly finds himself mistaken for a spy and menaced in all sorts of ways—most famously by an airplane.*

EYE OF THE NEEDLE

(1981), C, *Director:* Richard Marquand. *With* Donald
Sutherland, Christopher Cazenove, Kate Nelligan, Ian
Bannen, and Philip Martin Brown. **112 min.** *R*. Tape,
CED: CBS/Fox.

Eye of the Needle comes as a pleasant surprise for those
who have followed the career of Donald Sutherland. He
probably leads in the acting sweepstakes for appearing
in more box-office bombs than almost anyone else. This
excellent production is based on the best-selling spy
thriller by Ken Follett, and really is two stories in one.
Part of the film deals with the exploits of a ruthless and
resourceful German master spy in Great Britain during
World War II. The other half chronicles the unhappy
marriage of a young woman to an embittered cripple,
and their existence on a Scottish island. The tension in
the film's last 45 minutes develops when the spy and the
wife encounter one another by chance.

Faber (Donald Sutherland), the knife-wielding German spy, has learned of the Allies' deceptive efforts at
convincing the Germans about a false landing site for
the D-day invasion. In order to relay this information to
the German high command, Sutherland must travel
across Britain to a rendezvous point with a U-boat off the
Scottish coast. His small boat crashes in a storm and he
is washed ashore near the home of a sheep rancher
(Christopher Cazenove) and his sexually and emotionally starved young wife (Kate Nelligan). The lonely
Nelligan confides in the new stranger, and soon they are
having an affair. Cazenove learns of Sutherland's espionage activity, so Sutherland pushes him off a cliff to his
death. Nelligan finds her husband's body and decides to
escape with her son. When Sutherland catches up to her
he tells her that, "The war's come down to the two of us."
This combination of an espionage thriller and woman-
in-distress theme is an absorbing if violent tragedy.

GOLDFINGER

(1964), C, *Director:* Guy Hamilton. *With* Sean Connery,
Gert Frobe, Harold Sakata, Shirley Eaton, Honor
Blackman, Bernard Lee, and Lois Maxwell. **112 min.**
NR. Tape, Laser: CBS/Fox; CED: RCA VideoDisc.

Goldfinger is the third James Bond movie, and the
first to highlight the sophisticated spy gadgetry that has
distinguished the popular series for over 20 years. The
tongue-in-cheek attitude of *Goldfinger* looks suspiciously
like parody nowadays, but it all seemed very fresh when
it appeared back in 1964. Perhaps the reason behind the
series' success is that it walks a fine line between self-
parody and an adolescent wish-fulfillment straight out
of the pages of *Playboy.*

James Bond (Sean Connery) is not on the trail here of a
mastermind from criminal organizations, such as
SPECTRE or SMERSH, but an international financial
wizard called Auric Goldfinger (Gert Frobe). With the
espionage aid of Chinese nuclear scientists, Frobe
means to destabilize the world's gold supply and corner
the market with his own private gold reserves. Connery
is out to stop Goldfinger's planned atomic explosion at
Fort Knox, which would render the gold reserves radio-
active for more than 50 years. The spy chase takes Bond
from Miami Beach, to England, Switzerland, and Fort
Knox, where he does battle with Goldfinger's hulking
henchman, Oddjob (Harold Sakata). Along the way,
Bond pauses to bed down the "Golden Girl" (Shirley
Eaton) and Pussy Galore (Honor Blackman), who has
the greatest, least modest moniker of any Bond heroine.

Any reader of Ian Fleming's Bond novels will realize
that Sean Connery was born to play Bond. While the
Bond character is extremely appealing, it's odd to reflect
that in some respects he is rather a bungler as an intelligence agent. He always seems to be easily caught by the
villains, and in *Goldfinger* he is responsible for the deaths
of two innocent women. *Goldfinger* is, with its excellent
production values and galvanic pacing, great fun.

NORTH BY NORTHWEST

(1959), C, *Director:* Alfred Hitchcock. *With* Cary Grant,
Eva Marie Saint, James Mason, Jessie Royce Landis,
Martin Landau, Leo G. Carroll, and Philip Ober.
136 min. *NR.* Tape, CED, Laser: MGM/UA.

Alfred Hitchcock directed a number of superior films
about espionage, particularly in England during the
1930s. *The Man Who Knew Too Much, Secret Agent, The
Lady Vanishes,* and *The 39 Steps*, all have spies as the
main villain. *North By Northwest,* made over 20 years
later, is in many ways a remake of the latter film, except
that it is superior to its predecessor and is one of Hitchcock's greatest all-around successes. Two of the chief
reasons are the pulsating rhythmic musical score of
Bernard Herrmann and the rollicking tongue-in-cheek
attitude taken by Hitchcock and screenwriter Ernest
Lehman towards the cloak-and-dagger material.

A Madison Avenue advertising executive (Cary
Grant) is kidnapped by two spies who mistake him for
someone else. This begins a series of adventures for
Grant, such as his being unjustly accused of a political
assassination. He flees the spies and the federal authorities by taking a train half-way across the country,
where he meets, unbeknownst to him, a CIA agent (Eva
Marie Saint), and romances her. *North By Northwest*
includes the famous and chilling crop-duster sequence,
in which Grant is pursued by a predatory plane in an
empty field, and culminates with a suspenseful chase
atop Mount Rushmore—classic scenes in the spy genre.

As in a number of Hitchcock films, the theme is one of
mistaken identity, and as a result, an innocent man
must outwit both the criminals and the authorities.
Hitchcock's genius for narrative economy is showcased
in the last concentrated minute of the film. Within
seconds the pursuer of Grant and Saint is dispatched, the
chief spy (James Mason) is caught, and the couple are on
their way East on a train—married.

NOTORIOUS

(1946), B/W, *Director:* Alfred Hitchcock. *With* Cary
Grant, Ingrid Bergman, Claude Rains, Louis Calhern,
Reinhold Schunzel, and Moroni Oken. **103 min.** *NR*.
Tape, CED, Laser: CBS/Fox.

Notorious is a seamless mixture, part spy thriller and
part romantic melodrama. The plot deals with uranium
—one of the main ingredients of the atomic bomb—and
is thus an excellent subject for espionage. (When director Alfred Hitchcock was doing research on the story,
prior to Hiroshima, he was under surveillance himself
by the FBI.)

After World War II, an FBI agent (Cary Grant) convinces the daughter (Ingrid Bergman) of a prominent
late Nazi agent to undertake a clandestine mission to
Brazil, where she will infiltrate a group of fascist
refugees. A wealthy former associate (Claude Rains) of
Bergman's father is sheltering Nazis as they wait to
begin a new world order. When he proposes marriage to
Bergman, she accepts as part of her intelligence assignment. She and Grant find some uranium hidden in
Rains's wine cellar, and shortly thereafter Rains learns
she is an agent. Grant then takes it upon himself to save
Bergman, who is slowly being poisoned by Rains and his
jealous mother.

With that subtle streak of perversity he was famous
for, Hitchcock here creates both hero and villain in
shades of gray, which has since become the stock-in-
trade of spy novelists. Cary Grant is deeply in love with
Bergman, yet is manipulating her in a dangerous
assignment. This ambiguity in Grant's nature is at the
core of his singular appeal as an actor. (This light side/
dark side quality of Grant's is even more in evidence in
the first film he made with Hitchcock in 1941—*Suspicion.*) Claude Rains's Alexander Sebastian is a suave
villain, who, before he learns of his wife's betrayal, truly
loves her. The sympathy with which the character is
written and played causes us to fear for his safety, after
his cohorts learn he has been duped by spies and blown
their cover.

THE 39 STEPS

(1935), B/W, *Director:* Alfred Hitchcock. *With* Robert
Donat, Madeleine Carroll, Lucie Mannheim, Godrey
Tearle, and Peggy Ashcroft. **80 min.** *NR*. Tape:
Embassy; CED: RCA VideoDisc.

The 39 Steps was Alfred Hitchcock's first big hit in the
United States. It also is the first time he used the theme
of the innocent man blamed for a crime—a theme he
would return to in *Saboteur, The Wrong Man,* and *North
By Northwest.* As in the latter film, there is a sure sense
of fun to this engaging spy yarn, as logic is thrown by the
wayside in favor of pure emotional involvement with the
hero's predicament.

A young Canadian (Robert Donat) visiting London
innocently gives refuge to a female agent. After he finds
her murdered, Donat escapes from the spies who have
killed her, and learns that the police have made *him*
their chief suspect. He heads by train for Scotland,
where he meets a young woman (Madeleine Carroll).
They are handcuffed together by the spies posing as
policemen, but manage to escape. At first Carroll refuses
to believe Donat's improbable story. It is only after further adventures with him that she comes to realize the
truth. The climax, during a vaudeville performance at a
London theater, has become one of Hitchcock's set-pieces
of suspense.

No Hitchcock retrospective nowadays is complete
without a showing of *The 39 Steps,* although prior to the
early 1970s it was impossible to see it on American
television. Since 1960, the story has been filmed twice in
England, but neither version contains the combination
of menace, mirth, and intrigue that characterizes the
original.

WAR FILMS

War and film have been intricately linked since the first newsreel played in the theaters. The combination of the two has not always been for the better of the country or the world. It was war that first tapped into the great propaganda properties of cinema, turning film into a weapon of astounding proportions. But when handled responsibly, by independent artists, the War Film can heal and probe. Whether or not a War Film plays well on TV depends on the amount of spectacle (battlegrounds, airfights, etc.) incorporated within the movie. We chose films that do get their message across on the TV, although a few of them are among the greatest (and most expensive) spectacles in all of movies. Other War Films to consider include: *Breaker Morant, The Longest Day, The Red Badge of Courage, A Bridge Too Far, M*A*S*H, The Naked and the Dead,* and, in a factual vein, Frank Capra's *Why We Fight* series.

Sergeant York. *Alvin York (Gary Cooper, center) sets aside his religious convictions when his country calls him to war.* Sergeant York *deals squarely with the issues of personal conviction and duty to country.*

ALL QUIET ON
THE WESTERN FRONT

(1930), B/W, *Director:* Lewis Milestone. *With* Lew
Ayers, Louis Wolheim, John Wray, Slim Summerville,
William Bakewell, Beryl Mercer, Russell Gleason, and
Ben Alexander. **103 min.** *NR*. Tape: MCA.

Fifty years after it was made, *All Quiet On the Western
Front* still stands as the greatest antiwar film ever produced, with the most realistic portrayal of World War I
trench warfare (though *Paths of Glory* rivals it on both
counts). It's effective because it plays against our national sympathies by showing the human side of the
enemy—so much so that when we see American troops
surging forward, we identify more strongly with the
Germans shooting them!

In a faithful adaptation of Erich Maria Remarque's
famous novel, the film follows the life of a young German
volunteer, Paul (Lew Ayers), whose naive patriotism
turns to disillusionment and bitter resignation. Most
war pictures focus on the survivors, the victors, the un-
hurt. This one dwells on the dead, the wounded, the
broken—such as Paul's friend Albert (William Bakewell), who has his leg amputated, or Kat (Louis Wolheim), the hard-mannered but soft-hearted veteran
killed by shrapnel. And unlike other war films, which
justify or even glorify combat, *All Quiet On the Western
Front* completely demystifies it. There is nothing
romantic about having your leg sawed off. "When it
comes to dying for your country, it's better not to die at
all," says Paul.

When it was released, the film was prophetic as well as
historical, for Hitler had come to power the year before,
and Germans were once again daring to speak of defending the Fatherland. Among the many memorable scenes:
soldiers catching lice and burning them in a candle
flame, Paul pleading forgiveness from the corpse of a
man he has killed, and a love scene depicted only by a
still life and the sound of a scratchy Victrola.

APOCALYPSE NOW

(1979), C, *Director:* Francis Ford Coppola. *With* Martin
Sheen, Marlon Brando, Frederic Forrest, and Robert
Duvall. **139 min.** *R*. Tape, CED, Laser: Paramount.

The baroque surrealism of *Apocalypse Now* is, in its
own way, a realistic depiction of the Vietnam War.
George Trow of the *New Yorker* has said, "*Apocalypse
Now* is not so much a movie about Vietnam as it is a
movie about the world created by television"—that is,
the world created by ratings-conscious network pro-
grammers. *Apocalypse Now* conveys the striking dichotomy between the war as it was and the war as most
Americans experienced it. Vietnam was also the first
war to be fought by soldiers frequently on drugs, and the
film reflects this both literally and stylistically, from the
napalm-drenched opening nightmare of Captain Willard (Martin Sheen)—surely one of the most original and
haunting opening scenes ever filmed—to the hallucinatory sadism of renegade Colonel Walter E. Kurtz (Marlon Brando) at the end.
   The plot, such as it is, is loosely borrowed from Joseph
Conrad's *Heart of Darkness* and concerns the gradual
alienation of Intelligence Officer Willard as he travels
upriver into Cambodia on a secret mission to assassinate
Kurtz, whose "methods are unsound." In fact, Kurtz is a
genocidal maniac, but as Willard observes, "Charging a
man with murder in this place was like handing out
speeding tickets at the Indy 500." Willard's harrowing
journey hardens him, until ultimately there is little
difference between him and Kurtz, a realization that
seems to apply to America's conduct in the war (though
director Francis Ford Coppola admits that the film is not
effective as an antiwar statement, as it makes war look
too fascinating).
   Sheen gives the best performance of his career, and
Brando does wonders with an almost-impossible role.
Robert Duvall shines as a jingoistic colonel who loves
"the smell of napalm in the morning." Visually, the film
is like a Hieronymus Bosch painting as executed by
Rembrandt. A masterpiece.

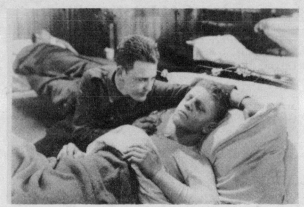

All Quiet On the Western Front. *Young soldier Paul Baumer (Lew Ayres) cannot bear to tell his buddy Albert (William Bakewell) that he has lost a leg. The film fearlessly details the many horrors of war.*

Apocalypse Now. *Captain Willard (Martin Sheen) emerges ready to perform the will of his superiors, and the will of his victim, Colonel Kurtz. He had his mission and "after it was over, he'd never want another one."*

BIRTH OF A NATION

(1915), B/W, *Director:* D. W. Griffith. *With* Lillian Gish, Mae Marsh, Henry B. Walthall, Miriam Cooper, Robert Harron, and Wallace Reid. **159 min.** *NR*. Tape: Budget.

It's odd to reflect that this 70-year-old epic artifact is farther removed from us than from the American Civil War it depicts. Even more amazing is how a picture made in the infancy of cinema can still look so good and work so well. In its portrayal of the ravages of war, and the smoldering hatreds that both cause wars and survive them, *Birth of a Nation* has no equal. It is not too much to say that with *Birth of a Nation,* D. W. Griffith almost single-handedly established film as a serious art form. Certainly no other director at the time had attempted a work of such depth and richness.

Griffith's self-appointed task is no less than the retelling of the causes, events, and aftermath of the Civil War, as seen through the intertwined fortunes of two families: the Stonemans from the North and the Camerons of the South. Friends at first, the Camerons and Stonemans take opposite sides in the great conflict, and the young men from each family end up fighting one another (and dying in each other's arms). The war also brings together and then divides the young lovers, Elsie Stoneman (played by a young and very beautiful Lillian Gish) and Colonel Cameron (Henry B. Walthall). The burning of Richmond shown here is painfully real and gripping. Its nightmarish intensity clearly influenced not only a later version of the same event in *Gone With the Wind,* but also the dreamlike night combat scenes in *Apocalypse Now.* And the scenes of hand-to-hand combat and musket fire are on a scale not matched since. Most interesting, though, is the turn the film takes after the surrender at Appomattox. No other film renders so movingly the tragedy of Lincoln's assassination and the subsequent rape of the South during Reconstruction.

Modern viewers should beware of the blatant racism that shows the Ku Klux Klan riding to the rescue like the U. S. Cavalry in a western and that depicts Blacks in sweeping stereotypes.

THE BOAT (DAS BOOT)

(1981), C, *Director:* Wolfgang Petersen. *With* Jurgen
Prochnow, Herbert Gronemeyer, Hubertus Bengsch,
Bernd Tauber, Erwin Leder, and Martin May. **150 min.**
R. Tape, Laser: RCA/Columbia.

There have been dozens, perhaps hundreds, of submarine films; some of them quite good. *The Boat* rises
above them all. It achieves a level of realism previously
unknown in the sub genre, and suspense to match. Like
All Quiet On the Western Front, it does this by revealing
our "enemies" as ordinary human beings laboring under
the extraordinary task of killing other men on order. As
a result, we find ourselves rooting for the laconic, cynical
U-boat captain (played with grim intensity by Jurgen
Prochnow) and his devoted crew. They are not Nazis, but
loyal Germans, willing to fight for their country although dubious of their Fascist leaders.

When the film opens, the tide is already turning
against Germany in the north Atlantic; the blockade of
Britain is failing; and many U-boats are being sunk by
the Allies. *The Boat* follows the fortunes and misfor-
tunes of one U-boat as it hunts and torpedoes Allied
freighters and suffers retaliation from Allied destroyers.
Along the way we get as detailed a look at submarine life
as we are ever likely to see: quarters so cramped that
even privies are crammed with supplies; rows of sau-
sages and breadrolls swinging overhead in the corridors;
crewmen driven to distraction by boredom, and then to
panic by claustrophobic terror when the submarine is
disabled by a depth charge; acts of bravery and camaraderie that are somehow fostered by these unhappy conditions. There are genuine comic moments, too, as when
the captain gives morale a boost by playing the World
War I British fighting song, "A Long Way to Tipperary,"
on the PA and everyone joins in singing; or when one
sailor remarks, "Mildew is good for you. It's the next best
thing to fresh-grown lettuce."

The dubbing is so accomplished that it's often un-
noticeable, and the script by Wolfgang Petersen (who
also directed) is subtle and superb.

THE DEER HUNTER

(1978), C, *Director:* Michael Cimino. *With:* Robert De
Niro, Christopher Walken, Meryl Streep, John Savage,
John Cazale, George Dzundza, and Chuck Aspegren.
183 min. *R.* Tape, Laser: MCA; CED: RCA VideoDisc.

If *Apocalypse Now* shows the inhumanity and insanity
of the Vietnam War, *The Deer Hunter* reveals the humanity of the Americans who fought it. Where *Apocalypse Now* is a grand but chilling spectacle, *The Deer
Hunter* is warm and moving. This is partly because it's
an actor's film, with an extremely strong ensemble of
actors, and partly because it's as much about the bonds of
friendship between men as it is about the war.

Robert De Niro, Christopher Walken, and John
Savage play Michael, Nicky, and Steve—three buddies
and co-workers from the steel town of Clairton, Penn-
sylvania, who enlist and go to Vietnam together. Technically De Niro has the lead, and he turns in a marvelous
performance as the stoical Michael. But Walken steals
scenes from him left and right, and in fact won an Oscar
(as did director Michael Cimino and the film itself) for
what is without doubt his finest role to date. This is also
the best work John Savage has committed to film, and
the last work of the late John Cazale, who plays Stanley,
a loser who wins by staying home. Meryl Streep is her
prettiest and most compelling in her first major film role
as Linda, Nicky's girl before the war, and Michael's girl
when Nicky fails to return.

Many words have been spent (and wasted) concerning
the war footage—particularly the scenes of Viet Cong
sadists forcing prisoners of war to play Russian roulette,
and later scenes in which Nicky plays it for money in
Saigon. Those who criticize this aspect of film because
"no one ever played Russian roulette in Vietnam" are
missing the point of the metaphor. Other cruel and per-
verse games *were* played in the war. And anyone who
has tasted the hospitality of a Vietnamese tiger cage will
affirm that *The Deer Hunter's* depiction of POW's is
otherwise all too accurate. If you want to know how the
war affected those who were there, this is the film to see.

KAGEMUSHA

(1980), C, *Director:* Akira Kurosawa. *With* Tatsuya
Nakadai, Tsutomo Yamazaki, Kenichi Hagiwara,
Jinpachi Nezu, and Shuji Otaki. **159 min.** *PG*. Tape:
CBS/Fox.

Kagemusha (The Shadow Warrior) is the magnum
opus of Japanese director Akira Kurosawa, whose *Rash-
omon, The Seven Samurai,* and *Derzu Uzula* have already established him as one of the greats of cinema.
Though it is many other things as well, *Kagemusha* is a
magnificent war film, an epic study of combat in an alien
time and culture: 16th century feudal Japan.

The complex plot involves three warlords vying to
take the capital city of Kyoto. When one of them dies, the
other leaders of his clan decide to keep his death a secret
by hiring a double to impersonate him for three years,
while they regroup. Kagemusha is about to be crucified
for thievery when the Takeda clan leaders hire him to
pass for the late Shingen Takeda. "It is not easy to
suppress yourself to become another," says Shingen's
brother. "The shadow of a man can never desert that
man." Kagemusha takes on the job reluctantly, yet does
what is expected of him and in the end uncovers his own
latent gift for leadership. As this personal drama unfolds, we also witness the backroom political dramas
that precede every war: secret alliances, secret plots,
secret betrayals. All of these threads come together in
the final 40 minutes of the film during the Battle of
Nagashino—a historical re-creation that resembles the
stuff of Arthurian legend. Colorful banners fly and men
do battle on horseback with lances and suits of armor
(this armor consists of ceramic chips). The Japanese
invented muskets, and there is no shortage of them here.

Like all of Kurosawa's works, *Kagemusha* is a moral
fable and a visual marvel that invites repeated watching. Note especially the schizophrenic perfection of
Tatsuya Nakadai in the dual role of Shingen Takeda/
Kagemusha, and the quiet strength of Tsutomo Yamazaki as his brother Nobukado.

PATHS OF GLORY

(1957), B/W, *Director:* Stanley Kubrick. *With* Kirk
Douglas, Ralph Meeker, Adolphe Menjou, George
Macready, Wayne Morris, and Timothy Carey. **86 min.**
PG. Tape, CED: CBS/Fox.

Of all the dark visions of director Stanley Kubrick,
Paths of Glory is the darkest. Its utter nihilism suggests
a world in which virtue is either nonexistent or irrele-
vant, in which it is impossible (or pointless) to do the
right thing. In such a world, it makes perfect sense for
the French high command in World War I to order an
attack against a German fortification purely for political
reasons, knowing in advance that the enemy position is
impregnable and the battle hopeless. *Paths of Glory* explores that cynical absurdity and all its tragic conse-
quences.

Adolphe Menjou is the coldly calculating commanding
general who gives the order. George Macready is the
glory-hungry General Mireaux, who has doubts about
the assignment but accepts it when he is told his pro-
motion hangs in the balance. Kirk Douglas is Colonel
Dax, the officer who must carry out the order and lead
the troops in the attack against the "Anthill," a heavily
guarded German fort, despite his own reservations. The
French soldiers fail to take the "Anthill," just as their
superiors expected them to. General Mireaux accuses
them of cowardice, and has three of them court-mar-
tialed and sentenced to death. Colonel Dax acts as their
defender, and the bulk of the film concerns their kanga-
roo trial and General Mireaux's failure to accept any
blame. In plot, *Paths of Glory* resembles *Breaker Morant,*
which also deals with an unjust court martial. But unlike that film, it contains some shocking battle scenes
with views of war's horrors that only Kubrick could
provide.

Douglas has seldom been seen at better advantage,
and Ralph Meeker is outstanding as one of the condemned "cowards." If you can't abide unhappy endings,
beware of this one, which has a doubly depressing twist.

PATTON

(1970), C, *Director:* Franklin J. Schaffner. *With* George
C. Scott, Karl Malden, Michael Bates, Stephen Young,
Michael Strong, Frank Latimore, James Edwards,
Lawrence Dobkin, and Tim Considine. **171 min.** *PG.*
Tape, CED, Laser: CBS/Fox.

"No poor bastard ever won a war by dying for his
country. He won it by making the other poor bastard die
for his country." So begins this sweeping epic which
glorifies war by glorifying one of the greatest modern
warriors, General George Patton of the U.S. Army. Patton as portrayed here is brave, bold, and brilliant—but
also egotistical, cruel, and quixotic: a fascinating
enigma of a man.

Francis Ford Coppola and Edmund H. North won an
Oscar for their exciting and often hilarious screenplay
(which made use of General Omar N. Bradley's mem-
oirs). General Bradley himself served as the film's chief
technical advisor. On screen he is portrayed by Karl
Malden. The film is as much about Patton's peculiar
character as it is about his artful and highly successful
campaigns in World War II. We see every side of this
complex man: the compassionate commanding officer
who kneels in prayer beside the bed of a wounded soldier,
and the fanatical taskmaster who slaps another soldier
for claiming to have battle fatigue—an illness that Patton swears is "a free ride that yellowbellies take to the
hospital." This slapping incident haunts the career of
Patton throughout the film, as it did in real life, and
serves to illustrate his contradictory nature.

Most World War II films are either long on action and
short on character, or vice versa, but *Patton* is magnificent in every department. The depicting of battles in
North Africa, Sicily, and Bastogne put similar efforts in
other films to shame. Towering above the entire worthy
production is George C. Scott as Patton—a role he seems
born to play. Some of Patton's cantankerous individu-
ality must have rubbed off on Scott, for he became the
first actor in history to refuse an Academy Award— for
his performance in this film.

SERGEANT YORK

(1941), B/W, *Director:* Howard Hawks. *With* Gary
Cooper, Walter Brennan, Joan Leslie, Margaret
Wycherly, George Tobias, Stanley Ridges, Ward Bond,
Noah Beery, Jr., and June Lockhart. **134 min.** *NR*. Tape,
CED: CBS/Fox.

World War I spawned a good many patriotic films, but
not many good ones. *Sergeant York* is one of the splendid
exceptions: a flag-waving tearjerker that upholds the
value of defending one's country without the implication
that killing is fun or the state is the highest authority.
Sergeant York helped convince young American men of
the 1940s that fighting Germans was a good idea.

It is the true story of Alvin York (Gary Cooper), the
World War I pacifist-turned-hero who single-handedly
captured 132 Germans and killed 20 others. We watch
York's transformation from a backwoods Tennessee hell-
raiser into a sincere Christian, and finally into a loyal
and brave soldier. If such a conscientious young fellow
can see his way clear to shooting at the enemy, the film
suggests, there must be something to it. Most of the
movie is spent setting up the crucial element: York's
character. Cooper gives an engaging performance in the
title role, while Walter Brennan plays pastor Rosier
Pile, the Baptist preacher who helps set York on the
straight and narrow. The religious theme is more than
an undercurrent; it's the pivot for the entire plot. York
converts after literally being struck by lightning, and
the script (in which John Huston had a hand) abounds
with biblical quotes and motifs. There is even a detailed
theological discussion between York and his superiors at
boot camp, after which he finds Christian support for the
soldier's duty in Luke 20:25 ("Render unto Caesar,
therefore, the things which be Caesar's . . .").

Only the last 40 minutes of the film deal directly with
York's life in the Army and his heroism during the
Meuse-Argonne offensive. The battle sequence is stirring and suspenseful, as director Howard Hawks meant
it to be. The sight of Cooper in uniform is as much of a
morale-booster as it was in 1941.

STALAG 17

(1953), B/W, *Director:* Billy Wilder. *With* William
Holden, Otto Preminger, Robert Strauss, Peter Graves,
Don Taylor, Harvey Lembeck, Richard Erdman, Neville
Brand, and Sig Ruman. **120 min.** *NR.* Tape, CED, Laser:
Paramount.

   The greatest tribute to *Stalag 17* is that every
prisoner-of-war film since has borrowed from it exten-
sively, from *The Bridge on the River Kwai* to *The Great
Escape* to *King Rat. Stalag 17* is the father of them all,
and it remains the finest film treatment of POWs.
   The story is simple: A group of American POWs in
Nazi Germany learn that there is a traitor among them,
a spy who is tipping off the Germans every time they
attempt a break. They must find the squealer before
more lives are lost and morale is completely broken.
They must also protect a new prisoner (Robert Strauss),
who is carrying valuable intelligence, from being tortured and killed by the Nazis. William Holden won a
much-deserved Academy Award for his portrayal of
Sergeant Sefton, the sneering pragmatist who trades
with the camp guards for scarce luxuries and has no
interest in escaping or helping anyone else escape. To
the other POWs, Sefton is the prime suspect. Otto Preminger, better known as a fine director, plays the Prussian
commandant. His performance has become the yard-
stick for actors playing sadistic Nazi officers.
   Director Billy Wilder, who also co-wrote and produced, achieves a near-perfect blend of comedy and
drama, which accurately mirrors the manic-depressive
nature of camp life. The theme of American POWs trying to keep their spirits up by engaging in covert combat
with the Nazis is still a powerful one, and the film is in a
class with *Casablanca,* in that it can be watched again
and again. And like *Some Like It Hot,* another Wilder
masterpiece, *Stalag 17* has one of the funniest closing
lines in film history.

WESTERNS

Although the Western itself is more a memory than an active filmmaking category, the themes of the Westerns live on in other cinematic forms. It's no secret that such popular modern films as *Star Wars* and *The Road Warrior* are really Westerns in disguise. This chapter salutes the real thing: those movies, many of them *the* blockbusters of their day, that singlehandedly dominated pulp cinema for decades. In general, Westerns are excellent home video movies, although it will be hard to simulate the feel of, say, a deep sunset over a rugged prairie. The fact that Westerns translate so well to prime-time television *(Gunsmoke, Bonanza, Little House on the Prairie)* testifies to the fact that they play well on the format. The Western lives on in videotape, and you'll be hard pressed to find better entertainment than those discussed in this chapter. Other Westerns to consider are: *A Fistful of Dollars, Fort Apache, High Noon, Little Big Man, The Long Riders, Melody Ranch, Rio Bravo, The Searchers, They Died With Their Boots On, True Grit,* and *The Wild Bunch.*

Tumbleweeds. *The stoic face of William S. Hart, the first great western hero.*

DODGE CITY

(1939), C, *Director:* Michael Curtiz. *With* Errol Flynn,
Olivia De Havilland, Ann Sheridan, Bruce Cabot, Alan
Hale, Frank McHugh, John Litel, Victory Jory, Ward
Bond, and Cora Witherspoon. **104 min.** *NR*. Tape, CED:
CBS/Fox.

This big, sprawling Warner Brothers' frontier epic is
the studio's best western ever. Under the surehanded
direction of Michael Curtiz, it reaches a height of adventure and a depth of feeling uncommon in the genre.
Errol Flynn, in his first western, appears as Wade
Hatton, bringing a herd of cattle and a wagon train of
settlers to Dodge City. Wade clashes with Abbie Irving
(Olivia De Havilland), who is headed there with her
family, when he's forced to kill her drunken brother
after he causes a cattle stampede. The girl wrongly
blames Wade and refuses to have anything to do with
him. In Dodge City, a gambler (Bruce Cabot) and his
gang of desperadoes defy all attempts at establishing
law and order. When Wade and his men vanquish the
baddies in a big saloon fight, he is asked to remain as
sheriff. *Dodge City* sports one of the biggest saloon
brawls ever filmed, with breathtaking staging and stunt
work, including two men crashing through a staircase to
the floor from a balcony, and others being hurled through
the saloon's plate glass window. From then on, the picture is loaded with action until peace breaks out.
Errol Flynn, known primarily for his swashbuckling
sword-fighting roles in *The Adventures of Robin Hood*
and *The Seahawk*, took to the western saddle with ease.
For Ann Sheridan, who plays Ruby, it was a step up from
being the "Oomph Girl" (as she was then known, cour-
tesy of Warner's publicity department). Well-known
character actors such as Frank McHugh, John Litel,
Victory Jory, Henry Travers, Henry O'Neill, Big Boy
Williams, and Ward Bond rounded off the excellent cast.

THE GOOD, THE BAD,
AND THE UGLY

(1968), C, *Director:* Sergio Leone. *With* Clint Eastwood,
Eli Wallach, and Lee Van Cleef. **161 min.** *NR*. Tape,
CED, Laser: CBS/Fox.

This film was the third, last, and most elaborate of
Clint Eastwood's "man-without-a-name" Italian westerns directed by Sergio Leone. The trilogy helped
establish him as a major star. Although it was filmed in
1966, it was not released in the U.S. until 1968.

Clint Eastwood (the "good") is a mysterious stranger
who saves Mexican bandit Eli Wallach (the "ugly") from
bounty hunters. The two concoct a scheme in which
Eastwood will collect reward money for capturing Wallach and will then rescue him in the nick of time before
the hanging. Simultaneously, vicious bounty hunter Lee
Van Cleef (the "bad") and a band of cutthroats seek a
fortune in buried Confederate gold, murdering and tor-
turing everyone in their path. Wallach and Eastwood
are captured and sent to a prison camp run by Van Cleef,
who has become an army sergeant in hopes that it will
lead him closer to the gold. The three men form an
alliance and eventually find their way to a cemetery
where the treasure is buried. There is a spectacularly
tense showdown between the three before the blackly
humorous finale.

This was the film that proved that the success of the
earlier Leone-Eastwood films (*A Fistful of Dollars* and
For a Few Dollars More) was not a fluke. It gave Eastwood the leverage he needed to return to Hollywood and
make the kind of movies he wanted to make—and
proved he could.

The critics found *The Good, the Bad, and the Ugly*
sadistic and repellent, but the public did not share their
distaste. The picture has many rousing action scenes,
terrific music by Ennio Morricone, awesome camera
work, outstanding performances by the three stars,
black humor, and spine-chilling shootouts. Who could
ask for more in a western?

THE MAGNIFICENT SEVEN

(1960), C, *Director:* John Sturges. *With* Yul Brynner, Eli
Wallach, Steve McQueen, Horst Buchholz, Charles
Bronson, James Coburn, Robert Vaughn, and Brad
Dexter. **127 min.** *NR.* Tape, Laser: CBS/Fox; CED: RCA
VideoDisc.

This American remake of *The Seven Samurai* is one of
John Sturges's finest efforts—and from the director of
The Great Escape, that's saying plenty.

In a small Mexican town in the post-Civil-War era,
seven professional gunfighters are hired by the townspeople to rid themselves of a gang of terrorizing bandits
(their leader played by Eli Wallach). When the gun-
slingers, trained and led by a black-clad gunman (Yul
Brynner), arrive in town, the natives are suspicious of
them yet unable to fend for themselves, making for some
painful conflicts. The gunman has recruited a motley
crew of outcasts. Lacking the emphasis of the original
Japanese movie on samurai honor and social responsibility, this version spotlights the various skills of the
seven men in overcoming seemingly impossible odds.
The film's success is in large part due to the characterizations, including Steve McQueen's humorous outlaw,
cool killers Charles Bronson and Robert Vaughn, and
particularly James Coburn's memorable knife thrower.
(Coburn struck a chord with audiences throughout the
world and especially in Italy, where his character
strongly influenced the spaghetti westerns.) Yul
Brynner's "man in black" was a departure for the actor,
who was not recognized for western roles.

As in the original, the combination of humor and
drama is most effective. Particularly poignant is the
gradual transformation of the townspeople from cowed
victims into courageous defenders of their homes and
families.

RED RIVER

(1948), B/W, *Director:* Howard Hawks. *With* John
Wayne, Montgomery Clift, Walter Brennan, Joanne
Dru, John Ireland, Coleen Gray, Harry Carey, Jr., Noah
Beery, Jr., and Harry Carey, Sr. **125 min.** *NR.* Tape:
Key; CED: RCA VideoDisc.

Only people who hate *all* westerns could dislike this
one. Howard Hawks's magnificent epic made a star of
Montgomery Clift, and prompted the director to state
unequivocally of John Wayne, playing his first downbeat character role after 18 years of epitomizing the
western hero, "He's one hell of an actor." *Red River*
remains, after 36 years, the ultimate epic of the cattle
drive.

The opening finds a group of wranglers gathered
around a makeshift funeral under a sky streaked with
ominous clouds, as Tom Dunson (John Wayne) reads the
words that could serve as the moral of the film: "We
brought nothing into this world, and it's certain that we
can take nothing out." Wayne is boss of the first cattle
drive over the Chisholm Trail, past the Red River into
Missouri, and on to Abilene, where the coming railroad
will open up a huge market for beef in the East. If he
doesn't make it, he and his fellow ranchers may starve.
This makes him ruthless, tortured, driven with pain,
and alienated from his men. His foster son, Matthew
Garth (Montgomery Clift), the person Dunson loves
most in the world, sides with the men. If Garth takes
over, Dunson feels he will have to kill him. Among the
most memorable sequences is the start of the drive in the
dawn's early light; the camera pans over the waiting
men and animals until the cry of each wrangler blends
into the vast moving mass of humans and beasts.

Director Hawks later commented of *Red River:* "We
were walking a tightrope in telling a story like that. Are
you still going to like Wayne or not? Fortunately, we
ended up with a good characterization and you did like
Wayne."

Shane. *Shane (Alan Ladd) proves his prowess with a gun while Joey (Brandon De Wilde) recoils at the noise. Oddly, Shane is a case where the video version is superior to the original theatrical version. Made in normal ratio, it was released in theaters as a wide-screen film (with the top and bottom parts of the image cut off). The video version shows the whole image, substantially as shot.*

SHANE

(1953), C, *Director:* **George Stevens.** *With* **Alan Ladd, Jean Arthur, Van Heflin, Brandon De Wilde, Jack Palance, Edgar Buchanan, Emile Meyer, and Elisha Cook, Jr. 117 min.** *NR.* **Tape, CED, Laser: Paramount.**

Director George Stevens's 1953 film remains the classic homesteader story, concerned more with the farmer than the cowboy. It is also the prototypical story of the "mysterious stranger" who arrives from nowhere, does what he has to do, and rides on—a plot device of countless B-westerns since then, but a classic battle of virtue over evil in the hands of a master director like Stevens.

Alan Ladd is the stranger, Shane, an ex-gunfighter who arrives at the Wyoming farm of the Sparretts (Van Heflin and Jean Arthur) and their eight-year-old son, Joey (Brandon De Wilde). Shane gladly accepts their hospitality and stays a while to help with the chores. Shane discovers that the Sparretts and other homesteaders are in a mortal struggle with Ryker (Emile Meyer), a cattle baron determined to drive them off their farms. After a rousing fistfight in the saloon, which sees the bullies vanquished by Sparrett and Shane, Ryker brings in a hired gunman (Jack Palance), who kills a farmer in cold blood. When another farmer's home is torched, the rest of the farmers decide that someone has to do something. Shane takes on the job. He rides to Ryker's hideout and kills the gunman in a duel. His mission accomplished, he rides off alone, the youngster's now famous cry of, "Come back, Shane!" ringing in his ears—and ours.

Filmed in Wyoming, beneath the peaks of the Grand Tetons, *Shane* is a rich and dramatic cinematic painting of the American frontier scene. The detailed authenticity of its costumes and sets separates it from the many other westerns with similar plot lines. An outstanding, if sentimental, angle is Joey's hero worship of Shane.

THE SPOILERS

(1942), B/W, *Director:* Ray Enright. *With* John Wayne, Marlene Dietrich, Randolph Scott, Margaret Lindsay, Harry Carey, and Richard Barthelmess. **87 min.** *NR*. Tape: MCA.

Among other classic moments, *The Spoilers* contains the biggest fistfight ever filmed. Top western stars John Wayne and Randolph Scott (the latter in a rare role as a villain) spar it out in a scene that makes other movie brawls look like kindergarten spats. It also boasts a first-rate cast, frontier-raw humor, and a sultry love interest.

Wayne plays Roy Glennister, the part-owner of a gold mine, who is strongly attracted to Helen Chester (Margaret Lindsay), niece of Judge Stillman (Samuel S. Hinds). A double-cross by Stillman causes him to lose the mine. When the town marshall is murdered, the new gold commissioner, McNamara (Scott), has Roy unjustly imprisoned. Marlene Dietrich plays the saloon girl, Cherry Malotte. Cherry is in love with Roy and tries to help him by proving that the commissioner, the judge, and the niece are conspiring to rob the miners. Richard Barthelmess, the great silent-film star of D. W. Griffith's *Broken Blossoms* and *Way Down East*, appears as the Bronco Kid, a gambler in love with Cherry. Roy escapes from jail and, with his partner, Destry (Harry Carey), reclaims the mine from McNamara's men. He then rides back to town, kills Judge Stillman, and engages McNamara in a mammoth fistfight.

This climactic fight hits the all-time high for brawling, with Wayne and Scott battling it out all over the saloon and into the street, among the horses, and in the mud. Wayne learned the technique of movie barroom brawling from Yakima Canutt, former rodeo champion, silent western star, and top stuntman. Wayne and Canutt perfected the technique now generally used in movie fights. They discovered that near-miss swinging punches, with the fist smacks dubbed on the sound track, looked very authentic when photographed at an angle.

STAGECOACH

(1939), B/W, *Director:* John Ford. *With* Claire Trevor,
John Wayne, Thomas Mitchell, Andy Devine, George
Bancroft, Louise Platt, John Carradine, Berton
Churchill, and Donald Meek. **99 min.** *NR*. Tape:
Vestron; CED: RCA VideoDisc.

"People don't make westerns anymore," RKO told
director John Ford when, having bought the story of
Stagecoach for $2500 after reading it in *Collier's,* he
sought financing. Eventually, independent producer
Walter Wanger signed Ford to make it for United
Artists, and Wanger wanted Gary Cooper and Marlene
Dietrich for the leads. "This is the kind of picture you
have to make for peanuts," Ford replied, as he cast John
Wayne in the role that would make him an "overnight"
star after ten years of toiling in low-budget westerns and
serials. The final budget for the film was $220,000. Need-
less to say, it made its money back, and won the hearts of
millions of viewers.

The film brings together (in *Grand Hotel* fashion) a
cross-section of characters traveling on the Lordsburg
coach through hostile Indian country, where Apache
chief Geronimo lurks with his band. Claire Trevor, a
good-hearted lady of dubious virtue, is leaving town by
popular request. Other passengers include John Carradine, a Southern gentleman and professional gambler;
Thomas Mitchell, a drunken doctor; the pregnant Louise
Platt, anxious to join her husband at the coach's destina-
tion; Berton Churchill, a crooked banker; Donald Meek,
a timid whisky salesman; George Bancroft, a sheriff; his
prisoner, the Ringo Kid (John Wayne); and the driver,
Andy Devine. Tense interaction among the passengers
points up their distrust of and snobbery towards Trevor,
whose sympathy lies with the Kid. The latter awaits his
chance to escape for a showdown with the outlaw Plummer boys. When the Apaches attack, everyone's true
color surfaces, and several meet their death before the
proverbial cavalry comes to the rescue. The Ringo Kid
proves himself, of course, in the final shoot-out.

TUMBLEWEEDS

(1925), B/W, *Director:* King Baggot. *With* William S.
Hart, Barbara Bedford, Lucien Littlefield, J. Gordon
Russell, and Richard R. Neill. **81 min.** *NR*. Tape:
Blackhawk.

Silent-film star William S. Hart was not only one of
the all-time screen greats, but also the first to make
westerns that were noted for their authenticity, aus-
terity, and strong characterizations. He often portrayed
a "good bad man." *Tumbleweeds*, his last film, and
among his three best, is here reissued with music, sound
effects, and a spoken prologue by Hart in his only sound-
film feature appearance.

Hart plays Don Carver, a fearless, hardened "tumble-
weed" who, with his sidekick, Kentucky (Lucien Littlefield), mingles with homesteaders heading West to lay
claim to the Cherokee Strip. Don encounters the Lassiter
family and falls in love with Molly (Barbara Bedford),
the eldest daughter. When he tries to stake out a home-
stead claim for himself and Molly, he is foiled by her
rascally half-brother and a crooked partner who attempt
to control the water rights and cause Don's arrest as a
"sooner."

Tumbleweeds was hailed by critics when it opened,
but a dispute between Hart and the distributor, United
Artists, fouled up its release, and the result was a box-
office disappointment. It was Hart's last feature film, but
in 1939 Astor Pictures reissued the film with a synchron-
ized sound track and a prologue by the star. The remarkably vibrant quality of Hart's voice and dramatic delivery was highly praised by reviewers who felt that, had
he been a younger man coming into pictures then, he
would have zoomed to the top. For film buffs today, it is a
unique opportunity to see Hart and hear him virtually
delivering his own epitaph. The spectacular scenes of the
land rush have never been equaled on the screen, and the
shots of Hart breaking out of the stockade where he has
been trapped, mounting his horse, and riding to out-
distance everyone (he was almost sixty years old at the
time), provide a rare thrill.

VERA CRUZ

(1954), C, *Director:* Robert Aldrich. *With* Gary Cooper,
Burt Lancaster, Denise Darcel, and Cesar Romero.
94 min. *NR.* Tape, CED: CBS/Fox.

Teaming two big action names proved highly successful in this production, both creatively and commercially,
with Burt Lancaster gladly taking second billing to get
the pull of Gary Cooper's box-office draw. Few westerns
pack as much suspense and character as *Vera Cruz*, but
a plot full of double-and-triple-crosses and amoral adventures angered the critics. The audiences, however,
loved it. It started a Hollywood cycle of trying to team
two big names in one picture, and anticipated the direction the Italian "spaghetti westerns" were to take later,
obviously influencing director Sergio Leone's films with
Clint Eastwood.

It is 1866, the time of the Mexican revolution. Benjamin Trane (Cooper) and Joe Erin (Lancaster), two American adventurers, will fight for whichever side pays
them the most. The fiery Nina (Sarita Montiel) urges
them to side with the rebels, while the Marquis de Lab-
ordere (Cesar Romero), an aide to the Emperor Maximilian (George Macready), wants them to fight for him.
At a ball in the lavish Chapultepec Palace, Trane and
Erin meet the Countess Marie Duvarre (Denise Darcel),
and agree to escort her on the dangerous journey to Vera
Cruz. Later, they discover that she is secretly transporting a gold shipment to Maximilian's troops. The
Countess offers to steal the gold and split it with the
Americans, but the Marquis, discovering their plan,
flees with the shipment. Trane and Erin assemble their
men and attack the fort, and Erin gets the treasure. Nina
persuades Trane that the gold belongs to the people, but
Erin refuses to give it up, and Trane is forced to kill his
friend.

In the midst of this complex but fast-paced story,
watch for Charles Buchinsky (later Charles Bronson) as
Pittsburgh, Jack Elam as Tex, Ernest Borgnine as Don-
negan, and Hopalong Cassidy's frequent nemesis,
Morris Ankrum, as General Aguilar.

MOVIE INDEX

Numbers in bold indicate photograph.